The Muslim Brotherhood and State Repression in Egypt

The Muslim Brotherhood and State Repression in Egypt

A History of Secrecy and Militancy in an Islamist Organization

Ahmed Mohamad Abou El Zalaf

I.B.TAURIS
LONDON • NEW YORK • OXFORD • NEW DELHI • SYDNEY

I.B. TAURIS
Bloomsbury Publishing Plc
50 Bedford Square, London, WC1B 3DP, UK
1385 Broadway, New York, NY 10018, USA
29 Earlsfort Terrace, Dublin 2, Ireland

BLOOMSBURY, I.B. TAURIS and the I.B. Tauris logo are
trademarks of Bloomsbury Publishing Plc

First published in Great Britain 2023
This paperback edition published 2024

Series design by Adriana Brioso
Cover image © Keystone/Hulton Archive/Getty Image

A catalogue record for this book is available from the British Library.

A catalog record for this book is available from the Library of Congress.

ISBN: HB: 978-0-7556-4660-9
PB: 978-0-7556-4664-7
ePDF: 978-0-7556-4661-6
eBook: 978-0-7556-4662-3

Typeset by Integra Software Services Pvt. Ltd.

To find out more about our authors and books visit www.bloomsbury.com
and sign up for our newsletters.

For Mohamad Abou El Zalaf

Contents

Acknowledgements

This book would never have become anything if not for the generous support of many institutions and individuals.

I am deeply grateful to the University of Southern Denmark and the Center for Modern Middle East and Muslim Studies whose kind support enabled me to launch this project. At SDU, I owe special thanks to my academic mentor and supervisor Professor Dietrich Jung, who has become a dear friend and a great inspiration. The support and endorsement that Dietrich Jung has shown me throughout the years are immeasurable and have offered me with indescribable impetus to fulfill this work. I also extend my thanks to Kirstine Sinclair for her great endorsement and kind support.

Further thanks go to the Faculty of Humanities and to the Centre for the Study of Nationalism, University of Copenhagen, for hosting me and for offering me facilities to conduct my research and to discuss my work with accomplished colleagues. Special thanks go to Mogens Pelt who since 2010 has encouraged and supported my work and untiredly assessed this work through its development. Mogens has carefully read and commented on anything I have asked him for, and I profited immensely from his remarkable knowledge and never-ending insights. The trust he placed in me and the support he has offered me have always gone hand-in-hand with an intellectual rigor that always pushed me to constantly improve my work.

I am most indebted to the Department of Culture Studies and Oriental Languages, University of Oslo, for hosting me as a visiting fellow. Here a special thanks go to Professor Brynjar Lia who received me with the greatest and most genuine generosity.

Among those I would like to express my gratitude to also are Professor Ulf Hedetoft for his hospitality and great endorsement, Jørgen Bæk Simonsen, Ehab Galal, Professor Marie Louise Nosch, Professor Bjørn Olav Utvik, Ulrika Mårtensson, and Thomas Hegghammer. They have all been a great source of inspiration throughout my academic life. I apologize to those I may have omitted here; you are not forgotten.

My thanks go to my editors Rory Gormley and Yasmin Garcha who readily accepted my book proposal and made this book possible.

I would like to express my deepest love and appreciation to my loving and devoted parents. Always prioritizing education, they offered me the delights of scholarship. I feel blessed and grateful to have them at my side. My wife was always supportive, loving and caring despite all my mental and physical absence. My siblings were a persistent source of support and encouragement—Thank you all.

Lastly, Mohamad Abou El Zalaf, my son, friend, and the best thing that has happened to me, this is for you.

Introduction

On October 26, 1954, while addressing a rally at al-Manshiyya square in Alexandria, to mark the signing of an evacuation agreement between revolutionary Egypt and the UK, an abortive attempt was made on Prime Minister Gamal Abdel Nasser's life. As a large crowd was listening to the man who, in the near future, would become the undisputed leader of Egypt and the symbol of Arab Nationalism, Mahmoud Abdel Latif drew a pistol and fired eight rounds at Nasser, only to miss his target. When apprehended and interrogated, Abdel Latif confessed to the assassination attempt and to being a member of the *Ikhwan* and its militant wing, *al-Niẓām al-Khāṣ* (the Special Apparatus).[1] Allegedly acting on behalf of the Special Apparatus, Abdel Latif conceded that his act had come as a reaction to the revolutionary government's signing of an agreement with the British.[2] The attempted assassination was, on the word of the thirty-year-old plumber, in retaliation for the Anglo-Egyptian agreement of October 19.[3] The agreement fell short of nationalist expectations and, according to Abdel Latif's testimony, amounted to a betrayal that justified the killing of its signatory.[4]

It was a cold Tuesday in Cairo when six members of the Muslim Brotherhood[5] walked to the gallows to encounter the vengeful justice of the revolutionary regime. Putting into effect the death sentences handed out on December 4, the executions were carried out swiftly on December 7,[6] 1954, in *Sijn al-Isti'nāf*[7] (Prison of Appeal) in Cairo. A court martial found the six defendants guilty of masterminding the Manshiyya incident.[8] Since the botched attempt, the military regime[9] had been determined to eradicate the Brotherhood in Egyptian society, thus complicating matters further for the *Ikhwan*. To do so, the regime's security machinery embarked on an uncompromising crackdown to uproot the organization and disrupt its activities. Thousands of active members were arrested and subjected to ruthless torture and mistreatment.[10] What followed the Manshiyya incident, in terms of repression and constraints, was consequently a reality of unprecedented persecution in the Brotherhood's history.

With the organization outlawed and its members either arrested or compelled to flee official persecution by escaping the country or being forced into a reality of clandestine adherence to the Brotherhood, its chances of survival seemed rather illusory. In consequence, contemporary researchers and observers reached the conclusion that the Brotherhood had definitely been exterminated at the hands of a stronger and more modern opponent, that is, the secular nationalist military regime embodied in Gamal Abdel Nasser. In the late 1960s, Richard P. Mitchell wrote "[o]ur feeling, for some time now shared by others, is that the essentially secular reform nationalism now in vogue in the Arab world will continue to operate to end the earlier appeal of this organization."[11] Gilles Kepel described the Muslim Brotherhood during the Nasserite era as an organization "already consigned to the past by the world's newspaper editors and diplomatic corps."[12]

For many Brotherhood members, the period of 1954–70 represents a focal point in the organization's history. The clash with the military regime in late October 1954 marked a radical change for the Brotherhood and its members; what occurred after that evening in late October was radically different for the *Ikhwan* in terms of persecution and restricted opportunities. This period left many deep scars, no doubt, but it also presented the Brotherhood with particular opportunities for development and continuation. Despite the monumental importance and centrality of this period in the history of the Brotherhood, there are a surprisingly limited number of studies dealing with its history in these crucial years.

Most studies dealing with the Brotherhood in the aftermath of al-Banna's death in 1949[13] have largely been dominated by investigations of the radicalizing role of Sayyid Qutb on members of the Brotherhood. A majority of these studies did so at the expense of focus on the *Ikhwan*'s organizational structures, and its social, political, and religious activities during years of political repression. In explaining the ideological evolution of the militant radicals that wreaked havoc in the Sadat era, authors traced their ideas back to Qutb and particularly his book *Maʿālem fī al-Ṭarīq*[14] (*Milestones*). A case in point is Gilles Kepel's seminal study *Muslim Extremism in Egypt, the Prophet and the Pharaoh* from 1985, in which he held that the indiscriminate and radical ideas of *Milestones* were a result of a writer that only knew Nasser's concentration camps.[15] Penned by Qutb while he was incarcerated, *Milestones* was conceived by Kepel, and others, as *the* guidebook for the life journeys of many Islamist militants. These commentators argued that it was Qutb's writings that put Islamist militants on a collision course with the secular postcolonial regimes. Along these lines, Sayed Khatab described Qutb as "the key figure of the Muslim Brotherhood, whose works were considered as the manual of the Islamic groups, al-Jamāʿāt al-Islāmiyya, in Egypt and abroad." Describing the Muslim Brotherhood in Egypt as essentially radical and violent, Khatab pointed to Qutb as imperative in paving this radical road.[16] Continuing in a similar vein, Fawaz Gerges maintained that "Qutb's memory and manifestos have nourished and inspired most subsequent waves of militant Islamists."[17] Thus, when studying the Muslim Brotherhood and state repression, authors offered an explanation correlating the radicalization of Qutb's ideas with his experiences in Nasserite jails. Doing so, several authors, as illustrated above, drew the conclusion that the prison experience of Islamist activists resulted in a radicalization and militarization in their ranks.[18]

In stark contrast to the abovementioned studies, a diverging body of literature broke with the perception of the Brotherhood as monolithic and necessarily radical. Drawing attention to the multiplicity of ideas present within an organization of the Brotherhood's proportions, these studies highlighted the role of Hasan al-Hudaybi (second *Murshid,* 1951–73) in leading the *Ikhwan* in a moderate direction. As understood by this current, the Brotherhood opted for a moderate path during the late 1960s and rebuffed the radical worldview of Qutb. Barbara Zollner, for one, argued that "al-Hudaybi played a major part in the re-establishment of the organisation. Although he died in 1973, his moderate and conciliatory ideas continued to be relevant." Continuing along these lines, Zollner maintained that "[i]n these terms, *Duʿat la Qudat* remains an important critique of radical thought."[19]

Thus, whereas the ideological outcomes of repression have been widely studied, especially with regard to the second *miḥna* and the imperative role of Sayyid Qutb,[20] the existence of the Brotherhood as an organized but secret mass organization during the two periods of repression known by *Ikhwan* activists as the first and second *miḥna* (ordeal/trial), that is, 1948–51 and 1954–70,[21] has been remarkably understudied. This has resulted in unanswered questions about the history of the Egyptian Brotherhood: What happened to the organization following the dissolutions in 1948 and 1954? And how did the Brotherhood continue its existence when the political opportunities were seemingly nonexistent in society? It has furthermore left us with an incomplete understanding of the *Ikhwan*'s historical development and political role in postcolonial Egypt.[22]

By looking into organizational features and the historical course taken during these two important periods in the Brotherhood's history, this study attempts to shed light on the *Ikhwan*'s history when it was forced underground.

When the Nasserite regime came to an end with Abdel Nasser's death in September 1970, the Muslim Brotherhood reappeared on the Egyptian scene, pointing, according to some scholars, to a "second founding" of the organization.[23] However, rather than regarding the development in the 1970s as a "second founding," this study points to this so-called "re-emergence" of the *Ikhwan* as clear evidence of the organization's continuity during the Nasserite era.[24] Consequently, rather than considering periods of state-authorized repression as a time of interruption in the history of the *Ikhwan*, I claim that the Brotherhood, from the earliest stages of its formation, created a duality in its organization. This duality rested on two reinforcing elements: on the one hand, the Brotherhood being a mass organization for overt public consumption and, on the other, it having a hidden side based on hierarchical cellular structures and an understanding of secrecy as *the* proper way to safeguard the organization in times of repression. This duality, according to the main argument of this study, accounted for the endurance of the Brotherhood during periods of intensified constraint.

Accordingly, I intend to concentrate on the development of the Brotherhood as an organization rather than focusing on the Qutbian influence, as has been the focus of prior studies. For this reason, the study at hand is an examination of the development of the Brotherhood as an underground organization in periods of repression. This book examines the way in which the organizational structures of the Brotherhood provide it with mechanisms to survive state persecution and enable it to endure as a secret organization inside and outside prison walls.

Put simply, this study suggests that the Muslim Brotherhood as an organization did not cease to exist following the suppressive campaigns of 1948 and from October 1954 but continued, in varying degrees, until the end of repression. As such, the Muslim Brotherhood is perceived as an inherent part of the political landscape of the first postcolonial order in Egypt which emerged following the military coup in July 1952. By looking at the Brotherhood as a clandestine organization in these periods, we can explore the continuation of the Brotherhood's social and political underground activism and understand how and why the organization survived the extensive suppression it experienced. Stated differently, I am interested in the continued activism of the *Ikhwan* in periods of oppression, in what happened when the organization resorted to clandestinity to endure repression.

I consider the Muslim Brotherhood as a diverse organization that is not an essentially radical and/or violent one; while some periods witnessed nonviolent activities, others did in fact see the Brothers use violence. By studying this particular phase, I can trace the ideological variations in the Brotherhood and the ambiguities its activists struggled with regarding violence and nonviolence. As I will show, the ideas espoused by Qutb in *Maʿālem fil-Ṭarīq* (*Milestones*) were not the only ideas of currency in the Brotherhood, and in the end, the *Ikhwan* opted for a divergent view, namely that presented by Hasan al-Hudaybi.

To gain an inclusive understanding of how the Brotherhood continued to exist during these repressive years, this study mainly involves two different but interchangeable levels of analysis. Consequently, I borrow the multilevel approach devised by Donatella della Porta[25] in her seminal study on clandestine political violence.[26] In her approach, della Porta distinguishes between macro-level features such as escalating policing[27] and structural political and social contexts, meso-level characteristics in which the organizational structures and mechanisms are in focus, and micro-level aspects where the individual motivations are emphasized.[28] While this study draws heavily on della Porta's multilevel analytical approach,[29] its main focus is on the macro and meso levels at the expense of the micro level. This preference in my analytical approach results from the specific focus of this study. As stated above, the intention of this book is to examine the Brotherhood's history during two periods of repression. Hence, the study centers its attention on the structural/contextual and the organizational aspects at the expense of micro-level considerations to understand the continuing existence of the Brotherhood during authoritarian years.[30]

In answering the question of how the Brotherhood continued its existence despite the repeated dissolutions, hangings, and persecution, one needs to understand the domestic and regional context, that is, the macro level at which this continuation took place. In view of this, I argue that the domestic, and at times regional, situation was relatively advantageous for the Brotherhood's ability to continue its existence despite repression. One such illustrative example is the "Arab Cold War," as the inter-Arab struggle during the 1950s has been termed by Malcom Kerr.[31] By looking at this geopolitical conflict that took place between the major players on the Arab scene, we can detect the political opportunities evolving for organizations like the Brotherhood when domestic political spaces are limited or closed on account of repression. As explained by Wiktorowicz, it is imperative to incorporate "the influence of external factors and concomitant structures of opportunity and constraint" in order to contextualize collective action and understand how changes in the surrounding political, social, and economic contexts affect a given organization.[32] I maintain that there are substantial links between the domestic policies adopted by the state toward the Brotherhood and the ways in which the Brotherhood structured its appearance in society.

One central theme of this study is to address the internal affairs of the Brotherhood, with a particular focus on periods of persecution and organizational secrecy. This focus, as is shown throughout this study, helps us to conceive a somehow overlooked but nevertheless crucial side of the Brotherhood's history, that is, the duality mentioned above. In that way, I link the macro-level analysis with the meso level, that is, the regional and domestic political opportunities and constraints with the concomitant development inside the organization. Accordingly, it is my argument that the semi-clandestinity of the *Ikhwan* has a long history going back to its formative years, when the organization, headed by Hasan al-Banna[33] (1928–49), constructed an idea and structure of secrecy.[34] Hence, I treat the Brotherhood in periods of repression as an organization that applies mechanisms of secrecy as a preemptive measure to continue its activism and survive repression.

It goes without saying that the study of a secret organization sets the researcher a difficult task. Because of their secret nature, these organizations try to stay out of sight, or under the radar, and they do their best not to be observed by the repressive state system under which they operate. This of course means that they very often do not appear in registers and archives, as their ultimate tactic is to remain unseen. Hence, the researcher faces the challenge of uncovering something that tries to stay hidden.[35]

In 1906, Georg Simmel's seminal study "The Sociology of Secrecy and Secret Societies" was translated into English.[36] In his study, Simmel offers a detailed analysis of secrecy and secret societies and presents a number of features that, according to his understanding, necessarily must figure in secret societies: Secrecy is gradual and can characterize entire societies[37] or be limited to only aspects of the society. These aspects, based on Simmel's exposition, can include the names of its members, its structural details, its sources of finance, its relationships to other actors, or its purposes. By hiding one or more of these aspects, the society/organization can protect itself from outside infiltration and avoid being subjected to persecution.[38] Furthermore, in Simmel's words, secrecy is a hierarchical construction designed deliberately to control the followers of the society that opt for secrecy.[39]

Pivotal for this study is the understanding of secrecy as a defensive mechanism. As understood by Simmel, secrecy is the choice of the weak; it is a response to the risk of suppression. Adding to this, he argues that "the secret society emerges everywhere as correlate of despotism and of police control. It acts as protection alike [*sic*] of defense and of offense against the violent pressure of central powers."[40] Thus, a secret society usually operates in an asymmetric power relation, the weak against the strong, and it goes without saying that the weaker side will be the one obliged to acquire secrecy to protect its existence.

In opposition to Simmel's insistence on hierarchy as an inevitable aspect of secret societies, Erickson and P. Gist argue that secret societies take different structural forms and are not necessarily hierarchical in their structures. Erickson draws our attention to the significance of looking into the social and political atmosphere surrounding the secret society in order to better grasp its structures. "If conditions include risk, as when the members of a secret society risk imprisonment or injury or death, the processes generating the society's structure are distinctive ones."[41]

My understanding of the Brotherhood as a clandestine/secret organization builds selectively on the concepts coined by, among others, Simmel, P. Gist, and Erickson.[42] I define a secret society in this book as a group of individuals united by a specific ideology or commitment to an organization with persisting relationships/membership and with some aspects of the organization deliberately hidden from people outside it.[43]

Secrecy is here understood in terms of graduality, which means that the degree and form of it can, and most probably will, change over time. In contrast to Simmel's insistence on hierarchy, I do not view hierarchy as an unavoidable and necessary feature of the secret society, but as we will see, hierarchy was an important component of the Brotherhood's organization. Yet, it is imperative to note that this book is a historical work, and my major focus is on studying the historical development of the Brotherhood rather than concentrating on secrecy as a phenomenon. Accordingly, while I certainly do discuss organizational problems that emerge as an outcome of clandestinity, my main focus is nevertheless on its historical development.

I apply this definition of secret society as an ideal type "formed by the one-sided *accentuation* of one or more points of view and by the synthesis of a great many diffuse, discrete, more or less present and occasionally absent *concrete individual* phenomena, which are arranged according to those one-sidedly emphasized viewpoints into a unified *analytical* construct," to borrow Weber's definition.[44] Furthermore, as put by Weber, "[i]n its conceptual purity, this mental construct (*Gedankenbild*) cannot be found empirically anywhere in reality."[45] By studying the *Ikhwan* in these years of secrecy through this specific understanding of secrecy and its historical traces in the Brotherhood's past, I will provide insight into the internal history of the organization during repressive periods.

Three terms appear prominently in the analysis and merit further elucidation: *radicalization*, *militancy*, and *de-radicalization*.

Radicalization is a process within a group or among individuals in which they undergo ideological and/or behavioral changes. This process leads to the approval or active adoption of "extremist"[46] actions "show[ing] disregard for the life, liberty, and human rights of others."[47] The question of "radical in relation to what?"[48] will commonly feature when one labels an organization or a person as radical. Thus, radicalization is understood as a transformation from one worldview or code of conduct considered in the historical context as mainstream or acceptable to another considered in the same context as unconventional.[49]

Militancy is understood here as the approval and/or execution of violence to support a cause. It refers to activism that applies or warrants one form or another of violent rhetoric or behavior. While radicalization does not necessarily entail militancy, I understand militancy as the application or approval of violence (by word and deed).

De-radicalization is a process of change in which a group or an individual witnesses a transformation of ideas and an alteration in behavior, thus moving away from the approval and execution of "extremist" actions as defined above.[50]

These conceptual tools, as broadly defined here, will be utilized in my analysis of the Brotherhood's development. On this account, throughout this study I refer to terms such as *violence/violent* and *radical/radicalized*. These terms will be applied heuristically to help us understand the history of the Brotherhood. Thus, I do not perceive the Brotherhood and its members as necessarily radical or violent, but as my study will illustrate, radicalization and militancy took place inside the Brotherhood within the specific historical context this book is studying.

Examining the above issues necessitated my working primarily as a historian. To a large extent, the work consisted of the historiographical enterprise of mapping, collecting, critically evaluating, and triangulating sources and studying the historical periods from different standpoints. However, in addressing the ideological and organizational developments of the Brotherhood, my work involved a more analytical approach. These two approaches are not separated into different sections but represent an organic part of my analytical and descriptive approach. As highlighted by Ludmilla Jordanova, "Historical work is based on identifying an issue that requires explanation,"[51] and along these lines, I combine traditional historical description with analytical approaches throughout the study to answer the questions posed in this book.

On account of the richness of primary sources, which will be listed below, historical method and source criticism were applied in order to reconcile sources and arrive at assessments. The primary sources studied in this book can roughly be divided into three categories: the Brotherhood's own accounts, the accounts penned by members of the military junta and other intelligence officers, and British and American intelligence and diplomatic sources. A discussion of these three categories will follow to evaluate their accuracy, biases, and importance for this study.

The largest and most crucial source for this study is the Brotherhood's own published and unpublished writings and other documents. This is a body of thousands of pages and several hours of recorded interviews or recollections consisting mainly of autobiographical accounts, memoirs, and shorter biographical narratives written by Islamist activists and published in magazines and books.[52] These accounts offer essential insights into the internal activities, ideas, and discourses that materialized during the "*sanawāt al-miḥna*" (the years of ordeal/persecution) and depict the way in which the *Ikhwan* factions understood and wished to present their own history and self-perception.[53] These accounts, which have not yet been exhaustively studied, offer a new source of knowledge about these periods of the Brotherhood's past and the life trajectories of more or less unknown Brothers. These are memoirs and accounts written by inner circle members of the Brotherhood who witnessed this period, many of whom had either been incarcerated or continued their engagement with the Brotherhood during the repressive years.[54]

In addition to this published material, I have collected considerable source material consisting of, inter alia, unpublished Brotherhood documents and other material, such as bylaws, letters, profile descriptions of and recollections by *Ikhwan* members, videotaped interviews, and recollections. These primary sources, which have not yet been studied, offer a deep insight into the internal affairs of the Brotherhood and make it possible to unearth key events in the periods under study. The unpublished nature of this material is of importance. Considering the fact that not every member of the Brotherhood was capable of writing proper memoirs, this form of recollection, in which the ordinary Brother is interviewed verbally, represented for many of them an alternative to the written text. Hence, these unpublished sources furnished me with a broader picture of the activities and thoughts of many ordinary Brothers. In other words, this unpublished material offers an account from the bottom and includes those Brothers who are not always heard.

This corpus is hagiographic and tends to present the Brotherhood as a victim of international conspiracies and unjust repression, which is why a critical assessment of the information presented in it is one of my main tasks.

In addition, as memoirs penned long after the events they intend to describe, they can naturally be affected by the filter of time and a need to explain and even justify, in hindsight, the actions of their authors. Nevertheless, as this is not the sole source of information available to me, the validity of these accounts can and will be checked against other sources in order to reach as accurate an account as possible. Apart from this, the principal problem of these memoirs and accounts is their accuracy, or the lack of it to be more precise. However, this challenge will be addressed by triangulation, by which the validity of facts, dates, and numbers can be checked and assessed when judged against other sources and data available to me. By triangulating sources penned by, say, *Ikhwan* members with contemporary archival material produced by British intelligence services, the CIA, and/or accounts by representatives of the Egyptian authorities who witnessed this period, I can substantiate the information these sources offer to a greater extent. However, in contrast to material authored by external actors, be it British and American diplomats or even members of the Revolutionary Command Council (RCC),[55] the importance of the Brotherhood accounts lies largely in their ability to offer an insight into the organization's inner workings and thinking, which are an exclusive feature limited to them as internal actors. The juxtaposing of *Ikhwani* accounts with the intelligence source material of British and US diplomats will by far be the key part of validating the Brotherhood sources. This is due to the contemporaneous nature of these intelligence sources and, to a greater degree, their impartial position (although not completely impartial), which renders them a more accurate and unbiased source of knowledge when compared to the other source categories.

In addition to the sources written by Brotherhood activists, I draw on memoirs and accounts written by non-*Ikhwani* activists and officers who also witnessed these years firsthand. These accounts are important, as they present me with a counternarrative to that of the Brotherhood.[56] Like the Brotherhood accounts, this corpus can also be influenced by the desire to legitimize the actions of the authors and will therefore be treated in the same way as the Brotherhood sources. My employment of this source material will naturally be more limited than my application of Brotherhood and intelligence sources. In view of their external position, RCC members and intelligence officers were not always aware of the Brotherhood's inner workings, especially in periods of secrecy. Hence, my implementation of them in validating the Brotherhood sources and discussing specific events will be of secondary importance.

Most of these primary sources are not easily obtainable. Because of their very old nature, and due to a lack of interest in them, most of the books have not been republished and are oftentimes hard to acquire. This difficulty made it almost impossible to get hold of all of them, as some of them were out of print. However, the nonsystematic nature of these sources has led me, since 2013, on some exciting and much-appreciated journeys to various countries to collect as many of the sources as possible. Beirut and Tripoli in Lebanon, Amman, Cairo, Alexandria, Marrakesh, London, Exeter, and Oslo were among the places I enjoyed visiting to obtain these sources. In Egypt, the Brotherhood was disbanded after the coup in 2013, and its adherents have been persecuted since that time, which is why posing any questions about the *Ikhwan* or its publications was no uncomplicated task. In Jordan, the Brotherhood's offices have been shut down since 2016, but in the dusty corners of old bookshops in central Amman, I was able to locate a number of Brotherhood publications as well as non-Brotherhood material. Yet, as one bookshop owner, himself close to the Brotherhood, told me, "these [*Ikhwani*] books have to stay in the corner, due to the political situation." Additionally, I either collected unpublished source material on the Ikhwan in these various countries or obtained it from the Brotherhood online database "Ikhwan-Wiki." To collect the sources, I also made contact with Brotherhood leaders and members outside Egypt,[57] in Istanbul, London, and Amman, which refined my understanding of this organization.

Finally, I rely on vital archival material from the two influential powers in this period: the United States and Great Britain. In contrast to memoirs penned long after the events they purport to present, diplomatic reports provide contemporary observations and assessments of events unfolding in their times. While their conclusions may prove wrong at times, their descriptions and estimates mirror the contemporary views and are therefore free of post-rationalizations and retrospective considerations. This renders them a unique source of information about the social, political, and economic situation in Egypt during the years under study. Designed to aid policymakers at home to grasp Egyptian circumstances and political developments in the region and thus to establish operative responses, diplomatic reports require meticulousness in accounts of conditions, developments, and discussions. Accordingly, in contrast to the Brotherhood and RCC sources, I found these reports at times more accurate with regard to figures and dates. A possible problem with diplomatic reports is, however, their external provenance. As outsiders, the intelligence officers and diplomats had at times to rely on descriptions offered to them by Egyptian police officers, military men, or policymakers, while at other times they had direct access to Brotherhood activists and sympathizers. Accordingly, their narratives and accounts constitute an interpretation based on what Egyptian sources were informing them. Furthermore, the assessments put forward by the diplomats were personal appraisals and interpretations influenced by their way of thinking and the time context in which they perceived the developments, and thus they were biased by the viewpoints of their authors. However, their accuracy, which was improved by the fact that they were written contemporarily, renders them an important source of knowledge and a vital source to validate the information presented by the Brothers.

This archival material was gathered in the British Foreign Office's National Archives and online from the CIA database, made available a few years ago. With regard to the CIA sources, they consist of, inter alia, Intelligence Reviews, Bulletins, Intelligence Estimates, and National Security Council briefings. The British sources consist of Foreign Office material FO 141 (Egypt: Embassy and Consular Archives) and FO 371 (General Correspondence), in addition to WO 201 (Military Intelligence Headquarters, Middle East) and WO 208 (Military Intelligence Middle East and Egypt).

Source-based skills, as defined by Ludmilla Jordanova, can be said to cover these considerations about the source material. These skills, as explained by Jordanova, include identifying the right sources, reading them critically, and then integrating them into a historical account. This approach methodologically guides my study. A central aspect of my work with this myriad of sources is to approach them critically, asking who, why, when, where, how, and so on each time I analyze and critically measure a source. As argued by Jordanova, "The manifest content has to be clearly understood, but so do any hidden agendas."[58] I argue that these "hidden agendas" are highly crucial for a historian to identify and understand in order to arrive at as close a reconstruction of events as possible. By this critical reading of sources, one can come to disclose the tendencies, biases, and values that necessarily exist in man-made sources and reach conclusions in this process.

The book consists of six chapters, which are ordered chronologically but concurrently include a thematic order so as to cover the subjects that characterize the different periods under study.

Presenting a historical discussion of the Brotherhood's construction of secrecy during its formative period (1938/9–45), Chapter 1 reviews the formation of secrecy within the ranks of the Brotherhood. Through a detailed narration of the Brotherhood's first "ordeal" taking place in 1948–51, Chapter 2 delves into the historical events that took place, leading to the Brotherhood's first experience of full-scale repression and consequently intensive clandestinity. Having shown that secret structures had already been constructed in the formative period, this chapter illustrates how this secrecy contributed to the organization's ability to continue underground.

Paving the way for the second *miḥna*, Chapters 3 and 4 examine the events and developments that affected the *Ikhwan*'s internal coherence and development. By studying the change in leadership following al-Banna's death and the leadership crisis that followed, we can trace serious ruptures, reconstructions, and challenges in the Brotherhood's internal affairs. Furthermore, examining the strained relationship between the Brotherhood and the military junta prior to the showdown, we gain a comprehensive view into the Brotherhood's internal deliberations. The showdown, as these chapters clearly demonstrate, did not occur suddenly but followed a protracted battle of wits between the erstwhile allies, the Brothers and the officers.

The clampdown on the *Ikhwan*, beginning from late 1954, represented the hitherto fiercest challenge to the Brotherhood's existence. However, as Chapters 5 and 6 demonstrate, the Brotherhood was not exterminated at the hands of the Nasserite regime. Beginning with a concise description of the magnitude of suppression directed at the *Ikhwan*, Chapter 5 continues with an excursion into the clandestine activities of the Brotherhood in the early period of repression (1954–57). Unfolding this account of continuation and secrecy, Chapter 6 takes a longer perspective and discusses the activities of the Brotherhood in the following period (1958–70), tracing the degree of activism, recruitment, and internal reflections that took place in this crucial period. This chapter also reflects in some detail on the role of Qutb in the Brotherhood.

1

Building Structures of Secrecy: The Brotherhood in Pre-revolutionary Egypt

In the evening of February 12, 1949, Hasan al-Banna was shot seven times just as he had entered a taxicab in the middle of Cairo. It was about eight-thirty Saturday evening when al-Banna and his brother-in-law Abdel Karim Mansour left the headquarters of the Young Men's Muslim Association (YMMA) having attended a meeting with representatives from the YMMA. Al-Banna had been invited to the meeting at the request of Prime Minister Ibrahim Abdel Hadi (r. 1948–9) with the alleged purpose of sorting out problems between the *Ikhwan* and the government. In what appeared to be a premeditated act, three assassins approached the taxi which al-Banna and his associate had just entered and shot both men. The Brotherhood's founder and lifelong leader was brought to the Qasr al-Eine hospital located on the bank of the Nile, where he drew his final breath within a few hours.[1]

The unexpected death of al-Banna at a time of crisis put the Brotherhood at a dangerous crossroads in its history. Since the beginning of 1948, the *Ikhwan* had found itself on a collision course with the Egyptian government, and the assassination of al-Banna came as the definitive culmination of this blood-stained strife between compatriots. Thus, the crisis, as I discuss at greater length in the following chapter, left the Brotherhood leaderless and subject to as yet unparalleled repression and persecution in the organization's history. Notwithstanding, the organization proved able to endure persecution and continue its activities and presence in society despite the unsurpassed crisis in which it found itself. At the point oppression abated, the Brotherhood reappeared on the public scene to take part in the nationalist struggle against the British in the Suez Canal Zone,[2] thus evincing its durability.

Against this background, I argue that the survival of the Brotherhood following the loss of al-Banna clearly demonstrates the importance of its sharply defined organizational structures, ideological framework, and working procedures.

These features of organization, as will be discussed below, were developed in the preceding years and became crucial in fortifying the Brotherhood's survival. Hence, I challenge the widespread understanding in parts of the existing literature that the success of the Brotherhood should be understood as exclusively linked to al-Banna's charismatic leadership.[3] Without disregarding al-Banna's role in the development of the Brotherhood, which cannot be overstated, I maintain that the modern organizational structures of the Brotherhood's mass organization as developed during al-Banna's lifetime signified the most important asset for its survival.[4] It was especially its dual nature, combining overt mass-organizational features with secret and hidden aspects of organization, that accounted for the *Ikhwan*'s ability to endure. These same structures, ideological frameworks, and methods would become crucial again during the Nasserite years, when the Brotherhood once again endured repression. In addition, I suggest that the dissolution and repression of the Brotherhood in 1948–51 gave the organization an understanding of and ideas for how to deal with and endure suppression.

In so saying, I do not claim that a calculated strategy was developed by the Ikhwan to endure repression. My line of reasoning is, however, that the valuable experience gained in the course of the formative years of the Brotherhood and more significantly during the first *miḥna* provided the Brotherhood's rank and file and leaders with a frame of mind preparing them to deal with similar repressions. And above all, it furnished the *Ikhwan* with specific operational procedures and practices which became vital, especially during the second *miḥna*. In this regard, it is imperative to note that the different waves of repression carried out against the Brotherhood obviously differed in severity and duration and contained varying degrees of political opportunity, which is why the reactions to them also differed. However, as the subsequent chapters illustrate, comparable operational procedures, a sort of pattern, can be discerned from the organization's reaction to different periods of repression. This crucial, if painfully acquired, experience created a set of recurrent patterns of methods to withstand repression, which were reapplied time and time again. Accordingly, this chapter examines the construction and rationale behind these structures. By looking into the ideas of organizational secrecy present within the Brotherhood, I illustrate that these features had been present since at least the early 1940s.

Three illustrative examples of secrecy in the ranks and organization of the Brotherhood are therefore presented in the following. First, I shed light on the general structures of the Brotherhood, and more particularly the *usra* formation, which I argue represented a bedrock of organization within the *Ikhwan*. Established in 1943 as a general formation to enlist every member of the Brotherhood, this cellular structure was built on an idea of secrecy, as is shown below. Second, I examine the Brotherhood's establishment of a secret and armed organization of Brotherhood civilians, the Special Apparatus (*al-Niẓām al-Khāṣ*). Third, I discuss the Brotherhood's recruitment of both army and police officers to form secret cells inside the army and police. As this inroad into the armed forces by the Brotherhood began almost simultaneously with the establishment of the Special Apparatus and was organically connected with the work of the Apparatus, it is accordingly studied as an event related to the establishment of the *Niẓām*.

The examples that follow are discussed in the light of the pervasive troubled reality the whole region was witnessing. I illustrate that the development inside the Brotherhood was closely tied to the domestic and regional problems facing Egypt, above all the Second World War and its implications for Egypt. Accordingly, these sections intend to demonstrate that during these years of world rupture and crisis, the *Ikhwan* developed a blueprint for how to engage secretly and developed structures that subsequently became crucial in surviving suppression. In this vein, 1941 presented the *Ikhwan* with the first, if limited, experience of repression and restraints when Hasan al-Banna was exiled and subsequently arrested. I thus suggest that it was from that particular time that the organization constructed a mind-set of secrecy as a protective measure against repression.[5]

Secrecy in the Ranks of the Brotherhood: Protection against Infiltration and Oppression

Founded in 1928 by al-Banna and a handful of men in the city of al-Ismailiyya, situated on the west bank of the Suez Canal, during the first half of the 1940s the Brotherhood managed to develop a well-structured organization consisting of welfare institutions, schools, a clearly defined hierarchical order with all members organized into cells, and an ideology and political vision in which Islam was reinterpreted and propagated as a modern thought system.[6]

What started as a small and inconsequential local reform movement in the Suez Canal Zone had thus become a nationwide organization of elaborate structures and a well-articulated ideology by the beginning of the Second World War. During the 1940s, the Brotherhood thus emerged from its early modest beginnings to claim a place as the largest Islamist organization in Egypt. In fact, during these years, the Brotherhood also expanded its existence beyond the borders of Egypt, hence becoming a regional player of sorts. The Brotherhood kept growing and refining its organizational structures through the war years, and by 1944 it had established between 1,000 and 1,500 branches throughout Egypt.[7] A systematization and structuring of the organization's hierarchies took place concurrently with the expansion of branches and membership, consequently resulting in a qualitative and quantitative development of the *Ikhwan*.

By way of illustration, in every province, the Brotherhood had established administrative offices (*Makāteb Idāriya*) with a senior Brother heading the organization in each province. This offered an effective line of communication between the central leadership in Cairo and the members in the provinces. These new structures outlined the organizational maturation of the Brotherhood and the attention it paid to attain a decentralized structure, which would be more effective in tying Cairo and the provinces together. This decentralization had the added effect of providing the organization with increased resilience in the face of state repression.[8] However, as this section shows, the Brotherhood combined these overt and public institutions and branches with structures and ideas of secrecy. The idea of keeping components of its organization and ideas clandestine represents an important aspect of the Brotherhood's inner workings, as I illustrate here.

Disgruntled by the British occupation of Egypt and fearing the oppressive potentialities of the Egyptian state, the Brotherhood began to prepare for secret structures and activities. Such preparations were intended as means to combat the British in Egypt and to protect the organization from undesirable intrusion. In the example of the Brotherhood, we can trace this construction of secrecy to the early years of its establishment. As a case in point, in 1932 the Brotherhood's bylaw made it an explicit requirement of the Brothers to keep their weekly meetings secret and "in secret places"—no one outside the Brotherhood was allowed to attend these meetings unless permission was explicitly provided by the meeting's head.[9] This deliberate exclusion of outsiders and the demand to keep meetings "hidden" account for what I understand as a duality within the Brotherhood. Such secrecy was soon to grow and encompass additional elements of the Brotherhood's activities, as we shall see.

In fall 1937, as a clear manifestation of its organizational progress, the Brotherhood established the *katā'ib* (plural; *katība* in singular: battalions or rover scouts). The battalions were devised as a vehicle for the *takwīn* (formation) and *tarbiyya* (education) of Brotherhood members on a broader and more structured basis. Aiming at reinforcing the bonds between members and creating a well-structured and systematized network for indoctrination, the *katā'ib* were established on the grounds of the growing enrollment in the *Ikhwan*. With its heavy emphasis on fraternizing and educating members, the *katā'ib* had a strong relationship aspect, and it was directly managed by Hasan al-Banna. A battalion consisted of ten to forty members, aged between eighteen and forty years, and was only accessible for individuals already enlisted in the *Ikhwan*. The purpose of this structure was to systematize the education and formation of Brotherhood members and to reach out to greater parts of the membership in a structured way. The battalion would usually begin at seven in the evening and continue until dawn. Being a body for educating and molding members, the battalion had a coherent program that included study of the Quran, prayers late in the night, communal eating, and a speech presented by the head of the battalion. These religious and social aspects were combined with "heavy emphasis on militancy and struggle in the ideological preparation [of the attendants]," and the program contained physical training in addition to strong focus on secrecy and serious-mindedness. In fact, the battalion had its own oath standing on three pillars: action, obedience, and secrecy.[10]

Thus, the perception of secrecy, loyalty, action, and obedience had been embedded in the organizational thinking of the *Ikhwan* since the 1930s and represented a crucial element of the education and indoctrination of its members. However, the importance of secrecy as a protective measure against repression became even more central in the early 1940s, when the war efforts brought forth an increase in repressive measures by the authorities in Egypt. Since 1941, the Egyptian governments,[11] in collaboration with British authorities, had restrained freedoms and tried to subdue oppositional voices in light of wartime censorship and as an attempt to fortify the Allies' positions in North Africa. From early 1941, the Egyptian border region had witnessed a German expansion headed by the brilliant general Erwin Rommel, commander of the "Afrika Korps." The German commander, known as "the Desert Fox," succeeded in swiftly winning spectacular triumphs against the British, pushing their forces back. Axis air raids on the Alexandria area were markedly increased, and alone during the summer of 1941, they killed 650 civilians. By July 1942, the "Korps" had advanced toward the Egyptian–Libyan border and was within 100 kilometers reach of Alexandria, forewarning something of a near collapse of the Allied forces in North Africa. The position and popularity of the Allied forces was decaying in light of these developments and as a result of the food shortages the Egyptians were suffering, for which ordinary people blamed the Allied forces.[12] The advance of Rommel's forces was therefore looked upon by some Egyptians as a possible salvation from the British "menace." It was not before November 1942, after two years of advance, that Rommel's exhausted forces finally were pushed back when he commanded an attack ordered by Adolf Hitler on Cairo and the Suez Canal area.

Against this troubled background, British officials contemplated drastic measures to address these mounting challenges. And considering the Muslim Brotherhood as a major source of unrest, some of these measures were directed against the organization and its leadership.[13] Measuring the proper ways of dealing with this tense situation, British officials talked about the greater need "for governmental action to control both the enemy agents and their dupes" and endorsed the arrest of Hasan al-Banna as an effective way of countering anti-British activities.[14]

In February 1941, and as an example of the political restrictions stemming from the above-sketched events, the authorities exiled Hasan al-Banna to the remote governate of Qena in Upper Egypt in an attempt to curtail his freedom and ability to influence his followers. Deeming the exiling of al-Banna as inadequate in curtailing anti-British activities, al-Banna was subsequently arrested in October of the same year alongside some of his lieutenants. Being apprehended for a month at the request of the British ambassador, al-Banna was accused of having held a public speech in which he attacked imperialism and expressed his "bitter" hatred of the British.[15]

In the same vein, and as a continuation of the policy of curbing oppositional voices of "anti-British elements," the Brotherhood, in this same period, was subjected to a number of repressing procedures. Among the restraints put on the Brotherhood were the banning of their meetings and the prohibiting of their publications.[16] When the Brotherhood decided to put forward a list of seventeen candidates headed by al-Banna for parliamentary elections in March 1942, Prime Minister al-Nahhas ordered al-Banna to withdraw his candidature and that of his Brothers, thus continuing these official restrictive actions against the *Ikhwan*. Al-Nahhas threatened al-Banna with arrest if he did not comply. Al-Banna gave in to the prime minister's demands in return for governmental consent for his organization.[17]

These incidents, which represented the Brotherhood's exclusion from formal politics and a limitation of its freedoms, embodied the restrictiveness with which the Brotherhood was met in this context of political disorder. As a consequence, we can henceforth observe a rising inclination to secrecy by the *Ikhwan* as an attempt to stay resilient in such times of restriction and oppression.[18] By way of illustration, when restrictions were put on the Brotherhood's overt meetings in the early 1940s, it was declared in a British report that "meetings attended by any of the leading members are stated to have taken place in one or other of their private houses." The report went on to say that "meetings there [in Ismailiyya] are now taking place in the greatest secrecy and only the most trusted members are admitted."[19]

Another decisive and far-reaching reaction to this restrictive context was the creation of the *usar* (plural; *usra* in singular: families) system as an all-encompassing organizational structure to include every member of the organization. The construction of this system can be said to signify an institutionalization of secrecy into the ranks of the Brotherhood. It was an organizational attempt by the Brotherhood to overcome the problems that had evolved from the restrictions it had been subjected to, particularly during 1941 and 1942. By developing this structure, the *Ikhwan* buttressed its ability to survive repression and the lack of centralized leadership which occurs in such periods of repression, as had been the case when al-Banna and his closest associates were put away. This was the manifestation of the Brotherhood's response to repression and came in the form of decentralized formations.

This fundamental feature of the organization, which was introduced in 1943, less than two years after al-Banna's detention, came as a replacement for the battalions and became imperative in the Brotherhood's organization and indoctrination of members. The *usra* was then, as it is to this day, a tightly knit hierarchical structure of cells composed of five members in each. Each *usra* is headed by a *naqīb* (chief) responsible for his "family." All cells in any given geographical area are organizationally put under the command of the local *shu'ba* (singular; *shu'ab* in plural: branch headquarters). In turn, the head of the local branch, who is selected by the General Guidance Office, is in command of all cells under his authority. The branches (*shu'ab*) in an area are in turn organizationally situated under the command of the local headquarters (*maktab idārī*),[20] which is organically connected to the *Murshid* and the headquarters (*al-Markaz al-'Ām)* in Cairo. In this way, the Brotherhood was able to effectively connect the organization's different branches and even the smallest units with the central leadership in Cairo, and concurrently ensure that every unit could continue decentralized activism and low-key connections in periods of repression. In other words, when the headquarters were shut down and the Brotherhood's freedom curtailed, the family system ensured that the *Ikhwan*'s activities could continue and that members were able to meet persistently notwithstanding restrictions.

The *usra*, which obligated regular weekly meetings, was an effective way of creating a sense of communality, mutual responsibility, and close-knit relationships between the various members of the cell, and in turn linked the organization together.[21] The introduction of this structure came at a time when the *Ikhwan* had experienced a rapid increase in membership but was concurrently going through restrictions and was lacking operational freedom. Accordingly, the restrictiveness of the political scene in Egypt and the simultaneous growth of the Brotherhood accounted for the establishment of the family system as an attempt to streamline the members' education and protect the members from repression. The *usra* structure was a deliberate attempt by the leaders of the Brotherhood to manage the membership, erect clear lines of command, streamline the activities of all members toward a specific goal, secure the loyalty of members, and ensure the secrecy and discretion of members.[22]

The establishment of the *usar* was in that sense a formalization of the Brotherhood's *tarbiyya* (education) of the growing number of members and at the same time a way of continuing the links of the members when under restrictions or repression. This was an effective way of putting every member of the Brotherhood into a hierarchical cell, which, in its original form, is centrally controlled and connected to the local branch headquarters, but which in periods of limited freedom can work independently and largely removed from direct control of the central leadership. Its working procedures, in times of political freedom and repression alike, included keeping its weekly meetings detached from the *shu ʿab* (branches). Instead, the meetings were to be held in private homes or similar "non-official" places, thereby enabling the members to persevere in their affiliation when the organization was proscribed and/or when members were prevented from meeting overtly. Since then, as illustrated in subsequent chapters, this structure has been key to affording the organization the means to endure repression and to continue effectively even when the branches were closed and the senior leadership arrested.[23] Asserting its importance, Mitchell pointed correctly to the *usar* system as "the real basis of the power" of the Brotherhood.[24]

Al-Niẓām al-Khāṣ (the Special Apparatus): The Brotherhood's Secret and Militant "Elite"

Established sometime between 1938 and 1940,[25] the Special Apparatus[26] represented another clear case of the occurrence of secrecy within the structures of the Brotherhood. Being also an armed wing that was, according to its own founders and members, aimed at combating the British, their "lackeys," and the Zionists, this structure came to signify a militarization inside the Brotherhood.

Al-Niẓām al-Khāṣ was founded to serve as an "Islamic army" assigned to fulfilling the obligatory application of *jihad*,[27] according to the justification offered by its commanders. It was, as explained by one of its founders, a translation of the Brotherhood's serious intent to "combat the British with the strength of arms until they withdraw their troops from Egypt."[28] In the following, I offer a concise excursion into the Apparatus's establishment, structures, and ideas. By so doing, I aim to shed light on one of the most controversial but understudied structures of the Muslim Brotherhood.

One account on the establishment of the Apparatus can be found in the memoirs of Mahmoud al-Sabbagh.[29] Al-Sabbagh joined the Muslim Brotherhood in 1939 after being introduced to the *Ikhwan* by Mustafa Mashhur, subsequently the Brotherhood's fifth *Murshid*.[30] Hailing from al-Sharqiyya in northern Egypt, the two men had moved to Cairo to study at the university. Like many of their peers, they epitomized the growing, upwardly mobile stratum known as the *effendiyya*, which represented a newly urbanized and educated middle class.[31] These young men, who had recently moved to metropolitan Cairo, abhorred what they perceived as a British occupation "subjecting Egypt through iron and fire." Worse still was what they observed as a lack of resistance to the occupation—if not even a direct collaboration between the major political parties and the British.[32] For the two men, as for many like-minded Egyptians, Cairo obviously symbolized what Frantz Fanon has coined as "the fortress of colonialism."[33] This had an expressly strong effect on their worldview, as we shall see.

At Cairo University, where they both studied at the faculty of science, they spent many hours discussing the lamentable condition in which they found their beloved Egypt and what steps could be taken to remediate the situation. Mashhur, who by this time was in touch with the Muslim Brotherhood, invited al-Sabbagh to join the organization. The Brotherhood was, Mashhur told his countryman, an organization that "seriously wanted to fight the British by engaging them in an armed struggle."[34] Mashhur talked of anti-British resistance in religious terms, describing it as a *jihad*, "obligatory for every Muslim man and woman."[35] Mashhur's words were felt most welcome by al-Sabbagh, who throughout his adolescence had looked for the appropriate way to work for the betterment of society. He therefore decided to visit al-Banna at the Brotherhood's headquarters to hear from the man himself. Upon his first encounter with al-Banna, al-Sabbagh immediately decided to join the Brotherhood. In his memoirs, al-Sabbagh relates this first meeting with the *Murshid* as captivating. Al-Banna, according to al-Sabbagh's portrayal, recited verses from the Quran "as if they had been tailored as solutions to our modern-time problems." And as it seems, it was especially the patriotism of Sabbagh that stimulated his early entrance to the Brotherhood.[36] Soon after joining the *Ikhwan*, al-Sabbagh was introduced to Abdel Rahman al-Sindi, founder and head of the *Niẓām*,[37] which at this time was in its initial phase.[38]

The establishment of the Apparatus, taking place in the late 1930s, came as a result of increasing anti-British sentiment among a segment of the Brothers. As the story of Mashhur and al-Sabbagh epitomizes, these young men came to see armed resistance as the sole means to end occupation. The establishment of the Apparatus was further stimulated by events in neighboring Palestine. *Al-Niẓām* was established at a time when the "Great Arab Revolt"[39] was occurring in Palestine, and its formation as an armed anti-colonial vehicle should therefore be seen in this context as well.[40]

On this account, *al-Niẓām*'s architects devised a syllabus combining religious education with political cultivation and military instructions. This syllabus was intended as a program for the refinement of the Apparatus's members. Its members, young and oftentimes well-educated men, were thought of as an elite force composed of the most zealous and ardent members of the Brotherhood. The initiated member, who was chosen on basis of his deep understanding of the Brotherhood's principles and eagerness to struggle for these principles, had to undergo a period of harsh testing to guarantee his desire to "give up his life for Egypt … and his ability to work inside the Apparatus."[41] Muhammad Mahdi Akef,[42] who became the seventh *Murshid*, recalls how he was introduced to the Apparatus by al-Banna with the aim of his becoming part of an elite group of the Brothers selected to accomplish special missions and to "erase the military-ignorance" of the Egyptian population.[43]

Accordingly, upon joining the Apparatus, the members would undertake a "deep and thorough study of the concept of *jihad* in Islam" merged with heavy physical training and instructions in the use of firearms. The activists would also be instructed in how to distribute pamphlets covertly, communicate clandestinely, and operate underground. This study program, according to al-Sabbagh, was arranged into four sequential stages, each containing a specific subject matter.[44] Secrecy and militancy were in other words the two main hallmarks of *al-Niẓām*.[45]

Erected as a hierarchical formation of tight-knit cells, the Apparatus was headed by a leading committee of the five Brothers: Abdel Rahman al-Sindi, Mustafa Mashhur, Mahmoud Al-Sabbagh, Ahmad Zaki Hassan,[46] and Ahmad Hasanein.[47] The main body of the Apparatus was organized into cells of five members,[48] with a leading Brother commanding each cell. It was a tightly constructed hierarchal order built on an idea of full secrecy and well-defined lines of communication and commands. The structures of the Apparatus had a strong presence in Cairo and some of the larger cities in addition to cities where the British had a strong presence, such as in the Suez Canal Zone.[49] Its formations were organized locally under the direction of the geographic Brotherhood branch. Thus, for illustrative purposes, in 1954[50] the Cairo sector was divided into seven districts, each of which contained a *faṣīl* (platoon) of the Apparatus numbering thirty members. Every *faṣīl* was directed by a senior commander. All seven districts with their platoons were centrally commanded by Ibrahim al-Tayyib, an attorney and middle-ranking member of the Brotherhood. Al-Tayyib was chief of the Apparatus in Cairo, and he was accountable to the Apparatus's head, Yusuf Talat. Instructions from the central leadership descended through this stratified order down to the rank and file of the *Niẓām*.[51]

The social background of most of its militants resembled that of its leaders, that is, young students or men with salaried jobs. With its tightly knit structure and covert nature, the *Niẓām* was kept under wraps, even from Brotherhood members and leaders standing outside its sphere.

As this discussion has illustrated, at least since the late 1930s the Brotherhood had worked toward the establishment of covert structures. These structures, being secret and militant at their core, were designed as a vehicle for anti-British activities and as defensive mechanisms to protect the organization in times of repression. I now turn to the Brotherhood's efforts to recruit followers inside the Egyptian armed forces. Seeing the army as a ready pool for the recruitment of armed and well-organized young patriots, the Brotherhood put a great deal of effort into recruiting young officers. In this way, this historical review points to another aspect of the Brotherhood's covert operations, this time in their attempt to awaken and utilize patriotic feelings within the armed forces.

Recruiting Secretly in the Egyptian Armed Forces

"Unless I hear by 6 pm [the following evening] that Nahhas Pasha has been asked to form a cabinet, His Majesty King Farouk must accept the consequences"—thus was the ultimatum presented by the British ambassador Sir Miles Lampson to King Farouk on February 1, 1942, with British tanks and infantry surrounding the Abdin Palace. Fearing the consequences, the king felt compelled to yield to the ultimatum. This event, representing a culmination of the crisis between the British and King Farouq, came as a result of rising tensions between the British and the king since early 1942. The British, being heavily preoccupied with battles in North Africa, as discussed above, had desired a Wafdist government for some time so as to secure a majority pro-British cabinet in Egypt.[52]

This incident[53] was enormously discrediting for the established political order in Egypt and came to unsettle the trilateral balance of forces: the king, the Wafd,[54] and the British. By bowing to British demands, the king had betrayed the country and exhibited unacceptable cowardice in the eyes of Egyptian nationalists—he had not stood up to a foreign intervention at a crucial moment in Egypt's history. As for the British side of the affair, their intervention in internal political issues had hideously displayed their disregard for Egypt's national sovereignty and autonomy. Yet, if the British and the king were discredited by the incident, the image of the Wafd was in every respect devastated[55] by what was perceived as an acceptance by the party to "come to power by the bayonets of the British."[56]

This particular episode in the history of Egypt, in which the sovereignty of Egypt was desecrated, stands out as a turning point in the lives of many nationalists, who, according to their own narratives, came to distrust the entire political elite and search for alternative ways to deliver Egypt from her misery.[57]

One segment of this discontented generation that began to look for other means to end the British occupation was disillusioned army officers. What they had in common with the remaining nationalists was their resentment toward the British and disillusionment with the political system, both buttressed by the Palace incident.[58]

As a result of the February 4 incident, the discredit of the established political system generally and the Wafd particularly undoubtedly played into the hands of radical anti-establishment organizations such as the *Ikhwan* and the Young Egypt society.[59] The Brotherhood, having been active in recruiting army officers to its ranks since 1940, saw this as an ideal opportunity for increased recruitment, an opportunity they were quick to utilize.[60] The intrinsic desire to change the status quo, get rid of the British, and establish a new order for Egypt was the common ground on which the officers, the Brotherhood, and the other nationalists could stand together side by side.[61] Those young officers, embodying the upwardly mobile middle and lower middle class, represented a social refashioning of the officers corps which had been taking place since 1936. In that crucial year in the history of the Egyptian army, but certainly also in the history of Egypt, the officer corps, formerly a small and closed circle dominated by the sons of elite families with traditions of enrolling into the corps, opened its doors to a wider segment of young recruits. What enabled greater numbers of young, lower-middle-class recruits to enroll was the significant reduction in or complete remission of fees for attending the academy. Hence, these changes brought into the Egyptian officers' corps young men characterized by nationalist sentiment who were experienced in anti-British and anti-establishment activities since their adolescence. The enrollment of "ordinary" Egyptians into the corps furthermore paved the way for this generation to acquire key positions in the army and consequently to take power less than two decades after this refashioning. It was also on account of this reorientation of enrollment criteria, and thereby the remapping of the social structure of the corps, that radical nonelite organizations such as the Brotherhood, the communists, and others acquired the ability to recruit from these hitherto elite institutions.[62]

Thus, from the early 1940s, but more outstandingly after the Abdin Palace "debacle", we can trace a deliberate strategy of the Brotherhood to contact and recruit young army officers to enlist them in its secret structures. The Brotherhood, like other radical groups, offered these discontented officers and young nationalists a platform—and opportunities—for working actively toward the betterment of what they perceived as an unbearable political and national situation in their revered fatherland.

Abdel Mun'im Abdel Rauf was one of those malcontented officers who joined the Brotherhood eager to change the existing state of affairs.[63] Impressed by what he perceived as an *Ikhwani* spirit, Abdel Rauf decided to join the Brotherhood in May 1942 to facilitate the "establishment of a group of army officers who adopt the principles of the Muslim Brotherhood, which is righteousness, strength and freedom, a group that will become a nucleus from which cells will extend to the entire army."[64] Abdel Rauf was assigned to work under the direction of Mahmoud Labib[65] to contact and recruit army officers to the Brotherhood.[66] Abdel Rauf was not the only young officer who was attracted by the Brotherhood at this time: Anwar al-Sadat, who served as president of Egypt from 1970 to 1981, recalls that "many of our [the RCC's] officers sympathised with the Brotherhood." It was the magnetism of nationalism and anti-establishment that attracted young officers to the organization, in Sadat's account.[67]

Gamal Abdel Nasser, who served as president of Egypt from 1956 to 1970, Hussein Hammuda, Hussein Kamal al-Din,[68] Husayn al-Shafi'i,[69] and Khaled Muhyiddin[70] were among the first officers recruited to the Brotherhood, according to Abdel Rauf's memoirs.[71] What started as a core group of officers soon began to grow, indicating the increasing appeal of the Brotherhood among these discontented segments. Pointing to this aspect, al-Sadat claimed the "Wafd had no attraction for the younger generation, being, at bottom, reactionary. The Brotherhood, therefore, absorbed these dynamic and explosive forces." The

Brotherhood was, to al-Sadat and many other officers, "a powerful group, and the only one with which we could safely co-operate in the difficult years which lay ahead of us."[72]

Attracted by the correlated nationalist and Islamic discourse of the Brotherhood, Hammuda recalls how he was introduced to the *Ikhwan* by Abdel Rauf after meeting him at the third infantry battalion in 1943. Lamenting the British occupation of Egypt, the corruption of the political elite, and the exploitation of the wretched people of Egypt, the two officers agreed that "an armed revolution prepared and executed by the faithful young men of the army and the people was the only viable way to rescue the Egyptian people from British occupation and the corrupt royal rule."[73] Hammuda joined the Brotherhood to achieve its goals "in reviving the glory of Islam and liberating the Muslim land from colonization and the implementation of shariʿa in Egypt and the rest of the Muslim world."[74] Joining the Brotherhood, Hammuda began eventually to recruit other officers to its ranks, thereby continuing a calculated attempt by the organization to enlist as large a number of officers as possible.[75]

However, despite the central position played by the Brotherhood in recruiting some officers, not all officers joined the *Ikhwan* on account of a full-hearted faith in its principles. Khaled Muhyiddin, who joined the Brotherhood in 1944, is a good example. Muhyiddin, maintains that what attracted him was not the religious discourse of the Brotherhood but the desire to liberate Egypt from the British. The Brotherhood provided this generation of officers and troops with a structured organization and a strong ideological framework enabling them to achieve their ends.[76] As recalled by Muhyiddin, "the nation needs sacrifice, and the Islamic trend is able to incite the spirit of sacrifice among the young."[77] Thus, while some officers were dedicated *Ikhwan*,[78] others were "just individuals who sought a way, we were not against the Brotherhood, on the contrary, we were with them, but we were not wholeheartedly with them," as Muhyiddin put it.[79] This was the beginning of a pragmatic relationship between these young officers and the Brotherhood, a relationship that built on a shared desire to combat the British and change the status quo in Egypt.[80]

Upon recruitment, the officers were enlisted to the Brotherhood's Special Apparatus, into which they were initiated by taking an oath of allegiance at the home of al-Sindi, the head of the Apparatus.[81] Muhyiddin describes how he and Nasser were brought to an old apartment in the neighborhood of Al-Darb al-Aḥmar in the vicinity of the well-known al-Sayyida Zaynab area in the southern part of Cairo. There, in a dark room with a person they could not recognize,[82] the recruits would take "an oath of allegiance on a Quran and a gun, pledging to obey the General Guide both in times of ease and hardship."[83] The oath introducing the officers to the Apparatus was taken on a gun and a Quran to symbolize the intrinsic correlation between the nationalistic patriotic duties represented by the gun and the obvious religious symbolism of the Quran.

Army officers joining the Brotherhood were organized into military cells (*usar*) falling under the command of the Special Apparatus.[84] These *usar* would organize weekly meetings in which the officers would discuss a variety of subjects, including political questions and religious and cultural issues.[85] When new officers were recruited, they were enlisted in military *usar* with each cell having an appointed commander. By enrolling the officers in cells, the organization could secure its ability to screen new members, instruct them in the ideas of the *Ikhwan*, and retain its ability to oversee their activities.[86]

The description presented in this section is a concise illustration of how the Brotherhood was organizing secret structures among its civilian and military followers at a time of domestic instability on account of the stormy events of the Second World War. All this leaves us with the picture of the Brotherhood as a well-structured organization that had acquired some success in recruiting among different social groups and that built a complex organization throughout Egypt.

Conclusions

To sum up, we can contend that during the war years the Brotherhood established secret structures to address the challenges it was facing in this period of world rupture. Within the framework of political restrictions and exclusion from the formal political scene, the Brotherhood opted for secrecy as a means to continue its activities in society. This became particularly visible with the establishment of the *usar* system, which appeared shortly after the *Ikhwan*'s first experience of arrests and restrictions. The *usar*, being a tight-knit, low-key organizational structure, became crucial to the Brotherhood's ability to endure persecution and continue in times of extensive repression. In addition, this period also witnessed a decentralization of the Brotherhood as a reaction to the repressive reality it faced during the war years. When the *Ikhwan* witnessed a lack of leadership due to al-Banna's forced exile and subsequent arrest in the period of 1941–3, it realized the importance of having clearly defined structures that can function even when the leadership is incarcerated. Accordingly, in contrast to many accounts which concentrate on al-Banna's charismatic leadership and his significance in all Brotherhood matters, I argue that, in these years of restriction, the Brotherhood built a well-structured organization which in subsequent years would account for its ability to endure repression.

The three examples of secrecy presented in this chapter, the *usar*, the Special Apparatus, and the secret cells among army officers, show clearly that the Brotherhood, at least from 1938 to1940, had adopted secrecy as an important feature of its organizational thinking. The construction of the Special Apparatus was also important, as it clearly shows the Brotherhood's intent to fight those whom they perceived as the "British occupation and their stooges." Indeed, during the 1940s, *al-Niẓām* would take the lead in a number of militant attacks against British facilities and personnel, thereby charting the course for later incidents of Brotherhood violence.[87]

2

Forced Underground: The First *Miḥna, 1948–51*

On May 5, 1949, in the leafy suburb of al-Maadi, south of Cairo, a well-organized cell of the Apparatus ambushed a person whom they perceived to be Ibrahim Abdel Hadi, the prime minister of Egypt. The cell, which had been waiting for the right moment and the appropriate spot for the assassination, made the attempt on that Thursday at the beginning of May. Armed with firearms and grenades and positioned in a well-chosen location from where they could observe Abdel Hadi's car, the covert cell opened fire on a car only to realize that the ambushed car belonged to Hamid Juda, head of the Lower House of Parliament. Juda's car was, to their misfortune, the exact same model as Abdel Hadi Pasha's. Ten of the militants were immediately apprehended and prosecuted.[1]

This botched attempt came at the height of an escalating conflict between the Muslim Brotherhood and the Egyptian state. It represented a link in the chain of a protracted tug-of-war that had been costly for both sides and claimed the lives of a prime minister and the founder of the Muslim Brotherhood. It is therefore important to shed light on the Brotherhood's development into a regional actor following the Second World War and their participation in the first Arab–Israeli War to understand the subsequent events that led to its dissolution and this violent development.

The Brotherhood had come out of the Second World War as a stronger organization. The war years had presented the *Ikhwan* with a formative period in which it had experienced growth in membership and branches and an institutional consolidation. Having built clearly defined structures of organization and leadership and formulated an ideology based on an Islamic discourse, the Brotherhood showed a considerable degree of organizational maturation during the war years. As I argued in the preceding chapter, the Brotherhood had developed duality in organization and a sort of blueprint for how to operate secretly and thus to survive persecution. By reorganizing its general framework, it had substituted its early reliance on the strong leading figure of Hasan al-Banna with a well-defined hierarchy and complex structures. As illustrated, these structures, starting from the smallest unit, the *usra*, all the way up to the General Guidance Office, the Brotherhood's executive authority, were constructed on an idea of "keeping the secrets."[2]

Consequently, this chapter starts with a brief presentation of the Brotherhood's attempts to expand the organization across national frontiers. In so doing, I intend to exemplify how the Brotherhood went from being a small and insignificant religious group among many equals during the 1930s to become *the* leading Islamist organization, not only in Egypt but in the Arab world too, less than a decade later. A discussion of this early growth of the *Ikhwan* beyond the borders of Egypt serves to illustrate how the organization looked to these "sister countries" from an early time as valuable sites for widening its outreach and developing its organization. Discussing the Brotherhood's expansion across national frontiers serves another purpose as well. I argue that by taking an active part in the conflict in Palestine, Brotherhood members attained the self-conception of being entitled to engage the "enemy" in armed battle. The clandestine units that had been established during the war years would turn into an armed vanguard of the Brotherhood during the post-war years. This armed faction would for its part engage in a number of armed conflicts and even a regional war, thus paving the way for the Brotherhood's first dissolution and repression, that is, the first *miḥna*, 1948–51.

The discussion of the *Ikhwan*'s role in the Arab–Israeli war therefore serves as an illustration of how events in Palestine militarized segments of the membership, who came to understand and define armed struggle against the British and the Zionists as an obligation of armed *jihad*. However, not limiting their violence to "external enemies," the militants turned their violent conduct to domestic targets, consequently engaging the Egyptian government in a protracted struggle.[3]

By briefly studying these events, we can reach an understanding of the Brotherhood's first critical crisis in which its very survival was on the line. By being dissolved and repressed, and having lost its founder, al-Banna, the Brotherhood faced a new and hitherto untried reality: its very existence hung by a thread. This was, as described in *Ikhwan* narratives, the first serious ordeal (*miḥna*) in the *Ikhwan*'s history. Yet, as this chapter establishes, it was by enduring this first *miḥna* that the Brotherhood further developed a mindset[4] of secrecy and a pattern of working procedures for how to endure waves of repression.

Expanding beyond Egypt's Borders: The First Arab–Israeli war

The Brotherhood's engagement with Palestine as an Islamic and Arab cause goes far back and can be said to represent the Brotherhood's first political engagement. From the early 1930s, Palestine began to acquire a principled position in the writings of al-Banna.[5] In 1931, al-Banna sent a letter to the Mufti of Jerusalem, Hajj Amin al-Husayni, commending him for his "*jihad*" in organizing the first "Muslim Conference," to be held in Jerusalem in December 1931. Directing his words to the conference attendees, al-Banna stressed that the "Brothers will take part in any decisions reached at the conference." He went on by listing a number of suggestions as to what the conference could practically do to assist the Arab cause in Palestine. Al-Banna emphasized "that speeches and protests were of no benefit." What was required, as far as al-Banna was concerned, was tangible work to rescue Palestine. Among the recommendations for such concrete activities was to "establish an Islamic monetary foundation" as an initiative to counter the "Jewish purchase of land." The Brotherhood would be the first to contribute to this foundation in the event the conference heeded their call.[6] To al-Banna, the struggle in Palestine was conceived as embedded in a greater and more far-reaching threat encircling all Muslim nations.[7] The aggression was collective: "They have all united against you, and they have coordinated their words on terrorizing you [the Muslim peoples] and even if they disagree in their greed and differ in their competition, there is one path they agree on and share [the responsibilities] to accomplish, and that is to put an end to Islam and the Muslims."[8]

What had thus begun as an early and insignificant outreach to neighboring Palestine increased during the 1930s when the Brotherhood embarked on a more determined quest to expand its influence in the region. In 1935, a delegation consisting of al-Banna's younger Brother Abdel Rahman, the Brotherhood's general secretary Muhammad As'ad al-Hakim, and the Tunisian nationalist Abdel Aziz al-Tha'albi visited Palestine to meet Amin al-Husayni, the Mufti of Jerusalem. This journey, which continued to adjacent Arab countries such as Syria and Lebanon, symbolized the intent of the *Ikhwan* to reach out and establish the organization in these "sister countries."[9]

Consequently, when the "Great Arab Revolt" broke out in Palestine in 1936, the Brotherhood seized the opportunity to advance the idea of an Islamic obligation to support the Arabs of Palestine and thus to further expand its outreach beyond Egypt's borders.[10] It was from this period that the Brotherhood began to actively engage in the conflict in neighboring Palestine, if we are to believe the *Ikhwan*'s own accounts. By way of illustration, Kamil al-Sharif[11] narrates that the Brotherhood began supplying the Palestinians with "what fell in their hands [in the way] of money and firearms" just prior to the revolt in 1936. Adding to this, al-Sharif relates that Brotherhood volunteers had fought alongside Izz al-Din al-Qassam[12] in northern Palestine in 1935.[13]

This early engagement with the revolt in Palestine is significant, as it shows that some Brothers had considered themselves entitled to engage in a transnational conflict and even take up arms under the banner of "pan-Islamism" as early as 1935–6.[14] Corroborating the above accounts, Martyn Frampton argues that the Brotherhood's participation in and propaganda for the Palestinian cause had been so significant that it made them appear "on the British Radar for the first time."[15] Consequently, from an early time, the Palestinian cause, being a contested and at times militarized issue, offered the Brotherhood an arena through which they could expand their presence across Egypt's borders.

Accordingly, when the revolt came to an end in 1939, Palestine did not evaporate from the *Ikhwan*'s rhetoric, maintaining its key position as an "Islamic" cause. In 1945[16] and as a manifestation of its regional expansion, the Brotherhood began to establish organizational branches in neighboring Arab countries. The establishment of branch organizations in Palestine illustrates this point clearly. Upon setting up its first branch in Palestine,[17] it quickly gained success in mobilizing a noticeable number of followers. According to an intelligence report from the CIA, the organization had obtained a membership of 20,000 adherents within the first six months of its establishment.[18] Pointing to the *Ikhwan* as "reportedly growing" in Palestine, the report singled out Said Ramadan[19] as the driving force behind this development.[20]

However, while greater attention was given to Palestine, a concomitant expansion took place in adjacent countries, highlighting a deliberate strategy by the *Ikhwan*.[21] Having made contacts and endeavoring to disseminate its ideas regionally from the early 1930s, the Brotherhood's expansion became more institutionalized following the war. This institutionalization took place in 1944, when the Brotherhood established a department tasked with "linking the Muslim countries together and reconciling their general policies." Named "The Department for Outreach to the Muslim World," it was established to increase and formalize the Brotherhood's contacts outside Egypt. Among the department's obligations, as formulated in its bylaws, was to "free these nations from every political, economic, military, cultural and social shackle" and to "establish branches of the Brotherhood in the various Arab and Islamic countries."[22] To organize the work of the department, it was divided into three geographical sections, each section operating within a delimited zone. Defining the sectors as the "Near East," the "Far East," and "Europe," the department was designed to reach out to "The Arab and Muslim peoples" and "the countries of East and Central Asia" in addition to Europe.[23] In 1945 to 1948, the Brotherhood founded branches in a number of countries, including Jordan, Syria, Sudan, Lebanon, Iraq, and Palestine. The first branch outside Egypt was surprisingly established in Djibouti, when a Djiboutian man who had visited the Brotherhood's branch during a stay in Egypt returned to Djibouti in 1932 to establish its first branch organization abroad.[24]

This deliberate strategy of the Brotherhood to achieve a transnational character and to expand its presence in the region is significant. As we see in the next section, the organization benefited enormously from this policy of "trans-nationalization," especially in times of restriction in Egypt. In addition, this transnational self-perception, which had started first and foremost with the Brotherhood's adoption of the Palestine case, made the organization enter the "*jihad*" scene from an early stage. This was the case when the *Ikhwan* militarized its discourse and presumably its actions to support the Arab revolt in Palestine from 1936. This engagement with the revolution, and the concurrent militarization of rhetoric and means, was a formative experience in which the ideas of *jihad* for the first time could be connected to a concrete case and realized on the ground. Now we turn to this "*jihad* experience" as it crystalized through the first Arab–Israeli war of 1948–9.

Within a few years of the end of the Second World War, the Muslim Brotherhood had become a regional actor, with branches spread throughout Egypt and in a large part of the Middle East.[25] The Brotherhood had also established a well-structured organization and succeeded in mobilizing a mass following consisting of thousands of active members. On an ideological level, the organization had formulated a program in which its political, social, and cultural visions were phrased as part of a holistic understanding of Islam. The *Ikhwan* had established itself as an anti-colonial organization during the 1940s, and it had established a duality in organization (as discussed in Chapter 1) combining these overt structures with others built on an idea of complete clandestinity. Consequently, when events began to escalate rapidly in Palestine following the Second World War, the Brotherhood was poised to take an active part in them.

The UN General Assembly's adoption of the November 29, 1947, resolution to partition Palestine into two states reignited a conflict that had been underway for some years and made war an imminent outcome. The UN resolution led to a bloody road paved with scattered violent incidents leading to regular war in mid-May 1948 following the evacuation of the British army as planned and the consequent declaration of the state of Israel on May 15, 1948.[26]

The termination of the British mandate for Palestine and the coinciding declaration of an independent state of Israel in great parts of what had heretofore been Mandatory Palestine triggered the intervention of the armies of five Arab countries.[27] However, notwithstanding the unrestrained and powerful rhetoric of the Arab armies and their pronounced goal to "push the Jews to the sea," the Arab forces "were incapable [of] and insufficient for taking over the whole country," as argued by Gelber.[28] What resulted from this "insufficient" Arab intervention in Palestine was a debacle that remains unresolved today. I now turn to the Brotherhood's participation in this regional conflict to illustrate how this particular event forged the self-conception of the *Ikhwan*, paving the way for its showdown with the Egyptian government.

Forecasting the eruption of war in Palestine, Hasan al-Banna announced in October 1947 that the "only way to rescue Palestine is by brute force," proclaiming that the Brotherhood would "marshal 10,000 of its best striving *(mujāhidīn)* members in the service of the Arab League as a first battalion."[29] Defining the struggle in Palestine as an individual responsibility for every Arab and Muslim, he described the decision to divide Palestine as an "opportunity to strive for reward in this life and dignity in the hereafter."[30]

Thomas Mayer has discussed the Brotherhood's overall contribution to the war, arguing that their "words spoke louder than action," adding that it was the *Ikhwan*'s propaganda that "encouraged the military intervention" of the Egyptian army in Palestine.[31] According to Mayer, its contribution lay chiefly in stimulating public awareness rather than engaging directly in the conflict.[32] However, the Brotherhood did more than stimulate public awareness and spread propaganda. While the organization admittedly failed to send the 10,000 men,[33] pledged by al-Banna prior to the war, the war in Palestine was wholeheartedly adopted by *Ikhwan*. As an example, various army officers belonging to the Brotherhood, such as Abdel Munʿim Abdel Rauf, Maʿrouf al-Hadri, Hasan al-Jamal, Hussein Ahmad Hijazi, Mahmoud Abduh, Ahmad Labib al-Turjuman, and Kamal al-Din Hussein, the future Minister of Social Affairs, volunteered to participate in the war, emphasizing the importance attributed to this involvement.[34] In total, the Brotherhood marshaled three *katāʾib* (battalions) to take part in the war. Muhammad Farghali and Kamil al-Sharif commanded the first battalion, which headed toward Breij in today's Gaza. The second *katība* under the leadership of Captain Mahmoud Abduh was sent to Qatana in southern Syria, where it received military training before heading toward Palestine. The third battalion obtained its training in the Huckstep camp in Egypt,[35] whereupon it entered Palestine under the command of the retired Lieutenant colonel Ahmad Abdel Aziz.[36, 37] According to Shadi, 100 were killed while approximately the same number were taken prisoner and some injured.[38] Prior to the war, the *Ikhwan* had established training camps to prepare Egyptian and Palestinian volunteers for the struggle, and by January 1948, together with the Young Egypt movement, they had recruited 500 volunteers.[39] These Brotherhood volunteers participated actively in various battles and took a leading role in some of the encounters, pointing consequently to their resolute intervention on the ground.[40] The organization also used every opportunity to declare its rejection of a ceasefire and to demand the continuation of the fighting.[41] The CIA underlined at the time that al-Banna continued "encouraging the members of the Lebanese and Syrian branches to resume fighting in Palestine" even after the dissolution of his organization in Egypt on December 8, 1948, which clearly indicates his and the Brothers' commitment to the war.[42]

Understanding their participation in Palestine as a *jihad*, many members had acquired experience of armed struggle and participated in a regional war. Death on the battleground had become "a much-coveted honor" for the Brothers, as described by al-Banna.[43] Another "battleground" would also develop in Egypt simultaneously with the struggle in Palestine, leading to a harsh domestic wave of violence in Egypt and strongly implicating the Brotherhood. The following summarizes a few illustrative examples of the *Ikhwan*'s violent conduct during this eventful period. These examples shed light on a crucial development in the history of the Brotherhood, when the Brotherhood, or a faction of Brothers, adopted political assassinations as a legitimate means to fight whom they perceived as the "stooges" of the British. Furthermore, by examining these tumultuous months, we can arrive at an understanding of how the first *miḥna* took place, leading to the *Ikhwan*'s first extensive experience of underground activities.

Toward Reciprocal Violence: Confronting the State

As he was heading to the court of appeal, Ahmad al-Khazindar was shot dead by two young members of the Special Apparatus on March 22, 1948. In the eyes of his assailants, Al-Khazindar, the deputy of the court of appeal in Cairo, had proved himself guilty of treason by convicting a member of the Brotherhood for attacks on British soldiers and sentencing him to prison.[44] The assassination of al-Khazindar triggered a strong reaction and brought forth strong condemnations, but most importantly, it was among the strongest incitements to the government's decision to disband the Brotherhood and try to uproot its presence in society. Consequently, against the background of the violent incidents and political turmoil characterizing 1948, the Brotherhood was dissolved on December 8, 1948.[45] The Saadist government of Fahmy al-Nuqrashi published an explanatory note summarizing the grounds for outlawing the *Ikhwan* organization. The note consisted of thirteen points of charges against the Brotherhood, among which were "its planning" to "overthrow the existing order" since 1942 and a number of violent incidents attributed to the Brotherhood.[46]

Arising directly was a wave of hitherto unparalleled repression of the Brotherhood, seeing 4,000 members detained and others driven underground or exiled to remote areas of Egypt or abroad.[47] Further complicating matters were the closure of Brotherhood headquarters and the confiscation of its funds and estates.[48] The spiraling of events seemed unstoppable and led to reciprocal violence that would reach unprecedented levels.

The violent reprisal for the dissolution of the *Ikhwan* was not long in coming. On December 28, 1948, as Prime Minister Mahmoud Fahmy al-Nuqrashi was entering the Ministry of Interior accompanied by his guards, he was approached by a young man. Wearing a police officer's uniform, the young police officer discharged three fateful rounds at the prime minister, leaving him severely wounded. The assassin was in fact Abdel Majid Ahmad Hasan, a 21-year-old student at the veterinary school and a member of the Muslim Brotherhood's *al-Niẓām al-Khāṣ*. The Apparatus had handpicked Abdel Majid to accomplish the undertaking of liquidating the prime minister in "his own den." According to the Apparatus's commanders, al-Nuqrashi Pasha had proved himself guilty of national perfidy and disloyalty toward the Palestinian cause and had committed an aggression "against Islam by dissolving the Muslim Brotherhood." For all of these, he had to be killed. Ahmad Adel Kamal, who at the time was a high-ranking commander of the Apparatus, recalls that the plan originally involved the subsequent assassination of Ibrahim Abdel Hadi and Abdel Rahman Ammar when they showed up at the crime scene. The latter part of the plan was aborted.[49]

The death of al-Nuqrashi Pasha paved the way for an increase in the spiraling violence. When Ibrahim Abdel Hadi Pasha, al-Nuqrashi's party colleague and former head of the Royal Cabinet, succeeded al-Nuqrashi, he swore to "stamp" out the Ikhwan and "complete their suppression."[50] And in what can best be described as another episode in this blood-soaked development of events, Hasan al-Banna was shot dead on the evening of Saturday, February 12, 1949, in front of the YMMA headquarters.[51] The passing of al-Banna was followed by a continuation of reciprocal violent incidents that undoubtedly took a toll on the *Ikhwan* and Egyptian society at large.

Furthermore, what evolved from the dissolution of the Brotherhood and the subsequent assassinations of Prime Minister al-Nuqrashi Pasha and al-Banna was a deepened transformation of the Brotherhood toward clandestinity, and a consequent radicalization of sections of the membership. Accordingly, before moving on to discuss the Brotherhood's secrecy during this first "ordeal" I highlight one example that illustrates very clearly how a segment of the Brotherhood came to understand their showdown with the Egyptian government as a justified battle against the "enemies of Islam." In this process, some Brothers explicitly justified the killing of al-Nuqrashi and similar events as a *jihad* sanctioned against those who were seen as in opposition to Islam.[52]

Yusuf al-Qaradawi, the renowned Azhari scholar,[53] recalled in his memoirs that the dissolution of the Ikhwan was perceived at the time to have been a result of Western pressures on al-Nuqrashi.[54] "We the young and students [of the Brotherhood] welcomed the assassination of al-Nuqrashi with relief and optimism" is how al-Qaradawi described the contemporaneous reception of the assassination of the prime minister, even though in retrospect he dissociated himself from political assassinations and violence. Al-Nuqrashi Pasha had done wrong by disbanding the Brotherhood, and he had to pay for this unforgivable mistake, according to the sentiments of this generation.[55]

Taking these attitudes into consideration, we can maintain that they constituted an early resemblance of the worldview put forward by Sayyid Qutb during his prison years. The perception of the state as an "enemy of Islam" would become a core of Qutb's dealing with the state, just as it was for these young Brothers.

Another immediate outcome of this first *miḥna* was the Brotherhood's first real experience of widespread secrecy as a means to survive persecution. I now turn to this particular experience to demonstrate how the organization reacted to the repression it endured following its dissolution.

Going Underground 1948–51

The claim of this chapter thus far has been that the momentous events of late 1948 represented a conspicuous instance of political repression directed toward the *Ikhwan* which led to a militarization of a current of Brothers.[56] Taking the form of the assassination of Egyptian political figures and the concurrent acceptance of such assassinations, this development was closely tied to the domestic and regional situation, which was strongly affected by war in neighboring Palestine.

Analyzing this first ordeal of the Brotherhood, Zollner argued that "the established network of personal relations saved the Brotherhood from disappearing into public oblivion. Political and personal relations spun in the 1940s were vital for the continuation of the Society underground."[57]

Whereas I agree that these personal networks undoubtedly played a vital role in sustaining the *Ikhwan*'s existence, I maintain that the organizational structures and the idea of secrecy integrated into these structures played an even more critical role in the Brotherhood's continuation and survival. To demonstrate this, I highlight different examples of continuation representing different patterns of how the Brotherhood reacted to this intensifying state repression.[58] Accordingly, I highlight aspects representing continuation of hierarchy, organizational structures, personal links, and international networks demonstrating how the Brotherhood sustained its existence in society. It is important to keep in mind that this section remains a sketch. I do not provide an exhaustive presentation of all the examples of Brotherhood activism during this period.

In keeping with Erickson's definition of "Secret Societies," such societies are required to involve "secret activities" and have "persisting structures," that is, to compose a "society" it is necessary that these structures and activities are not a "one-time collaboration" but include persistence. Hierarchy, Erickson tells us, is not a necessity of secret societies but can be one form of structure, and when hierarchical, the rigidity of this hierarchy can vary in degree.[59] In the case of the Brotherhood, we observe a continuation[60] of hierarchy, but not in a rigid way. One such example of this persisting hierarchy comes from the account of Ahmad Hasan al-Baqouri, one of Hasan al-Banna's closest associates. Al-Baqouri, upon the disbanding of the Brotherhood organization, was selected by al-Banna as his proxy and tasked with taking the reins of the organization while the *Murshid* was underground. Al-Banna, who was planning to stay out of sight to avoid persecution, denied leaving the Brotherhood leaderless, which is why he chose al-Baqouri as a temporary caretaker during his absence.[61]

I argue that the maximization of security[62] was the primary motive of the Brotherhood in these years and would become more so with every wave of harsh persecution. As an example of this, we learn from the *Ikhwani* accounts that the hierarchical structuring, as a modus operandi, continued when the Brotherhood leadership went underground as a reaction to repression. Thus, with a view to consolidate the organization's activities and presence in society, a hierarchical dimension operated within the Brotherhood. As an example, provincial representatives, consisting of lower-ranking Brotherhood activists, arrived in Cairo to meet with the interim leadership to discuss and plan future activities of the organization. Through these low-key activities and covert methods, the Brotherhood became able to sustain hierarchical ways of operation and maintained a line of command and action. Such meetings were held in secrecy as a means to maximize security, we are told by some of the Brothers who participated in them. And when leading members of the Brotherhood were arrested, others undertook the responsibility of the organization, thereby guaranteeing a degree of continuity.[63]

This is consistent with the development of the Brotherhood's structures in the 1940s as presented in the preceding chapter. For example, as previously highlighted, the lines of communication between the *usar* and the local branch organizations (*shuʿab*) were designed as a way of decentralizing the low-key activities of the members and enabling the organization to continue its undertakings in the event the upper echelons of the Brotherhood were obstructed from leading the organization. This came in 1943, in a period when the *Ikhwan* was experiencing the first restrictions and presumably as a direct response to these restrictions. This is also consistent with what al-Anani has described as a concomitant dynamic centralization and decentralization of the organization. As stated by al-Anani, while the *Ikhwan*'s hierarchical structures are centralized, a decentralization characterizes its extensive network, which offers the "local branches and offices" a freedom in "running the movement's activities according to current circumstances and needs without needing to confer with the leadership."[64] Thus, this dynamic continuation of hierarchy serves as an example of the organizational thinking which can be traced back to the formative period of the Brotherhood.

Interestingly, these methods were not confined to Brothers outside prisons, but were likewise adopted by activists in detention camps where we can observe a continuation of hierarchy and ongoing activities. We learn from al-Qaradawi, who was interned at al-Tur, that the Brotherhood members inside the prison camp established a hierarchical organization to manage their activism and coordinate their relationships. The camp *cum* detention center housed a large number of Brotherhood detainees who had been arrested in major parts of Egypt.[65] Al-Bahi al-Khouli, a senior member of the Brotherhood, was chosen as head of the Brothers in al-Tur, and when he was transferred to Cairo after a short period of detention, the inmates appointed Muhammad al-Ghazali as al-Khouli's successor. In so doing, the *Ikhwan* could regulate member behavior in prison and ensure that the members continued their affiliation with the Brotherhood. Furthermore, by appointing a leadership in every prison, they could streamline the activities of the members, represent the Brotherhood collectively vis-à-vis the prison authorities, and ensure their continuing communication with Brothers outside the prisons.[66] And while the hierarchy continued both inside and outside the prison walls, so did the Brotherhood's activism, to which I now turn.

British ambassador Sir Ronald H. Campbell pointed to this fact shortly after al-Banna's death. In his report, from March 1949, Campbell drew attention to "the high degree of internal organisation which the Moslem Brethren Society had attained, and which to some extent has so far survived the murder of the leader."[67] And as the following discussion shows, the Brotherhood was far from terminated as a result of al-Banna's demise and the concurrent repression of the Brothers and dissolution of the organization.

As an example of this incessant activity, Hasan al-Ashmawi, a jurist and one of the leading members in this period, narrates that prominent members of the *Ikhwan*, such as Munir al-Dilla,[68] Salih Abu Ruqayiq, and Abd al-Qader Hilmi, held regular meetings in Cairo to discuss and plan the Brotherhood's activities throughout this phase, thereby filling the gap left by al-Banna.[69] Al-Baqouri illustrates this continuity very clearly. In his memoirs, we are told that, despite the restrictions on the Brotherhood's freedom, he continued to meet with fellow *Ikhwan* to discuss the appropriate way of dealing with the crisis.[70] A similar account is offered by al-Sisi, who recalls that members of the organization continued to meet in mosques of the Islamist association *Anṣār al-Sunna*, where state shadowing was ineffective. In the mosques, meetings were held between leading members of the Brotherhood and representatives from the provinces to sustain a line of communication and orders.[71] As pointed to by Aminzade and Perry, religious institutions like mosques limit the state's ability to repress political activism and provide politico-religious movements with some shelter to avoid surveillance.[72]

Another way of overcoming security measures was by including the women's branch of the *Ikhwan* organization in "secret" activities. Up until this time, the "section of the Muslim Sisters" had been apolitical, limiting its undertakings to religious and social activities. However, this would now change because of the first *miḥna*, and the female members would henceforth acquire a vital role in carrying on the Brotherhood's activities in times of repression. This change is exemplified in the case of Amal al-Ashmawi, sister of Hasan al-Ashmawi and wife of Munir al-Dilla, both senior members of the Brotherhood. The severe treatment of arrested individuals had led to a situation where "families of internees often suffered financial hardship," according to Vatikiotis.[73] As a consequence, al-Ashmawi began organizing campaigns to support these families and began collecting money, which was distributed among the families of Brotherhood activists. Even more crucial, al-Ashmawi offered Brotherhood members a site where they could meet and discuss organizational issues.[74] This endeavor became institutionalized in the Sisterhood following the persecution, with official structures constructed to fulfill the task of sustaining the Brotherhood and supporting the bereaved families.[75] This continuation of various aspects of the Brotherhood's activities, though in secrecy, was also corroborated by contemporary British and American reports.[76]

Trying to clarify the reasons for this difficulty in wiping out the Brotherhood, a British report pointed to the *Ikhwan*'s numerical strength and its organizational complexity as the main grounds: "[T]here were 6 or 7 hundred thousand members and it would be necessary to arrest at least 5 or 6 thousand before the movement could in any way be considered as having been partly broken." He therefore concluded that this offensive against the Brotherhood felt "like looking for a nail in soft mud."[77] Sir Ronald Campbell, the British ambassador to Cairo, underscored in March 1949 that "[i]t was not to be expected that the issue of a proclamation dissolving the Moslem Brethren Society would *ipso facto*[78] ensure the cessation of subversive activity and planning by its more fanatical and extreme members."[79] For Ambassador Campbell, there was no doubt that the Brotherhood would continue its activities clandestinely. He reported, for instance, that the organization had had "a secret wireless transmitter stated to have been operated by Moslem Brethren for the purpose of communicating instructions and propaganda to their provincial branches, and perhaps also to branches outside Egypt." According to him, this "is an illustration of a determination on the part of some at least of the late Hassan al Banna's followers to continue their association and activities clandestinely."[80] This impression of continued activism was buttressed by the CIA. A report dated January 14, 1949, a month prior to al-Banna's assassination, asserted that "countermeasures" taken by the police against the Brotherhood had been "largely ineffective."[81] According to this report, the *Ikhwan* members continued their activities, and the funds of the organization were sustained through voluntary subscriptions, collection of jewelry from members, and contributions from labor syndicates.[82]

However, while this first "ordeal" undoubtedly resulted in heavy restrictions for the organization, from Brotherhood accounts we can also observe opportunities arising in such periods of repression. I therefore point to some of the opportunities that evolved out of this phase of repression to nuance my discussion of the first *miḥna*. However, in taking this position, I am by no means attempting to idealize repression or the Brotherhood's experience of repression, but I suggest that a discussion of the opportunities that emerge from such periods is vital to understanding the *Ikhwan*'s ability to endure.

One such illustrative example was the opportunities that emanated from the detention camps that housed large numbers of Brothers. We learn from a number of Brotherhood members that these camps, despite the difficulties naturally linked to them, presented the inmates with windows of opportunity. Al-Qaradawi, one of those detained in a camp in al-Tur in southern Sinai, recalls that as a consequence of the large number of arrested *Ikhwan*, the detention cells were overcrowded. Housing members of the Brotherhood from every corner of Egypt, the camp created a sense of communality among the incarcerated Brothers and brought them closer together. With seven or eight Brothers in each cell, al-Qaradawi recounts that they supported and amused each other, and even established courses to educate fellow Brothers in Quranic verses and other religious subjects, thereby making a "*minḥa*" (gift) out of the "*miḥna*" (ordeal). He also points to the fact that many Brothers became familiar with other members they had never met before, as the detention camp huddled *Ikhwan* together from various geographical areas and from different age groups.[83] This account is substantiated by Duh, who narrates that the many Brothers concentrated in the same camp became acquainted with each other and "lived as one big family" where they "studied aspects of [their] religion and *da'wa*."[84] Al-Tilmisani,[85] who became the Ikhwan's third *Murshid* in 1973, recollects that the Brotherhood inmates continued to organize "Tuesday Seminars," which had been the practice of al-Banna every Tuesday prior to his death.[86] Such accounts figure in abundance in *Ikhwan* memoirs, pointing to a continuation of activities inside the prisons. In other words, by concentrating many Brothers in the same place, the authorities unintentionally came to create ties among them.

In the biography of Fathi Osman,[87] authored by his daughter Ghada Osman, we find a similar account, but this time for Brothers outside detention. Based on her late father's experience, Osman describes how the government's attempts to scatter the organization by reposting its members to distant areas like Aswan in Upper Egypt "fostered new relations between them. These Muslim Brothers, often previously strangers to each other, now roomed together, with three or four to an apartment, creating a surrogate family and a new community."[88] Similar accounts are also offered by a number of Brotherhood members who underwent the same experience. Shadi, a police officer and high-ranking Brother, relates that he was transferred to Aswan, where he became acquainted with the "trustworthy missionary Fathi Osman." There in the remote Aswan, Shadi,

Osman, and numerous other Brothers created stronger links and continued their Brotherhood activities, according to their accounts.[89]

Another "window of opportunity" that presented itself in this period of expanding restrictions and repression[90] was the increasing transnationalization of the Brotherhood. Alongside the dissolution, the government had simultaneously issued an official declaration closing the organization's branch headquarters, seizing its money, confiscating publications and documents authored by its members, and prohibiting any Brotherhood gathering consisting of five members or more.[91] In response, an unknown number of Brotherhood members managed to escape Egypt to continue their activities from abroad. Some of these early exiles fled to Libya, where they were granted asylum by the Senussi order.[92] In 1949, and probably as a result of this interaction between Brotherhood exiles and Libyan society, the American Consul to Tripoli in Libya reported that "Moslem Brotherhood ideas and techniques are gaining importance" in the country.[93] According to al-Sisi, who was familiar with some of the Brothers who fled to Libya, they spent a period of time in neighboring Libya before they continued their journey of exile to Europe and, more particularly, London, where they established a presence.[94] British mandarins also reported growing *Ikhwan* activities in the Sudan at this time, which indicates that this searching for opportunities was crucial at this point.[95]

The Levant was also a destination for the Brotherhood's exiles in this period. At the end of December 1948, the CIA reported that more than ten members of the Egyptian Brotherhood had arrived in Beirut from Egypt, where they met with representatives of Islamic organizations in Lebanon and the Mufti of Lebanon, Muhammad Tawfiq Khalid. On January 5, 1949, meetings were reportedly held in Tripoli in northern Lebanon with representatives of the Islamist organizations there and with members of the Syrian Branch of the Brotherhood, among them Muhammad al-Mubarak, a well-known leader of the Brothers in Syria.[96] Pointing to the importance of this transnational aspect in ensuring the Brotherhood's survival, G. J. Jenkins noted, "If Egypt was the only country that had members of the Ikhwan it might be easier" to suppress the Brotherhood.[97]

Conclusions

Simmel describes secrecy as a "correlate of despotism and of police control. It acts as protection alike [*sic*] of defense and of offense against the violent pressure of central power."[98] With this understanding in mind, I have argued that the secrecy of the Brotherhood, beginning as a defensive mechanism, came to have a variety of effects on the organization and its trajectory. When the persecution began, first with the dissolution of the Brotherhood and then with the assassination of its leader and the detention of its active members, the structures of the organization were to a large degree transformed into secrecy in an attempt to survive persecution. This period has gone down in the *Ikhwan*'s own historical narrative as the first *miḥna*, in which a great deal of injustice and persecution was done to them.

As a well-organized and highly structured mass organization with grassroots structures, the *Ikhwan* did not merely disappear when persecuted but continued its activities covertly. Thus, this period revealed the "flouting of state authority and power by the Ikhwan," as underlined by Vatikiotis.[99] When the persecution peaked with the assassination of Hasan al-Banna and the arrest of an estimated 4,000 members of the organization,[100] the Brotherhood defied the Egyptian state, engaging it in an armed struggle. This was illustrated by the violent campaign executed by a fringe of Brothers in what they perceived as a *jihad* against an anti-Islamic regime. This early experience of armed struggle against domestic governments indicates that the idea of *jihad* against fellow Muslims was not merely invented by Qutb. As this chapter has shown, it in fact existed among some Brothers as early as 1948.

On July 25, 1949, Ibrahim Abdel Hadi left office, to be succeeded by the independent Hussein Sirri Pasha, who formed a caretaker government of all major parties to prepare for elections at the beginning of 1950. In January 1950, the Wafd was re-elected, with Mustafa al-Nahhas as prime minister, marking the way out of this first *miḥna*.[101] During the Saadist period, the Brotherhood had stood trial for different incidents,[102] such as planning the overthrow of the political order.[103] While the court found evidence of a "criminal conspiracy for murder and destruction," it acquitted the Brotherhood of the charges concerning an alleged conspiracy to overthrow the regime.[104] In his final statements, the judge announced that those accused had had "nationalist incentives, as sons of an occupied nation" and had been under the influence of the "Palestine catastrophe," declaring that the court "commends the principles of the Brotherhood." At a later date, this same judge announced, "I was prosecuting them, now I am one of them."[105]

The change of government and the acquittal on charges regarding a conspiracy to overthrow the regime marked the end of one period and the beginning of another in the history of the Brotherhood. What had forced the organization underground was now over, and the Brotherhood could return to the surface, demonstrating that it had not vanished due to repression.

3

A New Era: Hasan al-Hudaybi and the Muslim Brotherhood

Upon his appointment as *Murshid*, Hasan Ismail al-Hudaybi (1891–1973) formally announced that one of his main tasks would be to rid the *Ikhwan* of secrecy and militancy. As a conservative judge, a respected public figure, and an experienced man of sixty years of age, al-Hudaybi seemed the perfect candidate to fulfill this task. From a Western point of view, also, al-Hudaybi seemed promising. As someone representing conservatism and moderation, al-Hudaybi was looked upon as a person whose "first object appears to be to show that the Brotherhood is respectable" and as a man "of different type from the fanatical Hassan al Banna." This seemed to be the view of both American and British diplomats.[1] However, al-Hudaybi's task proved more complicated than he may have expected.

When al-Hudaybi was chosen as second *Murshid* in 1950, ending a leaderless period that had lasted for about two years, it soon became obvious that the "new Hasan" lacked the charisma and oratory skills of his predecessor, and, when compared to al-Banna, he seemed quite the opposite. Accordingly, when al-Hudaybi initially declared that he intended to rid the Brotherhood of its militancy and secrecy, a strong faction of the organization stood up to him. This chapter will therefore begin with a discussion of this change in leadership and strategy as personified in al-Hudaybi in his leadership of the *Ikhwan*. Omar Ashour has argued that al-Hudaybi "initially started a process that aimed to completely dismantle the SA [Special Apparatus]" but that upon facing "several obstacles" he "pragmatically changed the objective into the reformation, rather than the dismantling of the SA."[2] While I concur in understanding al-Hudaybi's initial task as ridding the *Ikhwan* of militancy, I argue that the change of heart by al-Hudaybi with regard to militancy and secrecy should be understood in the context of the continuing British presence in Egypt and the heightened anti-colonial struggle that emerged in the Canal Zone in late 1951, known as the War in the Canal Zone. Accordingly, by studying the engagement of the Brotherhood in the Canal Zone, I will critically assess the historical events that altered al-Hudaybi's initial objection to secrecy and militancy. What role did the War in the Canal Zone play in al-Hudaybi's change of heart?

A historical discussion of al-Hudaybi's early leadership and the Brotherhood's engagement in the Canal Zone is vital to an understanding of the history of the *Ikhwan* and their subsequent relations to the military regime in the 1950s. I argue that the continuation of the Brotherhood's secret structures, and particularly the Special Apparatus, which epitomized the militant idea of the *Ikhwan*, came to play a crucial role in intensifying the conflict between the military junta and the Brotherhood in 1954. In so arguing, I contend that the Brotherhood went into the postcolonial era as a militant organization that was prepared to use violence and had in fact constructed the necessary structures for the application of nationalist violence.

Hasan al-Hudaybi—A New Direction?

With the loss of Hasan al-Banna in February 1949, the Brotherhood was left without a leader to fill the gap left by the Brotherhood's founder. As we saw in the previous chapter, the organization had survived during the first *miḥna* on account of its highly structured organization and due to its hierarchical dimension, which saw different leading members assume responsibility to secure its continuity. However, the loss of al-Banna undoubtedly marked a leadership crisis in the ranks of the Brotherhood which lasted for two years. Hamed Abul Nasr, the fourth *Murshid*, describes the period that followed al-Banna's death as an "uneasy sea of confusion."[3]

Accordingly, the appointment of a new leader acquired high-priority status for the *Ikhwan* as soon as the political change had taken place with the dismissal of Abdel Hadi's government in late 1949 and the subsequent liberalization, although limited, that occurred with the election of the Wafd in early 1950.[4] Against this backdrop, four competing blocs evolved in the Brotherhood, each represented by a senior Brother:[5] (1) Abdel Rahman al-Banna[6], Hasan al-Banna's younger Brother, who claimed leadership by inheritance—his legitimacy stemmed from his blood relation to Hasan al-Banna and his early affiliation with the *Ikhwan*;[7] (2) al-Baqouri, a highly respected Azhari scholar and the de facto leader of the Brotherhood in the period of 1949–51, having been chosen as interim caretaker of the *Ikhwan* by al-Banna;[8] (3) Abdel Hakim 'Abdin, Hasan al-Banna's brother-in-law and the general secretary of the Brotherhood;[9] and (4) Salih Ashmawi, the deputy of the Brotherhood, editor in chief of al-Daʿwa magazine, and a close ally of the Special Apparatus.[10]

All vying for the position, the contenders could not agree on which of them to choose as *Murshid*, thus resulting in an increasing rivalry that threatened the very coherence of the *Ikhwan*. The perception at the time was that the appointment of one of the nominees, without the endorsement of his rivals, would split the organization.[11]

In an attempt to ease this tension, a fifth camp therefore evolved, consisting of upper-class Brothers headed by Munir al-Dilla. Al-Dilla's star had risen following the first *miḥna*, as he, his wife Amal al-Ashmawi, and his brother-in-law Hasan al-Ashmawi had played a central role in directing the activities of the Brotherhood and supporting the families of arrested Brothers.[12] This fifth camp, representing a camp of compromise, looked upon Hasan al-Hudaybi as a solution that could serve the *Ikhwan* in different ways. On the one hand, by picking al-Hudaybi as heir, the Brotherhood could internally reach a settlement without risking a split in its ranks.[13] On the other hand, as a respectable judge for more than twenty-five years who had served on the highest court in Egypt, the cessation court, and a respected figure with connections to the upper echelons of society, al-Hudaybi could help restore the good reputation of the *Ikhwan* after a period of political crisis in which they had been singled out as a terrorist organization.[14]

When first approached by senior Brothers in early 1950, al-Hudaybi refused the offer. With no experience in leading a mass organization, he cited bad health as one excuse and the disagreements between the leading figures in the Brotherhood as another.[15] However, sometime after this first approach and on the heels of a campaign to convince him to take over the position,[16] al-Hudaybi was informally[17] appointed the successor to al-Banna, thereby becoming the *Ikhwan*'s second general guide. Al-Hudaybi's appointment was made official on October 19, 1951, after a period of keeping it unofficial and concealed, as he was still serving as judge.

After his appointment, al-Hudaybi did not immediately convince the *Ikhwan*'s rank and file of his ability to lead their organization. He seemed to be diametrically opposed to al-Banna. While al-Banna had resembled many of his Brothers—from a newly urbanized, middle-class background, nonelite, and with a remarkable talent to address the masses[18]—al-Hudaybi was just the opposite. An upper-class judge, affiliated with the country's political elite and the palace[19] and characterized by introverted forms of behavior, al-Hudaybi lacked the very qualities that had distinguished his predecessor and made him a leader of men; in other words, the very attributes he had been chosen for became his initial disadvantages. Introverted in his outlook and behavior, al-Hudaybi "listened more than he spoke," and it was one of the difficulties that the Brotherhood members came across at the outset of his leadership.[20] He represented the classical bourgeois, which derived its autonomy from being sovereign, rational, tempered, and introverted.[21] Even more disadvantageous to al-Hudaybi was the fact that he had not been a regular member of the *Ikhwan*. The fact that he was looked upon by a majority of the Brothers as an outsider and a newcomer to the organization further weakened al-Hudaybi's position in the Brotherhood's ranks. Accordingly, at an early stage of his appointment, the British expected al-Hudaybi to be "a mere figurehead" who was "neither an impressive figure nor a particularly good speaker."[22]

Thus, al-Hudaybi, a conservative judge with no experience in mass politics, had acquired the leadership of a mass organization that was still hovering between an existence of secrecy and nonsecrecy.[23] Therefore, the senior Brothers who had fancied themselves as leaders of the *Ikhwan* prior to al-Hudaybi's appointment considered his role to be merely symbolic, leaving day-to-day administration of the Brotherhood to the already existing structures of leadership.[24]

However, shortly after his appointment, we observe a clear attempt on al-Hudaybi's part to consolidate his hold on the organization, which points to an early confusion about what role the new *Murshid* should play. This consolidation that al-Hudaybi attempted to push through was closely connected to the intention that he and his associates[25] had of moving the *Ikhwan* away from militancy and secrecy. Against this background, al-Hudaybi set about restructuring the leadership of the *Ikhwan*, effectively bringing it under his control. For example, he appointed Abdel Qader Uda as his new deputy, depriving Saleh Ashmawi of his hitherto powerful position as deputy.[26] This reshuffle in the higher levels of the *Ikhwan* by the new *Murshid* symbolized a clear challenge to the more radical faction of the Brothers, embodied in the Special Apparatus and its close ally and patron Saleh Ashmawi.[27] Uda, like al-Hudaybi, was a newcomer to the *Ikhwan* and shared both social background and the profession of judge with the new leader. The replacement of the radical Ashmawi with a conservative judge demonstrates the course al-Hudaybi had opted for at this early stage of his leadership. To further consolidate his influence, the *Murshid* demanded the appointment of a new General Guidance Office,[28] from which senior names were excluded, while close associates of his were elevated to key positions. As a case in point, Munir al-Dilla, who had played a key role in appointing al-Hudaybi as leader, became treasurer of the organization and a member of the Guidance Office. Remarkably, al-Dilla was also an upper-class magistrate, which implies that al-Hudaybi was attempting to change the social makeup of the *Ikhwan*'s highest leadership.[29]

What al-Hudaybi and his associates had in common was their disapproval of the Special Apparatus and their relative moderation in comparison to the radical faction endorsing the Apparatus and its ideas. Al-Hudaybi and many of his close associates saw the Apparatus at this particular stage[30] as the main reason why the Brotherhood had been dissolved and why al-Banna had been killed. Hence, I argue that al-Hudaybi's appointment, and his early attempts to restructure the leadership, came to deepen the rifts between different leading groups of the *Ikhwan*. In this regard, his early intention to dissolve the Special Apparatus and appoint newcomers to the leadership of the *Ikhwan* was considered especially high-handed and authoritarian, and thus explains why he faced strong opposition.[31]

Farid Abdel Khaleq, a close associate of al-Hudaybi, offered such an account. Abdel Khaleq maintains that the Special Apparatus had harmed the Brotherhood and through its mistakes had been partly responsible for the death of al-Banna. Abdel Khaleq added that he "as a member of the mainstream Brotherhood, like Hasan al-Banna before his death and Hasan al-Hudaybi as his successor, arrived at the conclusion that the Apparatus was inappropriate and secret activism should not exist."[32] Muhammad Khamis Hamida, deputy of the Brotherhood in 1954, offered a similar explanation. Testifying before Jamal Salem's[33] "people's court" in November 1954, he claimed that upon al-Hudaybi's appointment it was deliberately decided to disband the Apparatus. The reason for this, as explained by Hamida, was that the Apparatus had created a dichotomy inside the organization and in its decision-making mechanisms. So, in order to secure a streamlined leadership and cohesiveness, it was decided to dissolve the Apparatus.[34]

Consequently, according to statements of senior Brothers who were close to the *Ikhwan*'s decision-making at this time, shortly after his appointment, al-Hudaybi became determined to abolish the most potent structure of the organization, that is, the Special Apparatus. But as underlined by Hamida, this was no easy task considering that a sizable group inside the Brotherhood conceived of the Apparatus and its members as representatives of the obligation of *jihad*, an obligation the *Ikhwan* could not abandon.[35]

In February 1951, a few months after al-Hudaybi's appointment, it was noted that a split had occurred in the upper echelons of the Brotherhood, leading to two competing factions in the Guidance Office. This "definite split," as it is described by the CIA, occurred between Saleh Ashmawi and the new Guide.[36] This conflict, which took place shortly after al-Hudaybi's appointment, was unquestionably due to his initial desire to rid the Brotherhood of the Apparatus and his power struggle with its patron, al-Ashmawi. For the CIA, there were no doubts that two diverging factions existed in the Brotherhood, with al-Hudaybi, "the judge," looked upon as a moderating but still weak factor, pitted against the "fanatical" Ashmawi and the current he represented.[37]

Shortly after assuming leadership of the Ikhwan, al-Hudaybi set about a process of moving the Brotherhood away from militancy and radicalism, so my contention. There was a lack of consensus regarding this step, which led to internal divisions at various levels of the membership. By questioning the necessity of the Apparatus, al-Hudaybi ran into fierce resistance from a powerful faction in the Brotherhood. He had made it clear that "there is no secrecy in the service of God" and "there is no secrecy in the Message and no terrorism in religion"[38] in an explicit challenge to the Apparatus. More than that, the pro-Hudaybi faction perceived the Apparatus as an obstruction to a unified leadership of the entire Brotherhood. As long as the Apparatus existed, it would point to a duality (*izdiwājiya*) in the Brotherhood's ranks and leadership. Thus, the dissolution of the Apparatus was necessary in order to streamline the leadership, so ran the argument of the anti-Apparatus faction.[39] This in turn prompted opposition from those who considered themselves representatives of this Apparatus, which they deemed a vehicle through which the *jihad* obligation is fulfilled.[40] In keeping with their position, the very raison d'être of the Apparatus, that is, the occupation of Egypt, remained unchanged and hence the Apparatus continued to be a necessity.[41]

If al-Hudaybi was determined to dissolve the Apparatus shortly after his appointment, a decisive event took place which came to affect the political situation in Egypt, but also influence the decision of al-Hudaybi. That was the War in the Canal Zone.

The *Ikhwan* and the Canal War

Al-Hudaybi's well-known slogan "no secrecy in Islam"[42] signified the new Murshid's scheme to direct his organization away from secrecy and militancy. But as the leader of a nationalistic organization with a history of militant struggle against the British, the Zionists in Palestine, and at times against the Egyptian government, al-Hudaybi was soon to learn that the odds were against him. Violence at this point was not, however, an exclusive hallmark of the *Ikhwan* but characterized a trait of pre-independence Egypt. This trait was strongly influenced by the British occupation of Egypt. As pointed to by the British ambassador Sir Ralph Stevenson, the violent incidents which involved the Brotherhood were "symptomatic of a malaise deep-rooted in Egyptian life and politics. Every Egyptian political party has either used or connived at the use of violence for political ends."[43] In other words, it was a "signature" of the historical context and the spirit of the times.

Following a concise presentation of the historical events that led to what came to be known as the Canal War, I discuss how this war blocked al-Hudaybi's early efforts to dismiss violence, putting the *Ikhwan* on a path of direct confrontation with the British forces in Egypt and thereby escalating the *Ikhwan*'s self-perception as a group responsible for the execution of the *jihad* obligation. To do so, I discuss the Brotherhood's engagement in these crucial events and the ideological underpinnings of this participation. In concluding, I ask the question: Was al-Hudaybi himself won over by the *jihad* approach dominating the Brotherhood at this stage? In addition, the presentation of the crucial events that took place in this period, and more particularly my discussion of the role played by the Brotherhood, is significant for our understanding of the history of the *Ikhwan*. While these events that saw the Egyptian nationalists engage the British troops in guerilla-warfare were of pivotal importance in the history of Egypt and the Brotherhood, scholarly accounts of the role played by the *Ikhwan* are inadequate. The war, I argue, thwarted al-Hudaybi's initial idea of "dismissing militancy," causing the new *Murshid* to instead make it his intention to control and direct the secrecy and militancy of the *Ikhwan*.

Nationalism and the desire to rid Egypt of British colonization continued to characterize Egyptian politics, as had been the case almost since the occupation of the land on the Nile in 1882. Since being elected in January 1950, the Wafd had based its political program on achieving a solution to the national question, which ultimately meant the end of British occupation.[44] However, as the months went on without any notable results, popular sentiment became characterized by growing exasperation. This had become evident since early 1951, when nationalist fever had intensified and popular demands for the government to break off the negotiations with the British side were becoming thundering.[45] While not delivering any solution to the national issue, a general discontent toward the Wafdist government was felt among "all classes," which resulted in the impression "that the situation was thoroughly bad."[46] Therefore, as a consequence of the deterioration of public feeling and the widespread discontent, the Wafd began directing its energies against the British, presumably to satisfy public opinion and draw attention away from socioeconomic problems. As pointed to by Roger Louis, the Egyptian side, and especially the Wafd, had no choice but to demand evacuation of British troops from Egypt so as to satisfy popular claims. From the British point of view, on the other hand, the Suez Canal epitomized a crucial base for British security and global influence, which "seemed to be at stake" if any change to its status occurred.[47] Egypt was seen by the British as "the only country that fulfilled the strategic requirements of housing a base capable of supporting a major campaign in the Middle East."[48] On that account, an evacuation of this crucial base seemed inconceivable for the British authorities. This stiff approach by the British resulted in a "drift towards extremism," to borrow the words of a British report.[49]

By the summer of 1951, negotiations were characterized by distrust and disagreement, and the whole situation appeared to be moving toward confrontation. During talks between the Egyptian Minister of Foreign Affairs and the British ambassador to Egypt, the latter was told categorically that "unless satisfactory bases for negotiations [. . .] had been found by the end of the present Parliamentary session, the Egyptian Government would be compelled to publish the documentary exchanges and to declare their inability to continue the conversations." Responding to this, the ambassador warned him of the "seriousness of the consequences" if he did so.[50] In light of these confrontational attitudes, British forces in the Canal Zone began preparing for large disturbances from August 1951.[51] The following month, Sir Ralph Stevenson expressed to the Egyptian Minister of Interior, Siraj al-Din, his growing anxiety with regard to the Egyptian public discourse which had turned virulent against the British. As identified by Sir Ralph S. Stevenson, publications in various organs encouraged citizens "to undertake 'guerilla' or 'irregular' warfare against British forces in Egypt."[52] This development was "extremely disturbing" to the British and indicated the intensification of the Egyptian discourse against the British. The ambassador branded one author, "Maitre Sayed Kotb [*sic*]," whose violent articles appeared in, inter alia, the *Ikhwan*'s *al-Da'wa* magazine, as embodying this development. If this advocacy of violence continued unrestricted, it would "lead to violent attacks against British individuals."[53] This description of Sayyid Qutb in a British report as violently nationalist and anti-British suggests that Qutb in this period, much like the radical nationalists of this time, shared the anti-British sentiments and considered the Egyptian case as a key issue. It was the nationalist cause that predominantly occupied Qutb at this time rather than the Islamic nature of the state. It is interesting to note also that the *Ikhwan*'s publications continued to be a platform for anti-British agitation and radical discourses despite the moderating stance voiced by al-Hudaybi, which indicates that he had not yet been able to impose his will on the Brotherhood.

In September 1951, in a sign of the role played by the *Ikhwan* in intensifying the conflict, clashes were reported to have taken place between demonstrators and the police as anti-British demonstrations took place in major cities. A demonstration 10,000 strong, "largely under the control of members of the Ikhwan al Muslimeen [*sic*]," was angrily pointed to by the British ambassador, Sir Ralph S. Stevenson.[54]

By fall in 1951, the Egyptian government had reached the conviction that the "purpose [of the British] was merely to drag out the conversations," concluding that no resolution to the issue of the national question could be achieved except by "drastic measures."[55] These drastic, but highly anticipated measures arrived on October 8, 1951, when al-Nahhas uttered his historic words before the Lower House of parliament, "for Egypt I signed the defence treaty and for Egypt I abrogate it," thereby repealing the 1936 Treaty of Friendship and the 1899 Sudanese Condominium.[56] On October 16, the abrogation was approved in parliament, thus making the British presence in Egypt illegal in Egyptian eyes. The British diplomats lamented this unilateral step, maintaining that "the Treaty could not be unilaterally abrogated." Despite the British complaints, the Egyptian side went ahead with its decision, leading ultimately to a breakdown in diplomacy.[57]

By taking this bold move, al-Nahhas Pasha paved the way for what came to be known as the War in the Canal Zone, of 1951. The termination of the 1936 Treaty reinforced claims of the British presence in Egypt being an illegal occupation of another country, consequently leading to a hardening of popular attitudes toward the British and resulting on the ground in attacks on British troops and installations, sabotage of British utilities, and withdrawal of the Egyptian workforce from British bases.

It was in light of this development that the Muslim Brotherhood rose to the challenge and became a leading figure in the events that would develop from this point on. The British and Americans wasted no time in pointing to the Brotherhood as a main, if not *the* main, perpetrator of the resulting anti-British agitation in the Canal Zone and other parts of Egypt immediately after al-Nahhas' declaration. "[The] fanatic Moslem Brotherhood is planning to go ahead with a program of violence and terrorism" to be directed against the British, stressed the CIA on October 20, 1951. To fulfill this task, a Brotherhood group had acquired "25 machine guns" and made the necessary preparations to go ahead with anti-British violence.[58] To the CIA, it was beyond doubt that the "hypernationalistic Moslem Brotherhood [*sic*]" held "chief responsibility for a continuation of disturbances in Egypt."[59] The American ambassador to Cairo described the situation as a "dead-end loaded with dynamite" in which he thought his government should "not get involved."[60]

In broad agreement with the US assessment, the British considered the Brotherhood to be a main contributor to the escalating conflict in the Canal Zone. On October 11, 1951, a few days after al-Nahhas Pasha's announcement before parliament, the Brotherhood's students issued a proclamation urging the Egyptian government to announce that "Egypt was in a state of war with Great Britain" and asking it to declare the British forces as "enemy forces."[61] The students' statement went on to urge the government to allow the carrying of firearms and to deem attacks on the British unpunishable under Egyptian law.[62] The Brotherhood was asking the government to permit and even organize "[a]ttacks on the British," and the Brothers presented the idea of forming "a national guard of 16,000 volunteers, consisting of those who fought in Palestine," to accomplish the "Islamic Liberation."[63] And on October 17, the Ismailiyya branch of the *Ikhwan* declared *jihad* on the British, as a clear illustration of the developing events.[64]

On October 19–20, minor incidents were beginning to take place in the Canal Zone, such as the ambush of British vehicles and attacks on British bases.[65] On October 19, 1951, it was reported that Egyptian workers were not cooperating with their British employers in Suez.[66] The *Ikhwan*, according to the British reports, had threatened labor contractors not to supply a workforce to British installments, thereby using the workforce blockade as an effective measure against the British.[67] This seems to have been a highly effective tactic. On October 29, the Commanders in Chief Middle East maintained that "[v]irtually all our labour is leaving us on account of intimidation" exercised by the Brotherhood and the Egyptian police.[68]

Yet, from a British perspective, another more disquieting threat was developing. On October 23, 1951, a British report observed that the "[t]errorist pattern of the I.E.M. [Ikhwan el-Muslimin [*sic*]] [was] becoming more apparent."[69] The British were receiving reports of the Brotherhood collecting arms and believed that the "thing most to be feared was the rising danger of the Ikhwan El Muslimin [*sic*]."[70] British anxieties were growing by the day. On October 27, for example, it was reported by the British commanders in chief that there was "increasing evidence of preparations for terrorist activity by IKHWAN and Socialist Egyptian Party

[Young Egypt][71] extremists in the Canal Zone." With regard to the specific activities of the Brotherhood, the commanders in chief believed that about 1,000 *Ikhwan* members were training in Cairo "for operations in the Canal Zone."[72] Such rumors had to be taken with the utmost seriousness, according to British diplomats. Should such preparations continue undisrupted, an anti-British campaign would become "firmly established," and it could lead to a real threat to British security in the Zone, with "British lives [being] sacrificed."[73] Accordingly, British officials in Egypt saw no way out of an escalation of events unless they were immediately authorized to "arrest and detain ringleaders of Ikhwan and other terrorist organisations whenever they [could] be identified in the Canal Zone."[74] Such measures were out of the ordinary, as admitted by James Bowker, a British official, but they were necessary due to the immense threat posed by the Ikhwan to "the security of British forces and their families."[75] And just as forecast by the British and Americans, events did take a violent turn. By late October 1951, British troops were being attacked and casualties in their ranks were on the rise.[76] The British authorities informed the Egyptian side on November 28 that they would not "allow further British lives to be sacrificed without taking some counter action." Pointing to the lethal attacks on British lives, British diplomats contended that such attacks must be the result of Brotherhood cooperation with communists.[77]

The concrete decision by the Brotherhood to participate in this anti-British struggle was taken shortly after al-Nahhas' declaration in mid-October 1951. Kamil al-Sharif, a Palestine veteran of the Brotherhood, was chosen by the General Guidance Office to direct the Brotherhood's activities in the Canal Zone.[78] This decision was a translation of the widespread desire of the *Ikhwan* to combat the British. As a case in point, Hasan Duh, one of the Brotherhood's student leaders who took part in these events, recalls that "I believed and still do, that military power is the only tool and way to achieve our rights." The liberation of Egypt could only be achieved through military means, thus was the conclusion reached by Duh at the time. He therefore passionately welcomed the Brotherhood's decision.[79]

The Brotherhood's planning and preparations for the events had been fulfilled by three different Brotherhood sections: the students' section, under the leadership of Farid Abdel Khaleq; the Special Apparatus, under the leadership of Yusuf Talʿat;[80] and "the Units' section," consisting of military and police officers and headed by Salah Shadi. Erecting training camps in the areas adjacent to the Canal Zone and at Egyptian universities, the Brotherhood began preparing a cadre of militants to take part in the attacks.[81] These camps were tasked with instructing young men in the use of firearms, grenades, and mines, and with instilling them with a general military spirit, if we are to believe the accounts of their commanders. The camps were organized by students who had acquired military experience in the first Arab–Israeli war, and they were supported by army officers who volunteered to instruct the young nationalists.[82]

As a case in point, Muhammad Mahdi Akef, a member of the Special Apparatus and a student of the Muslim Brotherhood, became head of the camp organized at Ibrahim Pasha University (Ain Shams today). Akef, who throughout the late 1940s had been a dynamic student leader of the *Ikhwan* at the sports college, was in 1948 one of the Brotherhood's instructors who erected camps and trained volunteers in the use of arms in connection with the Arab–Israeli war. This enthusiastic young man had furthermore assisted the voluntary fighters in Palestine by collecting and transporting weapons to support their fight. Akef had thereby combined his sports education with military skills and acquired experience in smuggling weapons and instructing young men in the use of arms.[83] It was by dint of this background that Akef erected a camp at the faculty of engineering and came to lead the other camps at Ibrahim Pasha University. Tasked with "erasing the military illiteracy" among the Egyptian students and offering a forceful and serious program of training that combined rigorous physical exercises with education in terms of soldiery and the use of arms, these camps were numerous at this point. Perceiving it as the responsibility of Egypt's young men to prepare for the struggle against the British, Akef, who at the time was studying law, describes himself as a "zealous young man" who had acquired military skills through his engagement with the Special Apparatus. It was also through his ties to the Apparatus that Akef had access to arms. These weapons, which were necessary for the instruction of students and for use in the struggle against the British, were either passed to them by discontented army officers, purchased through underground channels, or collected in the Western Desert, where large quantities of the Second World War military equipment had been left behind.

University camps seem to have attracted a considerable number of young men bent on acquiring the necessary competences to fight the British. One thousand students joined the camp at Ibrahim Pasha University when the "door for preparation was opened," recalls Akef. Similar camps were erected at other universities, such as al-Azhar and Cairo University, and Brotherhood students likewise acquired key roles in these camps.[84] Hasan Duh, who at the time was a student leader of the Brotherhood, relates that the Special Apparatus played a coinciding role in mobilizing its militants and taking part in the training activities along with the actual battles in the Canal Zone.[85] It is important to note here that these different sections of the *Ikhwan* were not hermetically sealed from each other. As the case of Akef illustrates, a member could at once be a member of the students' section and a militant of the Apparatus, and this undoubtedly reinforced the Brotherhood's ability to mobilize young men for this task.

The units organized to participate in these events were to be known as "*Katā'ib al-Taḥrīr*" (Liberation Regiments) as a general designation for all the volunteer forces taking part in events. Corroborating the above accounts, Sir Willie Morris stated that "the bands in operation are probably Ikhwan, although Ibrahim Shukri, the Socialist deputy, is said to be in the Canal Zone with 80 volunteers."[86] It was against this background of intensifying militarization and an outspoken call for struggle against the British that violent incidents began to take place during the final months of 1951.[87] Throughout November, reports of attacks on British and other Western individuals seemed to be increasing, such as the attack on British soldiers, vehicle and facilities, resulting in the death of a number of British soldiers and officers.[88]

It was shortly before this period of escalation, which saw a group of Brothers undertake a militant agitation against the British, that al-Hudaybi had announced his intention to dismiss secrecy and militancy. Having just assumed the leadership less than a year before these incidents and without the prior experience of leading a mass organization, not to mention an organization active in anti-colonial *jihad*, he faced tremendous difficulties in carrying his plan through. Once the wheels of this crisis were set in motion, the Brotherhood's militant fringe saw no way back. As the following section discusses, the new *Murshid* did not stick to his initial vow of "no secrecy in Islam" but seems to have had a change of heart in light of the escalating nationalist struggle.

Al-Hudaybi and the Idea of *jihad*

As observed in the preceding section, upon his appointment, al-Hudaybi had resolved to disband the secret structures of the Brotherhood by dissolving the Apparatus and leading the *Ikhwan* toward deradicalization.[89] According to British assessments, al-Hudaybi intended at the beginning of his leadership to get the Brotherhood "out into the open as a political party" and away from underground activism.[90] To the US and British officials, al-Hudaybi initially represented a moderating factor. The British were, for example, told by Andraos Pasha, honorary economic adviser to the Royal Palace, that al-Hudaybi had assured the king that his organization "did not intend to use violence either against foreigners or Egyptians."[91] In December of the same year, Cecil Campbell referred to al-Hudaybi's advocacy "of peaceful measures and his denial that the Brotherhood were forming any Liberation Battalions."[92] In late November and at the beginning of December 1951, D. L. Stewart, a Foreign Office official, met with Farkhani Bey, a close friend and adviser of al-Hudaybi. In the report on their meetings, Stewart gave the same "uplifting" impression as that mentioned above. Farkhani had repeatedly claimed that al-Hudaybi "is an entirely different type from Hassan Al Banna." Farkhani also impressed Stewart as being truly pro-British, and he told Stewart that al-Hudaybi "is capable of leading the Ikhwan to much better purpose."[93] As regards the Americans, they had come to a similar judgment. On December 19, it was reported that "King Farouk and the powerful Minister of Interior have even conferred with the Moslem Brotherhood leader in an effort to gain his support for limiting violence."[94]

So, how do we understand this obvious discrepancy between the moderate utterances of people such as Farkhani Bey and al-Hudaybi himself and the events on the ground which demonstrated that a faction of the *Ikhwan* certainly took part in, if not led, the operations against the British. No doubt, when al-Hudaybi took over the leadership of the Brotherhood, he genuinely intended to lead it away from militancy and secrecy. This had already been observed in February 1951 when CIA reports perceived Hudaybi as a conservative judge, who on account of his background would be against the Brotherhood's application of "other means."[95] But as the events in the Canal Zone clearly revealed, al-Hudaybi quickly came to realize how difficult a task it was, and the domestic context only served to make it even more complicated. The self-perception of a group of *Ikhwan* as being representatives of a nationalist and Islamist anti-colonial organization, with a past of anti-colonial *jihad*, had taken root among many members. This is illustrated in numerous accounts of Brotherhood activists. This choir of *Ikhwan* highlighted their engagement in the violent campaign against the British as the natural translation of their being patriots. It was a translation of the much-coveted *jihad* obligation.[96]

Consequently, when the Suez Conflict was set in motion, the rank and file and many senior members of the Brotherhood understood it as an opportunity they had long waited for.[97] Therefore, despite al-Hudaybi's statements distancing his organization from violence in the Canal Zone, the Brotherhood *did* continue to be involved in the conflict. Cecil Campbell described the statements of al-Hudaybi as "inexplicable," for while al-Hudaybi publicly dissociated the Brotherhood from violence, intelligence reports frequently described violent operations involving the Brothers.[98] This contradiction between statements and actions indicates that the "militant choice" was preferred by a significant and powerful part of the Brotherhood. This may be an indication of the strength of the faction advocating *jihad* inside the *Ikhwan*. Thus, this continuation of the *Ikhwan's* involvement in violence in spite of al-Hudaybi's declarations to the opposite can be assessed either as a sign of his weakness vis-à-vis the militant segment or as his disguising his real position toward militancy. His first attempt to direct the *Ikhwan* in a new direction, one away from violence, had obviously failed, as the events signify. As explained by the Brotherhood lawyer Tahir al-Khashab in this regard, "the rule of the Ikhwan is for the Guide to submit to the decision of the majority … Therefore, if the Ikhwan as a body decided … to resort to violence, the Guide would have to submit to this decision."[99]

In later accounts, Brotherhood leaders such as Farid Abdel Khaleq and Kamil al-Sharif have clarified that al-Hudaybi's dismissal of violence against the British should be understood as a pragmatic, cautious, and diplomatic standpoint, which did not represent his genuine viewpoints. As argued by Abdel Khaleq, the *Murshid* was denying any responsibility for the ongoing events in the Canal Zone, while "the battalions of the *Ikhwan* were participating in battles of the Zone."[100] Kamil al-Sharif corroborates this perspective. Acknowledging that al-Hudaybi did utter conservative views with regard to the battles in the canal, al-Sharif highlight that such statements should be understood as a sign of al-Hudaybi's wisdom. "With his balanced and thoughtful nature, he does not resort to clowning and exaggerations, but he prefers to let the actions represent themselves," according to al-Sharif's clarification. Moreover, because of his lack of confidence in the government, al-Hudaybi feared that repressive measures would be taken against the *Ikhwan* if they publicly claimed responsibility for the events, and he therefore preferred to prepare and engage in the battle silently and secretly, letting others "deliver the thunderous speeches."[101] Interestingly, the British voiced similar doubts about al-Hudaybi's "real" attitude regarding the battle.

While some diplomats, understandably, seem to have believed al-Hudaybi to be a genuine moderate,[102] others suspected him of bending the truth. One such suspicion was voiced by Cecil Campbell, who pointed to the contradictions between al-Hudaybi's advocacy of "peaceful measures" and his simultaneous request that "arms be given to would-be assassins." One explanation offered by Campbell was that al-Hudaybi had probably "surrendered to the extremer Brethren."[103] Whether this is true or whether al-Hudaybi had been convinced of the necessity of *jihad* is difficult to say, yet we clearly notice that he had altered his initial position. Al-Hudaybi announced in January 1952 that "[w]e have no 'Liberation Squads', but we have men, of whom, each one is a squad in himself, armed with faith and resolution. If the Government wishes us to send them to the Canal we will send them, but we must have reassurance: we hesitate only for fear lest what has happened in the past should happen again."[104]

Along these lines, it is reasonable to assume that a change had occurred with al-Hudaybi as a result of the circumstances surrounding the Brotherhood. Bearing witness to this conceivable change of heart, Al-Hudaybi issued a public statement on December 14, 1951, backing the government's abrogation of the treaty. Commenting on the ongoing events, al-Hudaybi stressed that "[o]ur attitude from the Islamic point of view is also clear: if an enemy occupies any Islamic territory it is the duty of every Moslem to make war on him and expel him."[105] Interestingly and in univocal contraposition to his prior standpoint, al-Hudaybi declared that "it is our duty to make war on the British since they are enemies invading our territory."[106]

Whether al-Hudaybi turned into a genuine supporter of anti-British militancy or not is difficult to say. But in the eyes of those Brothers who actually took part in the battle, al-Hudaybi was certainly a supporter of their actions. Since al-Hudaybi was the leader of the Muslim Brotherhood, violent conduct could not have taken place without his consent, according to their argument. Explaining the discrepancy between his announcement as regards violence, the activists highlighted that this was a shrewd tactic to avoid repression and dissolution. To the British, these inconsistencies in al-Hudaybi's statements made his early dismissal of violence sound resoundingly hollow. And looking at the events on the ground, the *Murshid*'s words fell on deaf ears.[107]

Pointing to this imbalance between words and deeds, Stevenson proclaimed that, in spite of al-Hudaybi's statements to the contrary, one could not dismiss the role played by the Brotherhood. As he put it "the Egyptian is not particularly good at taking in instructions and he is always likely to interpret so as to suit his own situation and opinions." In other words, even if al-Hudaybi genuinely wanted to distance his *Ikhwan* from violence, Stevenson perceived that to be a complicated task. The Brotherhood was an organization with a past "smelling strongly of dynamite and gunpowder," and al-Hudaybi had been chosen to lead this organization. Stevenson would not exclude the possibility that al-Hudaybi's respectable reputation and background was being utilized as "camouflage by unrepentant terrorists who [had] learnt some subtlety through adversity."[108]

Conclusions

I began this chapter by arguing that al-Hudaybi undertook the task of ridding the *Ikhwan* of secrecy and violence, first behind closed doors upon his appointment as *Murshid*, in May 1950, and subsequently in the open, when his appointment was made public in October 1951. Exclaiming his maxim "there is no secrecy and militancy in the Islamic *da'wa* [mission]," al-Hudaybi vowed to rid the organization of both. To do so, he embarked on restructuring the Brotherhood's upper echelons to bring it under his direct command. In what turned out to be a far more complicated enterprise, al-Hudaybi tried to weaken the Special Apparatus, presumably on the route to dissolving it. He declared openly that violence and secrecy ought to be uprooted and that such elements were too dangerous. However, in so doing, al-Hudaybi touched a raw nerve with a strong segment of the *Ikhwan*.

This resolve to dismiss violence and secrecy resulted in a rift within the organization:[109] Al-Hudaybi and his closest associates advocated the maxim of "no secrecy and militancy in Islam," while a strong faction in the Brotherhood saw the struggle against the British and their "lackeys" as a religious obligation.[110] And this still pending struggle necessitated both militancy and secrecy, so their contention. They argued forcefully that neither al-Hudaybi nor anybody else had the right to dismiss the obligation of *jihad*. Consequently, when the war in the Suez Canal broke out in October 1951, just as al-Hudaybi's appointment had been made public, the idea of *jihad* resurfaced as an urgent task. Omar Ashour has argued that al-Hudaybi made his first attempt to deradicalize the Brotherhood over the period of 1951–3.[111] Yet, as illustrated in this chapter, al-Hudaybi did not unreservedly stand up against his organization's armed activism in the Canal Zone. In contrast to Ashour's argument that al-Hudaybi was against "any type of armed action," I have shown that al-Hudaybi's position vis-à-vis violence was more inconstant. Ashour is right in claiming that al-Hudaybi uttered antiviolent statements in the press, and may genuinely have been against violence, at least in the beginning of his leadership. However, as the battle in the Suez Canal escalated, al-Hudaybi began to alter his position toward a greater acceptance of militancy. Modifying his early statements, al-Hudaybi described fighting the British as an obligatory *jihad*.

Accordingly, when the revolution *cum* coup d'état broke out on July 23, 1952, the *Ikhwan* was looked upon and perceived themselves as a key political faction on the Egyptian scene. A significant number of the military officers who had planned and executed the coup d'état either had been in close contact with the Brotherhood or had themselves been previous members of the Brotherhood's secret structures.[112] Nasser and his fellow officers had also cooperated with the Brotherhood in their anti-British battles in the Canal Zone, which made the idea of a necessary cooperation prevalent.[113]

Yet, the initial harmony and expected cooperation between these two dominant actors rapidly turned into dispute and conflict. Thus, early partnership and the idea of shaping postcolonial Egypt together were replaced by acrimony and enmity. As a result, a radicalization of means came to shape the conflict between these recent allies, ending up with the persecution of the Brotherhood in late 1954. It is to this contentious relationship that I now turn.

4

The Route toward Conflict: The Brotherhood and the Officers' Revolution

Mahmoud Abdel Latif's botched assassination attempt on Egypt's postrevolutionary premier lieutenant colonel Gamal Abdel Nasser marked a watershed in the history of the Muslim Brotherhood and especially its Special Apparatus. With a past of political assassinations, secrecy, and underground activism, the *Ikhwan*'s Special Apparatus, and to some degree the Brotherhood itself, had acquired a reputation as a notorious group of lunatics responsible for countless violent incidents. Yet, with the unsuccessful attempt on Nasser's life on al-Manshiyya square in Alexandria, the Apparatus was moving toward its end. Its failures rather than any strategic planning seem to have ended its existence, as this chapter argues.

In what follows, I discuss how the Brotherhood entered into conflict with the military regime in division over its strategy. While a segment of the Brotherhood advocated coexistence and cooperation with the postcolonial regime, another fringe of the *Ikhwan* saw a showdown with the military regime as inescapable. In so arguing, I critically assess the contention that the radicalization of the Brotherhood in their struggle with the officers took place only from behind the prison walls and in some organically connected way to Qutb's worldview. Considering this conflict as one for Egypt's future, Gerges claimed that "[i]n one stroke, he [Nasser] sought to crush the only remaining viable opposition to his rule [the Brothers]." Gerges added that Qutb, in response to this attempt to crush the Brothers, "would resist Nasser's hegemony to the end, offering a revolutionary Islamist alternative. He would spearhead resistance to Nasser from behind the prison walls."[1] Similarly, Gilles Kepel argued that the radical worldview which interpreted the fight against the Egyptian state under Nasser, and subsequently under Sadat, as an Islamic *jihad* had evolved in "the Nasser regime's concentration camps." "In the Beginnings Were the Camps," argues Kepel.[2] Quite the opposite, I argue that a radicalization can be traced back to this pre-*miḥna* era, which indicates that Qutb's radicalization from the 1960s represented a continuation of previous thoughts. The idea of resisting the national regime violently did not start with Qutb but had its roots in pre-revolutionary experiences and continued among segments of young Brothers directly after the late 1954 repression, as is seen in the subsequent chapters. In so arguing, I do not deny that a radicalization took place in the prisons, but I contend that this was a continuum of an earlier radicalization taking place in this pre-prison period. Without this historic account, we are not able to understand how a fringe of the Brotherhood backed and even carried out violence against other Egyptians long before Qutb penned his well-known manifesto *Milestones*.

The facts of Mahmoud Abdel Latif's botched attempt remain contested. While Brotherhood accounts unanimously protest the organization's innocence and have done so ever since, claiming that the incident was staged by the regime to frame the Brotherhood, accounts penned by RCC members and antagonists of the Brotherhood refer to this particular incident as evidence of the organization's violent past (and present).[3] Some historical questions and dilemmas remain unanswered, and this may very well remain the case. Notwithstanding the veracity of the official story and the account offered by the Brotherhood, this incident marked a peak in the conflict between the Brotherhood and the military regime. Rather than being *the* root of conflict, the incident marked a highpoint of conflict between the junior army officers led by Gamal Abdel Nasser and the Brotherhood led by Hasan al-Hudaybi. This struggle, which took its most decisive turn on October 26, came to shape the Brotherhood's future, and even the future of Egypt and the Middle East if we are to agree with Fawaz Gerges.[4]

Therefore, rather than looking into the very incident and discussing the uncertainties surrounding it, I intend to study the path that led the Brotherhood toward this critical point of showdown with the regime. In so doing, I maintain that a radicalization of means took place prior to the notorious incident in Alexandria. The militarization of conflict did not happen abruptly and unexpectedly on that momentous evening of October 26 but was rather an ongoing process within a historical context in which the battle for a postcolonized Egypt had been going on for decades. The erstwhile informal allies, the officers, and the Brothers who had fought side by side in Palestine and in the Canal Zone ended up being the "last men standing" in an Egypt advancing toward independence.

The following section illustrates that the cordiality that marked the early relationship between the nascent military regime and the Muslim Brotherhood quickly began to sour, turning into bitter resentment. By so doing, I intend to show that this path toward conflict began shortly after the military takeover in Egypt.

The Brotherhood and the RCC: Between Cooperation and Conflict

The Brotherhood's first reception of the coup was friendly and welcoming. A few days after the military takeover, the Brotherhood issued a statement urging its members to back the new leaders of Egypt and describing them as "a genuine movement against corruption and [one that] was working for the good of Egypt."[5] And in a clear sign of this benevolence toward the officers, al-Hudaybi instructed at this point the Brotherhood's rank and file to support and assist the new regime after a meeting between him and General Muhamamd Naguib, lead figure of the junta on July 28.[6] On August 1 and as yet another example in this sequence of friendly utterances, the Brotherhood issued an official statement applauding the political change taking place in Egypt. The statement, which praised the "blessed movement" (*al-ḥaraka al-mubāraka*) of the army for opening the "gates of hope for the resurrection of the *umma* and the revival of its glory," publicized the reform scheme envisioned by the *Ikhwan*. Underlining that these reform suggestions were drawn from the Quran, the statement listed a number of aspects that were necessary for a sincere change of political regime. Among the proposed reform points were a complete and comprehensive purge of the political system and the abolishment of martial law and every law contradicting public freedoms. Furthermore, the statement declared that the military achievement which had delivered this "blessed movement, should work for the creation of virtuous individuals, achievable only through religious education." By so doing, Egypt could acquire a generation "embedded with the spirit of religion, ethics, and nationalism."[7]

This statement, which is the first written declaration of the Brotherhood in the postmonarchy era, is interesting, as it gives some insight into how the Brotherhood envisioned its role in this nascent order. Considering themselves a prime partner of the "blessed movement," the Brotherhood perceived its task to be counseling the young officers and guiding them on the right path of organizing society "Islamically."

As has been shown in different studies and noted by members of the RCC themselves, the junior officers who attained power had not yet developed at this early stage an ideological blueprint nor a clearly defined reform program to act upon.[8] Accordingly, the Brotherhood perceived themselves as the main political organization in Egypt embedded with the right and ability to authoritatively guide the new order and its reform program in an Islamic direction.[9] This, according to senior members of the Brotherhood, had been the arrangement agreed upon by the officers and the Brotherhood when preparing and coordinating the coup. The Brotherhood had sworn to stand by the officers and lend them their support on the precondition that the officers cooperated with the Brothers in applying Islamic law, which was the original "goal of revolution," as Brotherhood leaders contend.[10] In other words, the *Ikhwan* perceived themselves as equal partners with the officers.

The impression that the Brotherhood had had a hand in this development was held by British and American diplomats alike. For instance, a British report, directed to NATO on August 1, 1952, noted that "[t]he military group headed by General Neguib [*sic*] who are chiefly responsible for planning this coup d'état are probably connected with extremist elements in Egyptian politics and in particular with the Moslem Brotherhood."[11]

Therefore, when Ali Maher's government, which had been in office since the first day of the coup, resigned on September 7, 1952, as a result of disagreements over an agrarian reform proposed by the junta to limit the property of land to a maximum of 200 feddans,[12] it seemed that the fears the Western diplomats harbored with regard to an officer–Brotherhood "extremist alliance" were being borne out. Muhammad Naguib succeeded Maher and came to head a government of civilians. In this regard, special US and British attention was paid to Shaykh Ahmad al-Baqouri, a senior member of the Brotherhood who was appointed as Minister of Pious Endowments (*Awqāf*) by Naguib. Al-Baqouri came to symbolize this extremist turn which the British and Americans had been uneasy about. US ambassador Jefferson Caffrey noted, for instance, that "it is not pleasant to have men long on extremism and short on admin. Experience" in government. Among those referred to as "long on extremism" was not surprisingly al-Baqouri of the *Ikhwan*.[13] Thus, al-Baqouri's appointment in the post-revolutionary government was received as an indication of RCC–Brotherhood coalition.

However, despite the cordiality on the surface, the relationship between the Brotherhood and the RCC regime was beginning to show cracks at this early stage. I now point to a few points and episodes of disagreement that caused this deterioration in the relationship. Doing so, I maintain that this political conflict shaped the military–Brotherhood relationship and led to the bloodstained showdown between the erstwhile allies.

Rather than being actual proof of friendliness and alliance, as contemporary observers came to believe, Al-Baqouri's appointment as minister came to epitomize the first instance of disagreement between the two parties.[14] When approached by the RCC to join the new government on September 9, 1952, al-Baqouri did not hesitate to accept the appointment, seeing it as an opportunity he could not afford to let go.[15] However, in so doing, al-Baqouri had acted in direct opposition to a decision taken by the Brotherhood not to participate in government. Al-Baqouri, up until then a senior member of the Brotherhood who had been among the foremost candidates to succeed al-Banna, was dismissed from the organization on the grounds that he had transgressed the *Ikhwan*'s decision not to participate in government.[16] The dismissal of a personage of al-Baqouri's standing was perceived by the revolutionary regime as an act of animosity by the Brotherhood toward the nascent order and came to stimulate disagreements between them. As noted by Mitchell, by dismissing al-Baqouri, it seemed as if the Brotherhood was "withdrawing their support from the regime," an act that represented "a serious matter in those early days" when the military junta was in dire need of popular backing.[17] In addition, as explained by Mitchell, this "cabinet *débâcle*"[18] came to presage the personal antipathy between al-Hudaybi and Nasser, an antipathy that would characterize the conflict for the whole of this period. The antipathy between the two men had emerged following their first encounter. In the words of Farid Abdel Khaleq, barely a week had gone by after the coup before the relationship between Nasser and al-Hudaybi had turned lukewarm. At their first meeting, Nasser had made it abundantly clear that the Brotherhood would not acquire an advising prerogative in the new regime. Reacting to this, al-Hudaybi had intimated to his Brotherhood advisers that "this [coup] is not an Islamic movement (*ḥaraka islāmiya*) that follows the path and goals envisioned by the *Ikhwan*. It is at best a reform movement (*ḥaraka iṣlāḥiya*)."[19] In denying the *Ikhwan* an authoritative role, Nasser had, in the eyes of the Brothers, broken the deal they had struck. Being rooted in these early disagreements, this tepidity would develop into becoming an outright personal enmity.[20]

The second main cause of disharmony followed in early 1953. Martyn Frampton has accurately described 1953 as "the year of division."[21] The year started with the dissolution of all political parties on January 17—except the Brotherhood, on the grounds that the *Ikhwan* was not a political party. Concurrent with the decree of dissolution, the junta declared a three-year transition period during which Naguib would rule the country. In so doing, the military had de facto acquired the reins of power in Egypt.[22] It was at this point, argues Gordon, that the junta began to "fancy itself a revolution" and came to be called *Majlis Qiyādat al-Thawra* (Revolutionary Command Council).[23] In keeping with this, from early 1953, the RCC began formulating its own agenda in which it envisaged an unchallenged position for itself. The RCC "has complete control over the Egyptian Government" was the assessment put forward by the CIA in early 1953.[24]

Shortly after dissolving all political parties in January 1953, the RCC announced the foundation of a political body designated "to provide a new center around which political support for the new regime can be organized."[25] The "Liberation Rally" (*Hay'at al-Taḥrīr*), as this body was named, was envisioned as a political organization tasked with mobilizing popular support for the officers and arousing sentiment for the junta. Applying mass rallies and public events, the Rally attempted to fuel popular enthusiasm for the regime. Gordon has maintained that while *Hay'at al-Taḥrīr* "never succeeded in surpassing its rivals, the Wafd and the Muslim Brotherhood," as a grassroots political organization, it came to spotlight the officers' entrance onto the political scene.[26] The Rally was constructed as an organization with branches on campuses and in factories and with a hierarchical leadership aimed at disseminating the political visions of the junta. Muhammad Naguib was named president, and Nasser secretary, while other RCC figures also assumed leading positions in the Rally.

The Rally became a source of disharmony between the RCC and the Brothers since its inception. Seeing themselves as the civilian part of a civilian–military coalition, the Brotherhood viewed the newly minted formation as unnecessary competition to their envisioned position and as an attempt by the RCC to isolate them from real influence. Along these lines, Abdel Khaleq argues that Nasser and his military colleagues were unable at this point in time to drum up popular support and enthusiasm and were thus dependent on the support of *Ikhwan*-grassroots to obtain this backing. Therefore, in an attempt to find another source of support and free themselves from this *Ikhwan* dependency, Nasser set about creating the Rally. In his position as secretary of the Rally, Nasser invited the Brotherhood to join it, direct its programs, and in the end fuse with it. Seeing this invitation as a camouflaged attempt to subsume their organization into the newly formed body, the *Ikhwan* could not accept such a scheme.[27]

From the Brotherhood's viewpoint, its role was to be that of an equal partner, not a subordinated support group, and the *Ikhwan* thus refused to become second-tier members in their relationship with the officers. Lending support to this argument, al-Tilmisani points out that the Brotherhood had consented to back the "blessed movement" provided that the officers went on with the social, religious, and economic reforms agreed on with the Brothers prior to the coup. "Our popular assistance put the coup on a strong foundation in Egypt, but our backing was not an empty shell without meanings and viewpoints … we insisted on the application of Islamic law from day one."[28]

For the second time since the Baqouri "*débâcle*," the Brotherhood had exhibited its refusal to accept being a junior partner to the RCC. As explained by Shadi, the Brotherhood perceived such an inclusion in the Liberation Rally as a restriction to its influence and freedom, to which they could not assent.[29] From the viewpoint of the officers, however, the Brotherhood's reaction was understood as a declaration of war against the junta. Anwar al-Sadat, to give one example, saw these disagreements as clear evidence that the Brotherhood had the "obvious intention of overthrowing us and taking over the rule of Egypt."[30]

Notwithstanding, while the conflict was looming, both parties did their best to uphold a façade of friendship and harmony, although it obviously remained a hollow façade.[31] This was a battle of wits between erstwhile allies for the rule of Egypt. Despite the antagonism, however, there was no outbreak of hostilities during this first period of revolution. This veiled disharmony led, however, to a serious rift within the Brotherhood that weakened the organization vis-à-vis the regime, the discussion of which I now turn to.

A Divided Brotherhood: Hovering between Accommodation and Confrontation

The environment of competition, unease, and suspicion between the officers and Brothers led to a serious split inside the Brotherhood. Disagreeing internally on how to deal with the officers and the challenge they posed to the *Ikhwan*, this rift dominated the internal debates of the Brothers. As noted above, al-Hudaybi had been suspicious of the officers' intentions since the early days of the coup and had thus been cautious about going too far in relations with them. Yet, a strong faction inside the Brotherhood perceived these officers and their "revolution" to be an outcome of the Brotherhood's many years of anti-regime activism, and their post-monarchical regime as representing the dreams of the Brotherhood. Mahmoud Abdel Halim recalls, for example, that many Brothers celebrated the "successful movement [*cum* coup] completed by our officer-Brothers, as being their own."[32] Accordingly, the Brotherhood, as this section shows, was greatly divided as it entered the height of the conflict with the officers.

Al-Hudaybi's mandate had been weak since the early days of his appointment as *Murshid*. As noted in the previous chapter, lacking the personal charisma of al-Banna, al-Hudaybi failed to create harmony in the Brotherhood following his appointment. So, while his dealings with the officers were moving on the route of conflict, al-Hudaybi was also facing internal problems inside the Brotherhood.

The officers, many of whom had been in close contact with the *Ikhwan* for years before the coup, knew exactly what was going on inside the organization. And they were determined to utilize it to their advantage. Knowing of the internal divisions inside the Brotherhood, the officers began cultivating ties to al-Hudaybi's rivals within the organization. The *Ikhwan* was, at this point, split into three major factions headed respectively by al-Hudaybi, Abdel Rahman al-Banna (Hasan al-Banna's younger brother), and Saleh Ashmawi, the former deputy of the Brotherhood and the patron of the Special Apparatus.[33] The two latter factions were characterized by anti-Hudaybi sentiments and by an inclination to forge a friendlier relations toward the nascent regime. Thus, by cultivating closer ties to those two factions, the officers hoped to influence the course of the Brotherhood in a more pro-junta direction. This fragmentation within the Brotherhood had become an open secret during the early months of 1953.

In March 1953, and pointing unambiguously to this conflict, Ashmawi "castigated" the *Murshid* "for having forced Sheikh al Baqouri to resign from the Brotherhood on the grounds that he had accepted office without consulting the Supreme Guide and in a government not based on strictly Koranic principles."[34] Advocating a closer cooperation with the new regime, Ashmawi declared that the *Ikhwan* must "play an active role in the reform movement and exploit their influence as the most powerful organisation in the Middle East." Ashmawi maintained that this could not be achieved "while Al Hodeiby [*sic*] remained Supreme Guide," thereby unequivocally indicating that he preferred seeing the *Murshid* abandoning his position.[35]

These frictions affecting the internal cohesion of the Brotherhood show plainly that the Brothers had suffered a blow to their coherence following the coup. What can be asserted with confidence is that the Brotherhood, or at least its upper echelons, went into this crucial phase of conflict with the military regime as a divided organization. Consequently, when the RCC decided to dissolve the Brotherhood on January 13, 1954, in a clear intensification of the conflict, it did so to a fractured and therefore weakened organization. As a reaction to this dissolution and the concomitant repression of the Brothers, a section within the Brotherhood began seeing the conflict as heading toward an imminent showdown. Preparations for battling the regime were therefore made to ready the organization for what was to come.

Against this backdrop of division inside the Brotherhood, al-Hudaybi appointed a committee to reform the Special Apparatus. Doing so, al-Hudaybi and his close associates hoped to bring the Apparatus under their control, thus undermining Ashmawi's powerbase within the organization. Furthermore, and in light of the brimming hostility between the Brotherhood and the regime, this seemed like a Brotherhood act of mustering up force against the regime. Headed by Abdel Qader Uda, the deputy of the *Ikhwan*, and consisting of the five leading members of the Special Apparatus alongside Hussein Kamal al-Din and Husni Abdel Baqi from the Brotherhood's Guidance Office, the committee was tasked to explore appropriate ways of reforming and developing the Apparatus.[36] These attempts came at a time when the regime was demanding the abolition of the Special Apparatus as a step toward eradicating secrecy from the Brotherhood's ranks.[37] However, and in spite of these demands, al-Hudaybi was determined to keep the Apparatus. What al-Hudaybi had decided, in his own words, was not to dismiss secrecy, but to control it and put it under a leadership of his choosing.[38] For this reason, it was decided to merge the cells of the Special Apparatus with the *usar* system of the Brotherhood and to put both structures under the same command. By so doing, he envisioned a streamlining of command structures and communication, thus removing the dichotomy the Apparatus had created in the past.[39] However, the decision to keep these secret structures continued to be a point of contention and a root of strife between al-Hudaybi and the officers, but also between the *Murshid* and a strong faction within the Brotherhood. This faction, headed by Abdel Rahman al-Sindi, sensed in al-Hudaybi's scheme an attempt to wrest power from them.[40]

On November 19, 1953, Sayyid Fayez received a box at about 3 p.m. Offered to him as a gift on the day of the Prophet's birth, Fayez received the "present" believing it to contain sweets. Not knowing what the box really contained, Fayez opened the box just to realize that it was an explosive device intended to kill him. When the bomb went off immediately, it killed Fayez and left his apartment in Cairo a complete wreck. The victim, Sayyid Fayez, was a senior commander of the Special Apparatus and a close associate of the *Murshid*. By killing Fayez, the assassins wanted to derail al-Hudaybi's attempts to consolidate his control of the Apparatus. Fayez, Abdel Halim tells us, had grown tired of al-Sindi's "recklessness" and had therefore "decided to help the *Murshid* free the Apparatus from the authority of al-Sindi."[41] The assassination was thus understood as an inter-*Ikhwan* act, committed by the anti-Hudaybi leadership of the Apparatus against a fellow Brother. Ahmad Adel Kamal, a high-ranking militant of the Apparatus, was suspected of being behind the murder, and although no charge was filed against him, he remains under suspicion to this day.[42] Unprecedented in the Brotherhood's history, this event undoubtedly intensified the rift within the organization. Commenting on this issue, Nasser told the British embassy that the death of Fayez had come as a result of the latter's move to the Hudaybi faction "about a fortnight before his death."[43] According to a widely held story that is corroborated by Nasser's above account, on the day of his death, Fayez was scheduled to hand al-Hudaybi a report detailing "the long-concealed data on the Apparatus."[44] This information would have furnished the *Murshid* with crucial data, enabling him to take control of the Brotherhood's military wing. And this was what triggered the assassination of Fayez, according to this narrative.

At this crucial point when al-Hudaybi was balancing between putting an end to secrecy and controlling it, the Brotherhood accounts clearly indicate that the balance was tipping toward controlling and preserving it rather than ending it. The assassination would have deep repercussions for the Brotherhood and especially the upper echelons of the Special Apparatus. Shortly after the incident, al-Hudaybi dismissed four leading commanders of the Apparatus: Abdel Rahman al-Sindi, Mahmoud al-Sabbagh, Ahmad Adel Kamal, and Ahmad Zaki.[45] Ridding the Apparatus of some of its most authoritative commanders, al-Hudaybi could move in to replace them with commanders loyal to him.

Refusing to let their leaders' dismissal pass without resistance, al-Sindi's supporters stormed al-Hudaybi's home on November 27, 1953. The militants occupied his home, pressing for the *Murshid*'s resignation. When al-Hudaybi resisted all attempts to push him out, the mutineers left his house for the *Ikhwan*'s headquarters. There, in what seems to have been a coordinated plot, they joined a group of high-ranking anti-Hudaybi Brothers who had gathered in the headquarters, vowing to stage a sit-in until the dismissal of the four Apparatus commanders was overturned and an investigation into the matter completed. About seventy altogether, the group barricaded the headquarters' gates, thus making good of their threats. The incident continued throughout the night on that Friday but was resolved without bloodshed when the mutineers disbanded their occupation and left the headquarters at dawn. The crisis was resolved when an agreement was reached between the dissenting parties. While both sides pledged to quieten the situation and restore peace, it was agreed that an investigating body would be established to sort out differences. Yet the two sides would subsequently disagree over whether the investigation should relate to the four dismissed Brothers or to those who had occupied the headquarters. The former understanding was held by the anti-Hudaybi faction while the latter was invoked by al-Hudaybi and his followers. The following day, November 28, and in an atmosphere marked by excitement and anxiety, a general meeting was convened in the headquarters. Attended by a large number of rank and file from near and far, the assembled Brothers stated their support for the *Murshid* emotionally and en masse, and senior members repudiated the "coup attempt." The next day, twenty-one Brothers who had invaded al-Hudaybi's home were dismissed, while four senior Brothers were suspended until investigations could be completed. The four suspended Brothers were Saleh Ashmawi, Muhammad al-Ghazali, Abdel Aziz Jalal, and Sayyid Sabeq. The latter had been declared the new *Murshid* of the Brotherhood.[46]

The Fayez incident and its aftermath thus triggered a deep and lasting rift inside the Brotherhood, threatening to shatter the very coherence of the organization. Yet, Fayez's death and the subsequent insurgency were not all harmful for al-Hudaybi. The *Murshid* showed a willful ability to stay in control despite the threatening challenges he had faced. In the direct aftermath, he moved in to consolidate his grip on the Apparatus, and more generally to reinforce his position within the Brotherhood. Taking advantage of the crisis, the leader had dismissed the insurgent leaders, thereby purging the Brotherhood of some of his staunchest rivals.[47]

In the wake of this plot, al-Hudaybi continued his reconstitution of the Special Apparatus, naming Yusuf Tal'at its new commander. Tal'at was appointed by virtue of his esteemed position in the Brotherhood and its Special Apparatus, but also on account of his strong support of and loyalty to al-Hudaybi.[48] By appointing him in this role, Hudaybi once again showed that his initial idea of dismissing secrecy had been turned on its head.

The First Showdown: The Path toward All-Out Confrontation (January–October 1954)

As argued in the previous sections, since the early days of revolution the Brotherhood and the RCC had lived in an atmosphere marked by tension and mistrust. While the personal relationship between al-Hudaybi and Nasser is known to have been strained since their first encounter, the general relationship characterizing the military junta and the Brotherhood was also marked by apprehension and disagreement. Having overcome the plot against him, al-Hudaybi seemed to have secured a vital base of support inside the Brotherhood and rooted out the most serious internal challenge. By changing the leadership of the Apparatus and putting a loyalist at its head, he was on track to bringing the Brotherhood under his control. Therefore, as Mitchell maintains, al-Hudaybi's victory over the plotters was "a blow to the government" which "prompted its decision to dissolve the organization shortly afterwards."[49] Nasser, referencing the Brotherhood, intimated to the British shortly after al-Hudaybi's consolidation that the regime could not "tolerate a State within a State—he feared that there would be further trouble."[50] It was thus at this point in time, when al-Hudaybi had overcome the worst incident of division inside the Brotherhood, that the RCC "finally decided to dissolve the Brotherhood at the first suitable opportunity."[51]

On this account, I argue that it was this incident of repression, when the regime dissolved the Brotherhood and arrested 450 mostly senior members, including al-Hudaybi, in mid-January 1954[52] and again in February and March when other leading members of the organization were arrested[53] and Brotherhood officers were either court-martialed or fired,[54] that put the Brotherhood on a track of clandestinity and which brought about the final showdown in October 1954. In so claiming, I challenge the notion that the idea of confronting the regime emerged in the prison camps following the Manshiyya incident, as Kepel has argued.[55] This section therefore proceeds by discussing the deliberations which took place inside the Brotherhood on account of this first showdown in revolutionary Egypt. In this way, I intend to illustrate that this dissolution and the tense relationship with the regime more generally accounted for the militarization of conflict.

Therefore, as argued at the beginning of this chapter, regardless of whether the failed attempt on Nasser's life (the Manshiyya incident) was staged by the regime or ordered by the *Ikhwan*, the ensuing showdown came at a time when the Brotherhood had radicalized its means. In contrast to Kepel's account "[i]n the Beginning were the Camps,"[56] I hold that the "beginning" came before the "camps," although the subsequent treatment of the Brothers in the prison camps undoubtedly came to further radicalize a group of Brothers, as we shall see.

By dissolving the Brotherhood in January 1954, the regime had taken a drastic step against its erstwhile ally and partner. Following the dissolution, which was announced on January 15, 1954, the government issued a communique explaining its action and outlining its main accusations against the *Ikhwan*. Upon declaring the Brotherhood a political party, the communique announced that the Brotherhood was subject to the 1953 law of dissolution of parties. Charging the Brotherhood, inter alia, with efforts "to bring about a coup d'état under the cover of religion," endeavoring to infiltrate the army and police "in order to rouse opposition to the Government," and having contacted the Oriental Counsellor of the British Embassy while the Anglo-Egyptian negotiations were ongoing in April 1953, the regime showed an apparent intention of defaming the *Ikhwan*.[57] This was, as presented by the British embassy, an attempt to "smear the Moslem Brotherhood by showing that they [had] been intriguing with the British" against Egypt's interests.[58]

In the following days, a media campaign was launched against the Brotherhood highlighting their dangerous, malicious intentions. On January 17, 1954, the Minister of Interior issued a communique stating that "a secret store containing explosives and fire-arms to the value of £E 20,000 had been discovered on the estate of Hassan Ashmawi in Sharkiya Province."[59] The statement added that the discovered explosives "would have been enough to blow up an entire city." The government continued to release stories concerning the unearthing of dangerous elements of the Brotherhood and the discovery of quantities of explosives and other material such as wireless equipment belonging to the Brotherhood.[60] Additionally, regime-sponsored media continued besmirching the *Ikhwan*, accusing them of being a "reactionary force" working "hand in hand" with imperialism and exploiting "the faith of the masses in order to satisfy its lust for power."[61] The regime was making sure that the public should be under no illusions as to the Brotherhood's immoral and harmful intentions.

The dissolution and character assassination that the Brothers felt as unjustified triggered a reaction within the Brotherhood. Sensing an intention on the regime's part to root out their organization and to repress them, the Brothers, as they describe in their own words, began exploring the possibility of striking back at the regime. While this first dissolution and repression under military rule lasted for "only" two months,[62] we learn from Brotherhood accounts that to many of the Brothers it came to reveal the repressive and violent face of the postmonarchical regime, which induced a reaction on their part.

With the dissolution of the *Ikhwan* and the "deceitful accusations" with which he had charged the Brotherhood, Nasser had unveiled his true face and disclosed that he was "a dangerous man who [could] not be trusted, because he [had] no principles, morals nor religion" was the conclusion reached by Mahmoud Abdel Halim. Understanding the repression of the Brotherhood as a wrongful act, Abdel Halim reasoned that anyone "dealing with him [Nasser] should be cautious and in a cunning way, for one has to fight fire with fire." Against this background, while in prison, he drew the conclusion that the Brotherhood should take control of the country as soon as it gained freedom and totally "paralyze Nasser's maneuvering." To do so, it was necessary to undertake a "positive task, quickly," no matter the costs. This had to be done, according to Abdel Halim, to safeguard the people's aspirations. What Abdel Halim was envisioning was to confront the regime head-on, fearing that "Nasser would not give [them] time to rest." He relates confronting al-Hudaybi and other senior Brothers and lamenting their indolent reaction to Nasser's intrigues, as he puts it.[63]

Such anti-government sentiment and the desire to confront the authorities had become widespread among the rank and file of the *Ikhwan* following the dissolution. Symptomatic of this development, in late March 1954, a violent altercation broke out between Brotherhood members and the police. Yusuf al-Qaradawi recalls that the incident, which took place in his home village Saft al-Turab, in Gharbiyya province, had flared up when the local members of the *Ikhwan* had attempted to build a new branch house for the Brotherhood in the village.[64] Similar incidents took place in abundance in this period, indicating the deepening hostility and the hair-trigger response on both sides of the divide.

This reaction to repression also took a more organized turn at this point. Sensing a danger coming their way, Brotherhood members at higher levels began exploring ways and means to react to it. As a case in point, Abdel Munʿim Abdel Rauf, a former colonel in the army who had been exiled to Gaza in October 1952 and subsequently forced to retire in December 1953 only to be arrested in January 1954 and court-martialed, offers such an account.[65] He recalls a meeting with al-Hudaybi in which he warned the *Murshid* that the regime would "repress the Brotherhood's members" and it would "not abstain from erecting a prison camp in the desert to throw us in."[66] Concurring on the assumption that the regime would hit hard on the *Ikhwan*, al-Hudaybi tasked Abdel Rauf with organizing the Brotherhood officers in the army and to organize and train the members of the Special Apparatus. These preparations, Abdel Rauf recalls, were necessary to "deal the RCC a decisive blow." As a result of this meeting, which took place between late December 1953 and early January 1954, he began working with Yusuf Talʿat, the new commander of the Special Apparatus, to prepare a core group capable of confronting the regime.[67] On January 18, 1954, Abdel Rauf and other Brotherhood officers such as al-Hadri, Abdel Hay, and Hammuda were arrested, accused of subversive activities, and of recruiting officers to the ranks of the Brotherhood. This "unjust" arrest, as Abdel Rauf describes it, gave him the impression that there was no way back and led him to conclude that it had become necessary to conduct "a *jihad* against those despots" of the RCC. To fulfill this *jihad* and to "deal with this autocratic regime," he requested from Hussein Kamal al-Din, a member of the Brotherhood's General Guidance Office and leader of the Brotherhood in Cairo, 500 well-trained and fully armed *Ikhwan*. With this fully armed and trained "army," Abdel Rauf would lead a *jihad* against Nasser and his fellows. However, to his disappointment and "typical of the Brotherhood's leaders" as he lamentingly puts it, they did not live up to his request. Abdel Rauf, who had decided to fight the regime at any cost, sent al-Hudaybi a message asking for his consent to break out of prison and resist the "autocratic regime." Although he received al-Hudaybi's approval for escaping, Abdel Rauf did not receive an answer to the latter question. Aided by Muhammad Mahdi Akef, at that time an active member of the Brotherhood's Special Apparatus, Abdel Rauf escaped from prison in May 1954.[68]

Being at liberty, Abdel Rauf bemoaned what he lamented as the unpreparedness of the Brotherhood. He did not, however, cease preparing the Brotherhood for a confrontation. According to his account, he was at this time asked by Yusuf Tal'at and Ibrahim al-Tayyib (head of the Apparatus in Cairo) to prepare for "an Islamic coup." And he therefore set about making such arrangements.[69] Hence, in the words of leading members of the Brotherhood, this period witnessed a willingness and actual preparations for a showdown with the regime among a segment of Brothers.[70] As Abdel Rauf's story illustrates, a strong group inside the Brotherhood perceived the conflict with the regime as a zero-sum battle for which they had to be prepared.[71]

The prison experience no doubt had a significant impact on the Brotherhood and their perception of the regime. During the summer of 1954, in an atmosphere of pervading gloom, the Special Apparatus established a number of training camps to provide its members with the necessary training for an imminent encounter with the regime. Among the leaders of these preparations was Abdel Rauf, the fugitive officer who had, in his own words, decided to engage the "tyrants of the RCC" in an armed *jihad*.[72] Hindawi Diwayr (head of the Apparatus in Imbaba in northern Giza, who was later hanged by the regime in late 1954) points to these feelings of anxiety and the resulting preparations. Bearing witness before the "people's court" in late 1954, Hindawi stated that, fearing what was to come, the Apparatus's commanders reacted by expanding the body and incorporating many new members to its ranks. According to his testimony, this was to enable the secret structure to "fight the occupation and protect the *da'wa*."[73] "Protecting the *da'wa*" was more than likely meant as a protection against government repression. However, the hasty incorporation of large numbers of Brothers to the Apparatus without them having completed a challenging and extensive vetting and training process certainly created some significant problems for the maintenance of the Apparatus's rules and commands. Among the problems this expansion created were difficulties in indoctrinating and controlling the new recruits; many had never been a part of secret structures, and an effective line of command was lacking due to the novelty of these new structures. Another challenge was following the rules and commands regarding secrecy in practice. As a fragmented organization at this point, it was arduous to streamline these structures. Adel Kamal points to this challenge. According to him, the inner workings of the "secret" Apparatus were revealed to everyone outside the Brotherhood, which indicates that its "secrecy" was at least weakened.[74]

Meanwhile, the spiraling conflict between the Brotherhood and the regime seemed to find no way of ending. On May 4, 1954, al-Hudaybi sent a letter to premier Gamal Abdel Nasser denouncing the regime for breaking its promises made to the Brotherhood in late March 1954, and demanding social and economic reforms. Criticizing the government for its attitude toward the national cause, al-Hudaybi urged the government to prepare the army and people for the struggle against the British. Al-Hudaybi reminded Nasser that "speeches and declarations will not force the British to leave Egypt, what will, however, is a hard and long struggle [against them]."[75] This letter was also circulated as a pamphlet in the streets, strongly antagonizing Nasser and his fellow officers. This statement, circulated to the Egyptian masses, was understood as a clear challenge to the legitimacy of the nascent regime.[76] Hamed Abul Nasr maintains that Nasser perceived this letter as a threat, and thus his reaction was aggressive. American officials corroborated this view. They interpreted this statement as an indication of the Brotherhood's intention to challenge the regime, a challenge that most probably could include bloodshed.[77] Consequently, a wave of restraints was once again directed against Brotherhood members, many of whom were exiled to remote areas or fired from their jobs.[78]

At this time of increased tension and uncertainty, al-Hudaybi left Egypt in June 1954 for a tour of the Arab countries. Some leading members had come to consider al-Hudaybi as an obstacle to achieving better relations with the regime and thus hoped that his absence could help restore peace. Khamis Hamida and Abdel Rahman al-Banna, both leading members of the Brotherhood, met with Nasser to find a solution to unresolved issues. Hamida, the vice-*Murshid*, later established that al-Hudaybi's absence represented an opportunity to find a solution to the conflict with the regime.[79] The talks that took place between June 1954 and October of the same year between regime and *Ikhwan* representatives revolved primarily around the Brotherhood's Special Apparatus and their members in the police and the army. Nasser pressed for the dissolution of the Apparatus and the retirement of all officers belonging to the Brotherhood before a solution could be reached, but those were demands that these *Ikhwan* could not accept.[80]

These disagreements with the regime also resulted in a split in the upper echelons of the organization. Involving three different but powerful groups, the disagreements once again boiled to the surface. One group was headed by al-Hudaybi and his allies, such as Hasan al-Ashmawi, Munir al-Dilla, Farid Abdel Khaleq, and Salah Shadi. This faction had been the main force behind the appointment of al-Hudaybi in 1950 and was also bound together by family relationships. This first group was in control of the Special Apparatus and was strongly opposed to the government. A second group consisted of veteran Brothers such as Abdel Rahman al-Banna, Saleh Ashmawi, Muhammad al-Ghazali, al-Bahi al-Khouli, and others, who advocated close cooperation with the government and was at direct odds with al-Hudaybi, even calling for his dismissal as a step toward better relations with the government.[81] This faction had emerged shortly after al-Hudaybi's appointment but had become strong in its criticism of the *Murshid* during 1953, when veterans such as Ashmawi and Ghazali were suspended from the organization. A third group consisted of members of the Guidance Office, such as Khamis Hamida (vice-*Murshid*), Umar al-Tilmisani, Abdel Mu'iz Abdel Sattar, and others. This faction worked toward securing the support of a majority of the Brotherhood's General Assembly for closer cooperation with the government. In contrast to the second faction, however, this group did not explicitly challenge al-Hudaybi's legitimacy but envisioned nonoppositional policies toward the regime and wanted to achieve this by securing a majority in the Guidance Office and General Assembly.[82] Consequently, the rank and file of the Brotherhood was split between these different factions, each of which could command the support of a considerable group of Brothers. Al-Hudaybi's faction represented the confrontationists in this period, while the two latter factions were the accommodationists regarding their position toward the regime.

This fragmentation of the Brotherhood leadership became conspicuous in the organization's dealings with the government on the eve of the final showdown. While leading Brothers representing the accommodation factions were meeting with Nasser and other representatives of the junta to find a peaceful solution to the issues at hand, the Hudaybi faction continued to oppose the regime clandestinely. For instance, the confrontationist faction had been circulating a series of secret pamphlets[83] since late May entitled "The Muslim Brotherhood in Battle" (*al-Ikhwan al-Muslimin fi al-Ma'raka*). Harshly condemning the regime and propagating the ideas of the *Ikhwan*, the pamphlets were distributed by members of the Special Apparatus. These secret pamphlets denounced the regime among other things for compromising Egypt's national rights in its negotiations with the British.[84] The author of these pamphlets was Sayyid Qutb (1906–66), who had joined the Brotherhood in 1953.[85] The two pro-cooperation factions conceived such activities as dangerous and unnecessarily provocative. Yet, their requests for such activities to cease were to no avail.

In continuing the anti-government attitude, from Beirut al-Hudaybi strongly denounced the government's signing of a document titled "Heads of Agreement" with the British government. Being a preliminary foundation for a new treaty concerning the British presence in Egypt, al-Hudaybi's public disapproval of it in late July 1954 provoked the ire of the regime.[86]

Accordingly, and as a reaction to the *Ikhwan*'s continued opposition to the government, the Brotherhood became the subject of a strong media campaign during August 1954. Denounced as the "bearded charlatans" who trafficked in religion and who misrepresent the Islamic faith for their own gain, the Brotherhood once again became the target of verbal onslaught.[87] As a result, in the following period frequent violent clashes occurred between Brotherhood members and security forces. One such incident took place on August 27, when Hasan Duh, a prominent Brotherhood activists and preacher, reportedly denounced the regime from the pulpit of the Sharif mosque in Cairo. According to British reports, Duh had urged the worshippers to "oppose the present régime and [call] for violent action." Following his sermon, Duh led a demonstration into the streets which resulted in clashes with police and the subsequent arrest of Duh along with about "thirty to forty" Brotherhood sympathizers.[88] A similar incident occurred on September 10, 1954, when a violent clash erupted between Brotherhood members and the police, leading to the arrest of seventeen Brotherhood members and four people being injured. The clash was sparked by police intervention during the Friday sermon, where the preacher, who according to British reports was "surrounded by an armed bodyguard of Moslem Brethren," had described the RCC as "heretics."[89]

By September, the Hudaybi faction had come to the view that the government was committed to cracking down on the *Ikhwan*. In reaction, they began escalating their secrecy, seeking to avoid further repression. At this point, some 500 Brotherhood members had been arrested, and many had gone underground to avoid the same fate.[90] Anxious about the government's intentions to either arrest or kill him, al-Hudaybi went underground in early September. His going underground clearly indicates the level of conflict that had been reached at this stage. Hasan al-Ashmawi relates that Brotherhood leaders met at this time to discuss the proper way of dealing with the regime's policies toward them. But the Brothers failed to agree on a strategy to defend themselves. He lamented that "the revolutionary energy of a majority of them [the Brotherhood leaders] was an energy to endure persecution rather than confronting the oppressor to end his oppression."[91]

Such was the picture in September 1954, one month prior to the Manshiyya incident. On account of these tensions, a British report noted that the Brotherhood had decided to "take the strongest measures possible to gain their own ends." Among the measures suggest by the report was "the assassination of Colonel Nasser." According to Sir Ralph Stevenson "four Brethren are said to have volunteered for the task."[92] Nasser had stopped appearing publicly during this same period, thus forestalling a face-off of sorts.[93]

Hasan al-Ashmawi relates that the Brotherhood had decided to launch an anti-regime demonstration guarded by armed Brotherhood members to denounce the regime's autocratic nature and demand democratization. The demonstration was planned to take place on October 29. No plan, argues al-Ashmawi, was put forward to kill Nasser.[94] However, as this section has clarified, the idea of confronting the regime with violence had been present, at least among a faction of Brothers, prior to the Manshiyya incident. Accordingly, prior to the Manshiyya incident, the Brotherhood had developed the means to confront the government, as exemplified in their training camps and preparation for a showdown. This preparation and expansion of the Special Apparatus, as Talʿat testified before court in late November 1954, came as a correlate of the repression the Brotherhood had experienced in January 1954.[95]

Conclusions

Brotherhood accounts generally dismiss the Manshiyya incident as a fabrication, made up by the regime to frame the Brotherhood and use it as a pretext to repress them. It was a conspiracy (*muʾāmara*) and a staged act (*tamthīliya*) in which the Brotherhood played no role, argue most Brothers.[96] However, as this chapter has demonstrated, the lead-up to this pivotal moment of the conflict saw a militarization of means in which a section of the Brotherhood went toward radicalization in the conflict with the regime. As demonstrated in the accounts of leading members of the *Ikhwan*, such as Abdel Munʿim Abdel Rauf, Mahmoud Abdel Halim, and Hasan al-Ashmawi, some Brothers interpreted their conflict with the regime as an Islamic *jihad* against a despotic government which did not apply the rules of Islam, thus justifying the fight against it. I contend that long before its repression in late 1954, the Brotherhood had pivoted toward clandestinity and radicalization as a way of confronting the military regime. Accordingly, as a consequence of this development, it is arguably immaterial whether the Brotherhood was behind the assassination attempt or not. As shown in this chapter, the time was ripe for such an action, even if the Manshiyya attempt was concocted by the regime.

In parts of the existing research, there has been an underlying truism coupling the idea of *jihad* and the violent history of the Brotherhood with Sayyid Qutb and his well-known writings.[97] However, the period in the Brotherhood history studied above evidently disproves the notion that Qutb had the leading role in radicalizing the Brotherhood through his prison literature of the 1960s. On the contrary, senior Brothers such as Hasan Duh held the presumption at this early stage that a government which does not apply Islamic law should be perceived as "heretic" and can legitimately be fought.[98] One could therefore reasonably ask whether Qutb's affiliation with this radical fringe of the Brotherhood had resulted in his radicalization, rather than the other way around.

What I argue in the subsequent chapters is that, by experiencing the failure of "fighting the state" and the harsh repercussions this fight had brought down on their organization, many Brothers denounced anti-state violence and opted for nonviolent activism. However, a further attempt would first be made, as we shall see. The Brotherhood was wounded and split and many of the Brothers found themselves in prison, but they were by no means eradicated. To the Brothers, the aftermath of the Manshiyya incident represented the second *miḥna* (tribulation) in its history, in which the grim face of the military regime was unmasked. By being tortured, imprisoned, and hanged, the *Ikhwan* was subjected to a repression of unprecedented dimensions.

5

The Muslim Brotherhood Going Underground: Continuation under Suppression

As the momentous year 1954 neared its end, the Muslim Brotherhood seemed to be on its last legs. Having dared to defy the postcolonial regime without the necessary means to compete with it, the Brotherhood found itself hovering between life and death. *Al-Ikhwan* had gone into battle against Nasser and his fellows as a fragmented and therefore weakened organization. In the wake of Hasan al-Banna's death in early 1949 and the concomitant repression the Brotherhood witnessed, the formidable mass organization had experienced a blow to its coherence. Having named Hasan al-Hudaybi as al-Banna's successor, the judge-turned-mass-leader had failed to meet the expectations of his followers. The *Ikhwan* had therefore experienced multiple internal frictions and conflicts that had rattled its very foundation. In consequence, when the looming face-off between the Brothers and the officers took place, Egypt's new rulers managed to stamp out their last and most serious opponent with noteworthy ease. The date of October 26, 1954, would become historic in this tale about the one-time allies-turned-mortal-enemies. When on that day Mahmoud Abdel Latif discharged his eight rounds at the man who in the near future would become the champion of Arab Nationalism, he seemed to have sealed the destiny of his organization.

In the fatal weeks that followed, a sweeping suppression of the Brotherhood was set in motion, leading to the arrest of most of the senior members of the *Ikhwan* and the ransacking and subsequent burning to the ground of the Brotherhood's headquarters. Mobs attacked Brotherhood headquarters in different Egyptian towns, and properties known to be owned by Brothers were set on fire. In some attacks, machine guns and grenades were used, and those who attacked the sites were uniformed members of the National Guard. Such incidents, according to British intelligence, were "obviously organised."[1] On October 30, 1954, al-Hudaybi was arrested in hiding, marking what seemed like the definite defeat of the *Ikhwan*. Concurrently, a comprehensive propaganda campaign was set in motion against the Brothers, highlighting the "mischiefs" of this organization and its members. This media campaign, employing the pens of some of the most established authors in Egypt,[2] labeled the Brothers as wayward conspirators who "arrange death and fear" to their "Brothers in nation, religion and life" and describing them as those who traffic religion and utilize Islam to champion their misdeeds.[3] Ali Amin, in a mocking tone, described "*Ikhwani*-Egypt" had the assassination of Nasser succeeded as a country without banks, barbers, trousers, cars, foreign languages, or modern sciences.[4] As if this attempt at character assassination was not enough, daily reports of arrests and confessions revealing a "comprehensive and evil" conspiracy to kill the premier and overthrow the government filled the pages of newspapers almost every day in this period.[5] Buttressing the accusations against this organization that "justifies assassinations against all social groups in Egypt,"[6] the security apparatus presented "evidence" to demonstrate that the Brothers were agents of foreign powers and enemies of the nation.[7] Thus, facing mass arrests, dissolution, and becoming subject to a comprehensive media campaign intended to expose the "murderous face" of the *Ikhwan*, the organization was enduring its hitherto most serious challenge.

On November 1, the military junta established "the People's Tribunal" (*Maḥkamat al-Sha'b*) under the direction of Gamal Salim, the RCC's "wild man," together with Anwar al-Sadat and Hussein al-Shafi'i. Set up to prosecute those responsible for the botched attempt on Abdel Nasser's life, the tribunal became another tool of collective punishment of the Brothers and a platform for insulting them and their ideas.[8] When legal proceedings were commenced on November 9, they were broadcast live, and a clear attempt to character assassinate the Brotherhood and its leaders took place. Gamal Salem, in a grotesque manner, behaved like a chief prosecutor rather than a judge, intimidating the prosecuted and at various times threatening them. The officer-cum-judge, who seemed to be engaged in a personal vendetta, set witnesses against each other, insulting them and making the audience ridicule them. A great part of the questioning was irrelevant for the particular case, being applied instead to present the Brotherhood as "merchants of religion" and "lackeys of foreign powers." This may indicate that the court was generally thought of as a platform to discredit and break the Brotherhood, its leaders, ideas, and history, rather than actually indicting those responsible for the assassination attempt. Accusing the Brotherhood of considering Hasan al-Banna a "prophet," for instance, Salem described them persistently as a group of *munāfiqūn* (hypocrites).[9] The tribunal was essentially utilized as a vehicle to bring down the Brotherhood and eliminate what popularity it might still have among the general population.

Looking at the Brotherhood from this vantage point, the organization effectively seemed to have been eradicated or moving toward its imminent conclusion. Following the arrest of al-Hudaybi on October 30, other high-ranking members were brought in throughout November. Khamis Hamida, the vice-*Murshid* was arrested on November 11, and the following days witnessed the arrest of Ibrahim al-Tayyib (head of the Apparatus in Cairo) and Yusuf Talʿat (general leader of the Apparatus). The latter was arrested on November 14, signaling an almost complete breakdown of the Brotherhood's covert structures. By the end of November, the government announced that it had arrested 1,000 members of the Brotherhood. When brought before Salem and subjected to his harsh verbal assaults and unrestrained intimidation,[10] most Brothers seemed unable to stand up for themselves or their organization. That most members and senior leaders were unable to respond to Salem's accusations and insults certainly strengthened the impression of the Brotherhood as a group lacking the will and capacity to put up a fight. But the lack of resistance on the part of the Brothers was not simply due to a lack of will. As observed by Mitchell, the "speedy collapse of the organizational fabric was partly due to torture in the prisons."[11] The rough treatment of Brotherhood prisoners accounted for a great deal of the *Ikhwan*'s bewilderment at this point. The Brothers were taken aback by the unexperienced degree of mistreatment they were met with, as is shown below.

On December 4, the first verdicts of the "People's Tribunal" were pronounced, attracting considerable interest in the media and leading to anguish among the *Ikhwan*. Seven members of the Brotherhood, among them al-Hudaybi, were sentenced to death, while seven other members of the Guidance Office received life imprisonment with hard labor, and two members of the Office were sentenced to fifteen years in prison. On a cold Tuesday in December, six of those sentenced to death walked their last but certainly most heavy steps toward the gallows. On December 7,[12] 1954, in a mood of desolation, the Brothers uttered their last words before breathing their last breath. Having challenged the military regime, the *Ikhwan* had thus experienced the coercive face of Egypt's new rulers, paying the ultimate price.[13] Al-Hudaybi's death sentence was commuted to life imprisonment with hard labor. After the hangings, the work of the tribunal was assigned to three courts headed by junior officers assigned to prosecute other lower-ranking members of the *Ikhwan*. By February 1955, approximately 1,000 Brotherhood members had been tried.[14]

Under these circumstances, most contemporary observers and scholars perceived the Brotherhood as an organization of the past, ultimately broken by the "secular, tolerant spirit of the times in Egypt" personified by the young officers.[15] Commenting on the Brotherhood's ability to endure, Harris argued that the Brotherhood's organization "had been broken up, without any likelihood of resurrection in the foreseeable future."[16] Writing in the 1960s, Christina Harris viewed the Brotherhood as eradicated and did not expect it to re-emerge in the near future. Going even further, Richard Mitchell asserted that the *Ikhwan* would play no further role in the future of Egypt or the Arab world. "[T]he essentially secular reform nationalism now in vogue in the Arab world will continue to operate to end the earlier appeal of this organization."[17] Gilles Kepel has argued in a more recent study that following the suppression of 1954, the Brotherhood "began a sojourn in the desert that was to last two decades in Egypt."[18] Accordingly, while I disagree in understanding the *Ikhwan*'s history during these important years as a "sojourn in a desert," I attempt to historically present an insight into what happened to this organization, and how it continued during these repressive years.

However, with President Abdel Nasser's unexpected death in September 1970 and the concomitant termination of the Nasserite regime, many observers came to see the re-emergence of the Brotherhood as imminent. By way of illustration, in May 1971 a telegram from the British Embassy in Tel Aviv reported rumors of "more power for the Moslem Brotherhood."[19] Inquiring about the Brotherhood's position in Egyptian society, the embassy asked whether the *Ikhwan* had influenced al-Sadat's (then president of Egypt) "corrective revolution" of May 15, 1971, in which he purged Nasserite and leftist elements of the government. The telegram added that there were repeated rumors that "Sadat was formerly a member of the Brotherhood and that they [the *Ikhwan*] may even have been behind his actions."[20] Underpinning the notion of a reappearance of the Brotherhood, the British Embassy in Cairo discussed at length the organization's position in Egypt in July 1971. Assessing the prospects of a Brotherhood resurgence in Egypt, Richard Ashton Beaumont, British ambassador to Cairo (1959–73), stressed that his Egyptian contacts had "been telling" him that the Brotherhood was becoming "a force to be reckoned with."[21] Echoing the above, the ambassador referred to rumors saying that "Sadat is trying to encourage the Muslim Brethren to recruit again, as a possible antidote to Communist infiltration," and that "a Muslim Brother has been placed in each battalion of the army to inculcate correct religious ideas in the impressionable young." Beaumont, who advised caution in believing such reports, did conclude, however, that

"Sadat seems to be using the basic appeal of the Brotherhood for his own ends."[22] Reports to the same effect explicitly noted that a significant number of Brothers had been released and repressive measures against the organization had been brought to an end as part of a policy designed "to balance Leftist influence in the new A.S.U. [Arab Socialist Union]."[23]

The appearance and frequency of such rumors less than a year after Nasser's death clearly suggest that the Brotherhood had continued to exist despite the repression it had encountered during the Nasserite years. As soon as Nasser's regime had come to an effective end, rumors of an imminent resurgence of the Brotherhood became abundant. That being so, I intend to study these crucial years in the history of the Brotherhood that followed the repressive events of late 1954. In so doing, I contend that through a historical study of these years, we can trace a continuation of the Islamic modernist school that "strove to establish a balance between Islamic authenticity and Western-inspired modernization."[24] Accordingly, this chapter and the next aim to bridge the history of the Brotherhood by shedding light on this understudied period in the *Ikhwan*'s history. In arguing that the Brotherhood continued its existence during these years, I challenge the general presumption that the organization disappeared and then "re-emerged" following the demise of the Nasserite regime.

This chapter will examine the first part of this era, that is, 1954–7, during which the first period of repression forced the organization underground and left a majority of its rank and file separated from senior leadership. This discussion will be taken up again in the following chapter, where I will discuss the eventful years of 1958 to1970. In dividing this period into two subsequent chapters, I attempt to show how in the first period the Brotherhood continued on the agency of individual and often young members who perceived it as their personal obligation to continue working in the ranks of the organization. My main focus will be on those young and often inexperienced members who decided to continue their activities after the imprisonment of most of the active senior activists and leaders despite the risks entailed. I discuss the organizational developments at this time but also the ideological reactions to the harsh repression to which they were subjected. Furthermore, I discuss developments in the prisons, because I maintain that the Brothers did not cease to be *Ikhwan* when imprisoned, but more often than not they continue to play a role from inside the prison walls. Chapter 6, which is a chronological continuation of this chapter, deals with the nationwide reorganization of the Brotherhood, known in the research as "Organization 65" and the role played by Sayyid Qutb in these events.

Repressed yet Enduring (1954–7)

On a quiet and somber day in December 1954, despite widespread appeals for clemency from the Syrian government and popular pleas from a number of Arab countries, the death sentences were carried out on six members of the Brotherhood. Representatives of the press, including a number of Western correspondents, witnessed the execution on December 7 and were, in the words of a British report, "impressed by the bearing of the six men in their last moments." Muhammad Farghali refused to express any anxiety, declaring forcefully moments before his execution, "I am ready to die, I welcome the meeting with God." Abdel Qader Uda, the magistrate and former deputy *Murshid*, declared reproachfully, "Praise be to God that He has made me a martyr, and may He make my blood a curse upon the men of the revolution." Yusuf Tal'at in last-moment insight and valor proclaimed, "[M]ay God forgive me, as well as those who have done harm to me."[25] Yet, apart from the strong bearing of the executed men, there were no signs of outright resistance by the *Ikhwan* to the harsh crackdown it had become an easy target of. It seemed as if the Brotherhood had accepted its destiny at the hands of a stronger opponent, that is, the military regime. According to Mitchell, the hangings were received with "stunned and horrified silence." Mitchell, looking at the organization as being utterly destroyed, perceived this silence as a sign of its inability to react in any vigorous way.[26] Besides protests in neighboring Arab countries, by and large organized by the local branches of the Brotherhood,[27] virtually no objections were voiced in Egypt—the Egyptian Brotherhood remained almost silent, displaying its ultimate death. Or so it seemed at least for contemporary observers. As noted by Mitchell, the aftermath of the hangings was "anti-climactic."[28]

However, as this chapter discusses, this anti-climactic course of events was not so much an indication of the Brotherhood's termination as a reflection of the rough repression inflicted on the *Ikhwan*. This crackdown had taken place at a time when the Brotherhood was experiencing a broken coherence and major cracks inside the organization, which certainly did not buttress its ability to react or defy the postcolonial regime.[29]

The chapter proceeds as follows: after a short exposition of the repression faced by the *Ikhwan*, I move on to describe the continuation of the Brotherhood inside the prisons and on the outside.

Directly stemming from Abdel Latif's botched assassination attempt, an unrelenting wave of persecution directed against the Brotherhood took place. Besides the abovementioned executions of six members, an unknown number of members were incarcerated under cruel conditions. James Toth has claimed, for instance, that "thousands of its members [were] rounded up and jailed," while Zollner holds that the numbers made official only represent a "glimpse of the scale of the persecution" faced by the Brotherhood.[30] Such descriptions, despite their imprecise nature, indicate the hitherto unseen degree of repression directed at the *Ikhwan*. Brotherhood accounts offer even more bleak accounts, putting the figure of arrested Brothers at tens of thousands.[31] Be that as it may, on all accounts the degree and nature of persecution was of unprecedented scale in the Brotherhood's history.

In the first phase following the arrests, when the interrogations were still ongoing, a majority of Brothers were brought to the notorious *al-Sijn al-Ḥarbī* (the Military Prison). Known for its severe torture and mistreatment of inmates, the military prison presented many Brothers with unexperienced torments. Abbas al-Sisi, a middle-ranking Brother from Alexandria, recalls entering the military prison. "You were met by torturers, it was like entering a human slaughterhouse."[32] Muhammad Hamed Abul Nasr, at that time a member of the Brotherhood's Guidance Office, describes in his memoirs these painful early days of arrest. He was arrested on November 19, 1954, in Manfalut, his hometown, to be brought to the military prison in Cairo for interrogation. This was the beginning of a journey of torture, abuse, and subsequent imprisonment that would last for twenty years. In an atmosphere of intimidation and humiliation, upon entering the prison gates he was met with a beating meted out by a group of prison guards.[33] The experiences of Abul al-Nasr were prototypical for many of the *Ikhwan* at this time. These "welcome sessions," as they are described by the Brotherhood inmates, were a common practice inflicted on most newcomers to this prison of sinister reputation.[34] This "welcome" was an attempt by the authorities to break the confidence of the prison's residents and to subject them to the new reality they were expected to concede to. To the anguish of many Brotherhood members, however, this "welcome" only marked the beginning of a period of painful interrogation and repression, in which the oppressive state unveiled its most violent and brutal face. Brotherhood accounts describing the first phase of the second *miḥna* are replete with stories about the cruel treatment they were exposed to, especially under interrogation. Those arrested were subjected to a variety of harsh treatments and torture, including, inter alia, the extraction of fingernails and toenails, whipping, beating with clubs, being held in a room filled with cold water for hours, being kept awake under questioning for prolonged periods, and being subjected to attacks by dogs. The treatment had reached such ruthless levels that an unknown number of Prisoners had succumbed to it. According to a report compiled by the oppositional "Committee for Free Egypt" in July 1955, this had led to the death of many inmates under torture.[35] Farid Abdel Khaleq, who witnessed this suppression firsthand and on his own body, accounts that twenty-nine Brothers had died under torture between late October 1954 and early 1955.[36]

The torture, maltreatment, and humiliation were not purposeless. Looking into the methodical ways of mistreating and abasing the Brothers,[37] it would appear that this molestation was intended to break them down. By mistreating them, the authorities hoped to shatter the members' confidence in their organization and to push them away from previously held convictions. As an example, *Ikhwan* members were lined up in vast numbers as an orchestra in the prison yard with al-Hudaybi standing as maestro. The inmates-cum-chorus were forced to sing "Gamal [Abdel Nasser] oh symbol of nationalism, our most beautiful holidays were when you survived on the day of Manshiyya … ." This prison-yard spectacle was monitored by guards surrounding the yard who scourged the prisoners if they failed to sing, thus ensuring their partaking in this humiliating act.[38] In further attempts to break senior members of the Brotherhood, leading Brothers were given severe beatings in front of their followers, and some of them even had their beards pulled off or burned.[39] In a few instances, some of them were even mockingly photographed in a sack being interrogated by surrounding army officers. These photos were then made public, probably as an attempt to discourage any idea of opposition to the regime.[40] Mohammed Mahdi Akef looked back at the experience in the military prison as "black and miserable." Of its brutality he noted that no one's "imagination can understand the cruelty of that torture."[41] Al-Qaradawi, who like many other *Ikhwan* experienced this persecution on his own body, recalls his first impression upon entering the prison: "We were welcomed with whips, cursing and to a gruesome spectacle."[42] It was a vicious spiral of savagery and cruelty that the Brother would quickly come to fear after entering this "inferno of the war prison."[43]

One could discount these accounts as mere propaganda written in retrospect by Brotherhood members to discredit the Nasserite regime and portray it as inhumane. Evidence, however, points to the credibility of these accounts. In 1957, when a group of army officers were standing trial alongside leading members of the Wafd party, some of the officers described the same forms of torture as had been applied to the Brothers. Charged with preparing a coup d'état against the regime, the officers lamented in detail how they had been treated in prison, corroborating many of the stories the Brothers described. In one example, army officer al-Islambouly withdrew his confession before the court. Al-Islambouly, who was standing trial for conspiracy, claimed that his confessions had been obtained under torture. Interestingly, talking to the judge, al-Islambouly declared, "They [the interrogators] threatened me: 'If you do not tell us everything we will imprison your wife and your children will remain without food. You know what happened to the Moslem Brothers—you know we have the whip and other means.'"[44] Thus, during the latter part of the 1950s, the example of the *Ikhwan* and what they had experienced in prison had become an intimidating lesson for other actors in Egypt. What happened to the *Ikhwan* was something to be avoided. Contemporary British reports also stand as another corroborating source to this narrative of cruel mistreatment. According to these reports, to extract information about the Muslim Brotherhood, the Egyptian police used "unorthodox and ruthless" methods. Describing the methods applied by the Egyptian authorities to "disrupt" the Muslim Brotherhood, the British noted that no effort had been made to conceal "this forcible interrogation."[45]

Following the initial period of interrogation, and when the verdicts against the Brothers had been meted out during late 1954 and early 1955, the question of accommodating such a large number of prisoners was raised. To solve this issue, the authorities sent leading members of the Brotherhood, such as members of the Guidance Office and leading militants of the Special Apparatus who had been sentenced to long prison terms with hard labor, to Liman Tura.[46] In this prison, located just south of Cairo, the Brotherhood inmates were put to work crushing stones and other kinds of forced labor. The treatment in this prison was characterized as the most rigorous and harsh, only exceeded by the early experiences in the military prison. Al-Hudaybi and the members of the Guidance Office began serving their sentences in "department 1" of Liman Tura but were soon transferred to a desert camp in the Wahat al-Kharja, located in no-man's land about 600 kilometers south of Cairo. Presented as a "concentration camp for political prisoners," this camp came to serve as a remote exile for Brotherhood leaders. By placing them as far from their followers and families as possible, the authorities were making sure that they were unable to influence events.[47]

Younger and lower-ranking Brothers who had been sentenced to between five and ten years in prison were sent to provincial prisons such as al-Qanatir, Qena, al-Minya, Bani Swief, and Asyut.[48] In addition, a number of Brothers—estimates put the figure at about 1,000—were incarcerated without being brought before a judge or after receiving suspended sentences. These Brothers remained under arrest in the military prison or *Sijn al-Qalʿa* (the Citadel Prison) for about two years before being released.[49] In this way, the authorities intended to cut off the rank and file from the leadership by putting the leading and instrumental members as far away from influence as possible.[50]

However, even at this time of harsh repression, which by all accounts represented the darkest moment in the Brotherhood's history, the *Ikhwan* had not been terminated—clearly speaking to the organization's vitality. With the purpose of reaching an understanding of this persistence, I now proceed by shedding light on the Brotherhood's continuation. Taking into account the Brotherhood's continued organization and activities inside prisons, this section shows that prison walls did not necessarily disrupt the *Ikhwan*'s ability to continue as an organized body.

Inside Prison Walls: Hardships and Continuation

By the late 1954 and early 1955, the world's largest Islamist organization in modern times had been defeated by a stronger opponent. Nasser's postcolonial military regime had outmaneuvered and outclassed it, leaving the Brotherhood crumbled. The persecution, rough-handed and unyielding, had cost the lives of an unknown number of Brothers and the incarceration of many others. To cut off leading members from their followers, the authorities had transferred leading and commanding Brothers to the newly established concentration camp. However, as we shall see in the following, these tribulations, albeit severe and menacing, did not disrupt the Brotherhood's presence and engagement.

Presenting a detailed and sometimes romantic account of life in prison, Muhammad Mahdi Akef offers us an illustrative review of the continuity and endurance of this period. Akef, who was sentenced to death by the People's Tribunal but had his verdict commuted to life with hard labor, was a long-term inmate.[51] The seventh general guide, known by the Brothers as "the prisoner of all eras," was held in prison for twenty years, remaining in incarceration until 1974, almost four years after Nasser's demise in 1970.[52] As a militant of the Special Apparatus in Cairo, he had taken part in the first Arab–Israeli war and in the anti-British activities in the Canal Zone in 1951. Against this background, the young Akef had acquired a reputation for courageousness and militancy. An ardent believer in the Brotherhood's ideals, Akef did not shy away from challenges, as his activities clearly evidenced. These attributes and this resume taken together meant that upon his arrest he was transferred to Liman Tura alongside 200 of the leading members of the organization. In Tura, Akef shared a cell with al-Hudaybi and Abdel Aziz Atiyya, a member of the Brotherhood's Guidance Office.[53]

Tura, Akef remembers, was a trial for the newly arrived inmates at the beginning. With shackles on arms and legs, they were assigned to hard labor, such as breaking heavy stones and transporting them in searing heat. As a maximum-security prison, Liman Tura had very stringent rules. Inmates were prohibited from having ordinary everyday necessities such as tea and sugar and civilian clothes. "We were given threadbare clothes that hardly covered our bodies" was Akef's description of their prison uniforms.[54] What made life even harder there was the harsh treatment and severe restraints to which they were subjected. No doubt, by putting the influential members in such circumstances, the authorities were attempting to break them. However, it was not all bad, if we are to believe Akef's account. The *Ikhwan*, he recalls, soon began unearthing ways to get around these restrictions and to continue a life despite the difficulties. For example, it did not take long before a "secret" life had developed in prison in which Brotherhood members began smuggling a variety of foods and other "forbidden stuff" into the prison.[55] Even more consequentially, however, the inmates erected communication structures to activists outside the prison walls. "We had people inside the prison who helped us smuggle a variety of things in and out of the prison," Akef recalls.[56]

Judging by such accounts, the Brotherhood quickly became able to reach out to individuals outside the prisons, and even to uphold contact with inmates in other prisons through such structures of communication.

Shortly after being sent to Liman Tura, the Brotherhood began organizing itself hierarchically inside the prison. Akef, who had gained experience from his establishment of training camps in 1951 (see Chapter 3), was elected "head of the Brothers" in the prison. Tasked with organizing the everyday life of the *Ikhwan*, Akef was to take responsibility for this group of inmates. "We organized ourselves in a clearly structured way," Akef recounts. Having a direct channel of communication to al-Hudaybi and other key leaders, Akef became a link to the members of the Guidance Office through Saleh Abu Ruqayiq, himself a member of the Office. Besides directing communication between the Brotherhood's different layers, Akef also organized day-to-day activities within the prison. On this, he relates that prison became a "permanent camp" of the Brotherhood. Turning prison into a hub of knowledge and exercise, Akef set up circles of Quran studies and organized sessions of physical training for the Brothers to gain the most benefit from their time in imprisonment.[57] Akef, as head of all the Brothers inside this notorious prison, was aided by a committee of leading *Ikhwan* tasked with arranging the inmates' cultural and financial affairs. Arranged in a hierarchical order, the Brothers in each prison cell were organized in *usar*, resembling the systems that existed before incarceration.

Consequently, it became possible to rationalize communication and to proceed with unambiguous organizational structures within the prison walls.[58]

Liman Tura was indeed a frightening place, where hardcore criminals were incarcerated, and where inmates were assigned to do forced labor and were treated badly, according to Abdel Rahman al-Bannan's description of his initial emotions when he arrived at Liman Tura. Al-Bannan, who at the time of his arrest in 1954 was a 22-year-old humanities student at Cairo University, was sentenced to fifteen years in prison with hard labor. He served some of the time in Liman Tura, where he and his like-minded Brothers were set to crushing stones on the nearby mountain. Yet, despite these miseries and hardships, the prison, in the words of Abdel Rahman, was turned into a "camp of knowledge, culture and new human experiences, it was a bizarre but at the same time enjoyable period."[59] These accounts are illustrative, and we find similar narratives from other prisons where lower-ranking Brothers were interned.[60]

In May 1955, about six months into their term at Liman Tura, 100 leading members of the Brotherhood, including Akef, were transferred to the remote Wahat al-Kharja prison camp.[61] This concentration camp which, as seen above, was erected to house political prisoners became the home for many leading members of the *Ikhwan*. Intended presumably to further isolate these influential Brothers from the *Ikhwan*'s rank and file, this transfer placed them in the desert beyond the reach of any activists. Among the exceptions to this transfer was Sayyid Qutb, who had been sentenced to fifteen years in prison with hard labor. On account of his bad health and his consequent need for systematic health care, Qutb stayed in the Liman's infirmary. At the infirmary, the diligent writer found himself undisturbed by everyday issues outside prison. In his secluded spot, Qutb found solace in the company of fellow Brothers and the Quran. He affirmed as much in his magnum opus "*In the Shade of the Quran*." Commenting on life "in the shade of the Quran," as he dubbed it, Qutb penned passionately, "Life in the shade of the Quran is a blessing, a blessing that only those who have tasted it will comprehend. It is a blessing that elevates, sanctifies, and ameliorates life."[62] Finding an amelioration of life within these narrow walls of his imprisonment, Qutb set about penning a number of books, most noteworthy of these being *Milestones*.[63] Highly revered by his fellow inmates, the eloquent author became an acclaimed figure among those who came to know him in prison.[64]

In other words, the continuation of literary production and discursive interaction illustrates that a functioning network existed at this point in time, with the Liman Tura infirmary at the epicenter. Inmates who were transferred to the Liman Tura for treatment carried messages to and from their own prisons, thus continuing the lines of communication.[65]

When the leading members left Liman Tura to be relocated in the desert, other lower-ranking *Ikhwan* replaced them in the hierarchical order, thus ensuring that no vacuum evolved in the Brotherhood's hierarchy. Ahmad al-Bess, a member of the Special Apparatus, was appointed head of the commanding committee, thus replacing Akef as head of Brothers in Liman Tura.[66] Being a middle-ranking but highly esteemed Brother, al-Bess took charge of managing "*Ikhwani* activities inside prison."[67]

In al-Wahat, a similar organization of activities and systematic structuring of members emerged soon after the Brothers' arrival. The prison camp assembled a significant number of Brotherhood leaders and active members such as Mustafa Mashhur, Umar al-Tilmisani, Akef, Muhammad Hamed Abul Nasr, Salah Shadi, Hussein Kamal al-Din, and many others. With its isolated and outlying location, this concentration camp was no doubt a burden for many Brothers, who became displaced and cut off from their families and personal networks. However, as with life in Liman Tura, al-Wahat came to host a variety of activities such as sporting events, teaching of illiterate Brothers, and religious seminars, which offered the Brothers solace. Akef, who spent about nine years in this unapproachable site, looked back at the years in the Wahat as a time replete with activities, sports, and lectures.[68]

A similar account is presented in a poem composed by Mustafa Mashhur at that time while in prison. The poem, which urges courageousness and offers a sarcastic account of life in prison, reveals that the Brothers were preoccupied with discussions on different issues and engaged with training sessions, football, and basketball matches.[69] Furthermore, in letters he sent to his family during his prison years, Mashhur describes the prison experience as God's ordained tribulation and a test of the Brothers' belief in their cause. The ardent Mashhur was convinced that this suffering of the *Ikhwan* would be rewarded in the afterlife. The only condition was, however, that they withstand hardship and endure it in the name of Islam. Thus, comprehending his mission and his endurance as a Godly ordained duty, Mashhur encouraged patience and fortitude. This stands clear in the letters he sent home during these difficult years of tribulation.[70]

As such accounts clearly reveal, a continuation of Brotherhood structuring, activities, and relationships lived on inside prisons. However, these accounts stand in marked contrast to the descriptions of the first period of arrest and interrogation in the notorious military prison. When depicting their experiences in the military prison upon arrest, most Brothers agree in describing it as a period of humiliation and despair in which "most inmates were submissive and passive, unable to voice a 'why', never mind a 'no.'"[71] In the words of a Brother, "the military prison was pure hell."[72] We can ascertain from such descriptions that what Zollner has described as a "mood of despair"[73] was very present at the early stage of arrest, where "the atmosphere of pain and horror" was predominant.[74] Abbas al-Sisi gives a similar description. He explains that the hanging of six Brothers left the members of the *Ikhwan* in a state of "astonishment, silence and grief."[75] However, this state of mind did not remain constant throughout the prison period, as the descriptions cited above indicate. On the contrary, when the first period of extraordinarily rough duress was over, concomitant with the conclusion of legal proceedings in early 1955, we observe a relative normalization of conditions in prisons. This normalization, which occurred when the *Ikhwan* began serving their prison terms, gave the Brothers breathing room, which they utilized to continue their *Ikhwani* activities. Al-Tilmisani points to the continuation of the Brotherhood despite persecution, explaining that "the Brotherhood continued [upon the dissolution] as if it had only been dissolved on paper [...]. When two Muslims meet to sit down and study the Quran, or to get trained in the prophetic *Sira* (biography), Islamic jurisprudence, Quranic exegesis or to discuss the conditions of the nation and population, such activities cannot be prohibited by law."[76] Such meetings, which took place discreetly, continued inside and outside the prison walls.[77]

Thus, the prison period was not constantly characterized by the same degree of hardship as had been the case of the extraordinary treatment the internees had been subjected to in the military prison. "When we entered prison, no one dared to talk back to the interrogators [...] but soon we began meeting and talking to each other and criticizing the regime," relates Ahmad Raif, a Brotherhood activist who was interned in the military prison.[78]

To Support or to Defy the Regime? Deliberations inside the Prisons

By 1955, all the sentenced Brothers had been transferred from the internment camps to prisons where they would serve their terms. It was at this juncture that one of the more serious issues appeared among the Brothers and came to preoccupy a great deal of the *Ikhwan*'s thinking inside the prisons. Having been arrested and repressed on account of their opposition to the nascent military regime, the Brotherhood members found themselves in an agonizing position at the end of 1954. Upon consolidation, Nasser's postcolonial regime had uncloaked its true face to its opponents. As a populist, authoritarian regime, the military junta vehemently exhibited that it was not prepared to allow any form of political pluralism, let alone opposition. This was vividly felt by all oppositional groups when the Nasserite state began exposing some of its hardhanded methods, meant to subdue all voices and secure "consensus" in society. The Brotherhood, being the largest and most potent political force at the time, came to feel the lion's share of the regime's repressive capabilities.

Importantly, however, as was discussed in Chapter 4, not all Brothers had been staunchly against the regime prior to the showdown and the subsequent repression. On the contrary, many of them had seen Nasser as a Brother and the "revolution" as their own. These were the Brothers I described in the previous chapter as the accommodationists. In addition, as staunch nationalists who had perceived themselves to be the vanguard of a nationalist *jihad* against British colonization, the Brothers were faced with a fundamental dilemma when the Suez Crisis erupted in the fall of 1956. The crisis, historic and vital in Egypt's modern history, eventuated in the final demise of British colonization of Egypt. The beginning, however, came with Nasser's momentous nationalization of the canal on July 26.[79] The Suez Crisis, or the tripartite aggression as it is known in Arab historiography, amounted to a full-scale attack on Egypt, first by Israeli forces, then followed up by a British–French intervention. The British and French intervention turned into a debacle when the invaders were forced to withdraw from Egypt following warnings from the US government. This historic event has been thoroughly studied elsewhere, and therefore I do not need to recapitulate its story here.[80]

The assault on Egypt triggered a dilemma in the ranks of the Brotherhood. Pondering whether to state their support of the Nasserite regime or to stay on the sidelines was no easy decision to take. In the eyes of many Brothers, the Nasserite regime had committed atrocities that could not easily be forgotten, let alone forgiven. An offer of support was perceived by one group of Brothers as being an implicit endorsement of a regime that had killed fellow *Ikhwan*. But, at the same time, Egypt was being attacked by three foreign armies, and the Brotherhood had to make its stance unequivocally clear, so the contention of another group of Brothers. This discourse became the order of the day in the prisons and resulted in divergences among the Brothers. These discussions inside the Brotherhood resemble the accommodationists versus confrontationists split prior to the repression of late 1954 (see Chapter 4).[81]

Understanding it as a patriotic duty to endorse the regime under these conditions, a group of Brothers chose to state their support of the regime. Hasan

Duh, who was serving a 15-year term with hard labor, recalls organizing a meeting in Liman Tura to discuss the inmates' standpoint regarding the aggression. After long deliberations where Brothers voiced their strongly differing views on this question, they agreed to send a letter of support to the government. Rather than expressing their unconditional support of the Nasserite regime, the Brothers decided to state in the letter that they would volunteer as recruits to fight alongside the army, but in a separate "Ikhwan regiment." In a frank recollection, Duh recalled that "we expected to be released … but our hopes perished."[82] This accommodationist or pragmatist faction attracted a number of Brothers in various prisons but became particularly popular in al-Wahat prison camp, where the circumstances were severe and where many Brothers suffered deprivation. Incarcerated in this remote concentration camp, these Brothers felt badly isolated from their families and the outer world. This, certainly, was excruciating for a number of them. Ahmad al-Bess, who experienced life in this desert camp, pointed to the appalling conditions the Brothers experienced there. Some Brothers were lured by the promise of freedom offered by the regime, "falling off along the wayside and supporting the regime."[83]

However, underscoring the differences in the Brotherhood's ranks at this time, another group rejected sending letters of support to the government under any circumstances, seeing that as a ratification of the regime and a repudiation of the Brotherhood and its leaders.[84] This group of hardliners was headed by al-Hudaybi and other leading members of the *Ikhwan* who took an uncompromising stance against the military regime.[85] According to sources, al-Hudaybi was approached during this period by representatives of the government to work out a deal between the Brotherhood and the regime. The deal would allow the Brotherhood to return to normality provided that it renounced its oppositional stance and agreed to support the government.[86] Contemporary US reports, corroborating this account, noted that government officials had made an advance toward senior Brotherhood leaders to see if they could arrive at a joint understanding. In response, al-Hudaybi had taken an unyielding stance, rejecting any such arrangement. Al-Hudaybi's firm reply had been that Nasser should discuss issues with Abdel Qader Uda (who at that time had been hanged by the regime).[87] The refusal of senior Brothers, such as al-Hudaybi, al-Tilmisani, Hamed Abul Nasr, Mustafa Mashhur, and Mahdi Akef, to reach an agreement with the government stood in marked contrast to the abovementioned accommodationist current.[88] Sami Sharaf, an intelligence officer who in 1955 had become a close associate of President Nasser and his secretary, points to these attempts at reconciliation between the Brothers and the government. Sharaf mentions that Mustafa al-Sibai, leader of the

Brotherhood in Syria, approached leading Brothers in Egypt and urged them to end their opposition to Nasser, but to no avail. This overture came, according to Sharaf, after the Sibai's meeting with Nasser in Syria, which may indicate that the Egyptian side had tasked al-Sibai with this mission of mediation.[89] It is interesting to note that all these hardliners reached the top of the Brotherhood's hierarchy, all becoming general guides, which points to the appreciation of such "steadfastness" among the Brothers. According to Hussein Hammuda, who was among those who sent Nasser a support letter, a great majority of the Brothers in prisons refused to give in to the regime's demands. This segment of the Brothers was headed by members of the Brotherhood's Guidance Office in prison.[90] Corroborating this argument, Joel Gordon has maintained that "for the Muslim Brothers, no such reconciliation [in contrast to the remaining political parties] was conceivable .... Leading Brothers convicted by the People's Tribunal remained in prison until shortly after Nasser's death."[91]

Trying to subdue oppositional voices within the *Ikhwan* and to push through declarations of support for the regime, the authorities launched a program of "re-socialization" of the Brothers. The program was set in motion in most prisons at this time and was intended to rehabilitate inmates, but it was understood by the *Ikhwan* as an attempt at brainwashing.[92] This "re-socializing" included religious sermons by Islamic scholars who offered religious reasons for the obligation of supporting the government. These religious sermons were combined with political lectures that dealt with national issues. Pointing to the regime's patriotic and religious credentials, the sermons urged the *Ikhwan* to take a positive stance toward it. When this rehabilitation failed in winning over the hearts of the *Ikhwan*, the authorities offered promises of parole and threats of punishment as inducements to convince the Brothers to declare their support, but again without much success.[93]

On this account, I argue that such attempts to enlist the support of the Brothers for the government and to sow dissent in the *Ikhwan*'s ranks by punishing those who opposed the regime and promising parole to those who supported it indicate that the regime still perceived the Brotherhood as a potent actor. That further measures were still needed may indicate that the Brotherhood was not perceived as fully broken.

In 1956, presumably as the regime began to feel itself more consolidated in power, it began to release Brotherhood members who had been sentenced to short terms in prison or had been arrested without trial. Having lived through several years of incarceration and hardship, these Brothers could finally see this chapter in their lives as concluded. Now a new journey was to be undertaken outside prison, to which this discussion now turns.

Continuing Underground in Society

What had befallen the Brotherhood during the final months of 1954 amounted to a tough blow, which certainly weakened the organization extensively. The degree of repression, savage mistreatment, and draconian sentences they were subjected to could not but signify the darkest days in the Brotherhood's history hitherto. Notwithstanding, even during these years of tribulation, the Brotherhood did not cease to exist in society. Having previously built a mass following consisting of hundreds of thousands of members, the Brotherhood continued to retain a great number of those even during this second *miḥna*. During these years of proscription and repression, the *Ikhwan* retained an estimated membership of 250,000 to 300,000 "secret adherents."[94] Discussing the prevailing political system in Egypt under Nasserite rule and the potential political opponents to his government, Maxime Rodinson pointed to the Brotherhood as the only "dangerous" element in society at that time. While he maintained that the Brotherhood may "have lost many supporters" due to the military regime's violent crackdown, he underlined that it had continued its existence. This continuation had been due to it being, in Rodinson's estimate, a "well-organized" group. With reference to the Brotherhood's persistence, Rodinson remarked that its "civilian supporters can occasionally express their ideas in disguise: e.g. when writing in defence of Islamic values and traditions."[95]

The Brotherhood had thus on no account been thrust into oblivion. The purpose of this section is therefore to offer a historical excursion into the Brotherhood's underground history in these years of restraints. In so doing, I aim to shed light on an understudied period in the Brotherhood's history. While affiliation with the organization became "secret" in order to avoid repression, this excursion will show that efforts to keep the Brotherhood alive and active occurred in abundance. Perceiving the Brotherhood as a vehicle through which they could live an Islamic life, many young men overlooked the dangers inherent in working within the ranks of a disbanded and outlawed organization.

The first tangible indication of the Brotherhood's resolve to continue working in society, albeit underground, came in early 1955.[96] In January 1955, as a manifestation of this resoluteness to carry on, a group of *Ikhwan* individuals were arrested and brought to trial. Drawing attention to the fact that the *Ikhwan* had not just disappeared, this represented the first of numerous indications of its continuity. Arraigned for colluding to revive the disbanded Brotherhood organization, the group consisted mainly of younger and less-experienced Brothers who had come together shortly after the crackdown in late 1954.[97]

Having joined forces to redress a perceived "falsehood," according to one of them they represented a network that had spread widely in Egypt. Fully aware of the risks such activities entailed in this atmosphere of constraint, the Brothers defied fears of retaliation to fulfill what they felt themselves duty-bound to do, according to their depictions. Collecting donations to support bereaved families was combined with housing Brothers on the run and feeding those Brothers who were not able to work due to persecution. In addition, by forging identity cards for their fleeing peers, these activists provided the fugitives with an opportunity to endure in the underground, albeit in a limited fashion. Most importantly, however, this network[98] widely distributed propaganda pamphlets in large parts of Egypt. Describing the atrocities of the regime and agitating against it, these pamphlets were certainly important in giving the public and the Brotherhood's own followers the impression that the *Ikhwan* was still present and alive.[99] The CIA described such propaganda campaigns at the time as increasing "tensions [against the regime]" and further alienating it.[100]

Thus, this early "reorganizing" of a group of young Brothers clearly points to the tenacity of the Brotherhood and the resolve by a group of members to "fulfill my part of *Jihad*," as Abdel Halim Khafaji's characterized his activism at this stage. Barely two months had gone before a new Brotherhood organization was uncovered in March 1955. This time consisting of about 200 members, the organization was dubbed "the Funding's Organization."[101] With a broad presence in nine different geographical areas, this organizational structure, like its predecessor, enlisted mainly junior Brothers. Muhammed al-Sarwi notes that most of its members were below the age of twenty. As with the case of Abdel Halim Khafaji, these young men knew quite well the dangers such activities entailed, but went ahead, nonetheless. Their belief was that they were fulfilling a religious and patriotic duty, as attested to in their personal accounts.[102] Registering more than sixty students and university graduates in its ranks, the organization's personnel points to the active role of these young, well-educated, middle-class men in opposing the regime.[103] Taking upon their shoulders the task of keeping alive their organization and defying the regime, this segment was particularly active in this period.

The geographical scope of this and subsequent organizational structures offers an informative view into the domestic situation at that time. We notice from available data that activists had a considerably higher margin for maneuvering in remote areas when compared to the large urban centers. Thus, while persecution was noticeably rigorous in Cairo and to a similar extent in Alexandria, repression was pursued less vigorously in more remote provinces, where opposition was considered less threatening to the regime. This provided the activists with extra leeway to keep their work functioning.

Such an account we find in Ali Ashmawi's memoirs. At the time a young militant who had escaped arrest due to his young age and junior ranking in the Brotherhood, Ali began working underground soon after the repression of the Brotherhood. The young student, who knew that staying in Cairo to work in the ranks of the Brotherhood involved a high risk, moved back to his hometown Mit Ghamr to live close to his family. A rural area located in the Dakahlia Governorate northeast of Cairo, Mit Ghamr was in many ways isolated from the center of events. In Mit Ghamr and its environs, Ali Ashmawi found fertile ground to resume his work within the ranks of the *Ikhwan*. On account of their remote location, these rural areas had escaped extensive waves of persecution, leaving a considerable number of Brothers at large. Ali relates, that the Brotherhood organization in these areas had been left virtually untouched. This enabled Ashmawi and his Brothers to set up a number of activities and to resume their organizational activities, albeit in secrecy. Meeting to discuss political events and to evaluate the eventual role of the Brotherhood in view of events, these young men began roaming outside their own villages to visit Brothers in adjacent areas. Ali Ashmawi, whose memoirs offer a detailed account of activities in this period, recalls that such visits were conducted after dusk, so as to remain inconspicuous. Organizing themselves into three groups in the Dakahlia area upon their contact with a significant number of Brothers, the activities of these young men offer an illustrative example of how the clandestine underground was taking form at this time. It was built on an idea of close-knit connections, low-key activities and complete clandestinity.[104] A similar story can be found in Medhat Abul Fadl's account.[105]

In July 1955, a new Brotherhood network was unearthed by security forces, adding further evidence to the *Ikhwan*'s continuation. The regular uncovering of organizational structures, as had been the case since early 1955, signifies the continuing reorganization of the Brotherhood since its dissolution. Like its predecessors, this July network consisted mainly of university students who met secretly in small cells to discuss the affairs of the Brotherhood and continue its activities secretly.[106] Set up as a hierarchical order of *usar*, the network comprised 475 members, which at this time represented a relatively large number in view of the circumstances. With more than ninety percent of its members being below the age of thirty years, the organizational structure was led by a command group consisting of five middle-ranking Brothers. Sulayman Hajar was chosen head of this network, which represented a link in the Brotherhood chain of organizational structures cropping up clandestinely. The social composition and age of members and leaders of this group represents a pattern in the *Ikhwan*'s working procedures when its senior leaders are imprisoned or exiled. As the previously mentioned organizational structures illustrate, when senior members were hindered in directing *Ikhwan* activities, second-string rank and file took over the initiative. This is clearly demonstrated by the case of Sulayman Hajar, who, alongside other junior Brothers, assumed responsibility and took control of activities in society, thus ensuring the continuity of activities.

The July 1955 structure differs in one key aspect from the previous organizational structures unearthed in early 1955. The two former networks had aimed at continuing Brotherhood meetings, supporting bereaved families, agitating against the regime, and housing Brothers on the run. Yet, in contrast to these relatively benign aims, this new iteration of the organization aimed at avenging what it perceived as the unjust dissolution of the Brotherhood and mistreatment of its members since October 1954. Observing what had befallen their fellow Brothers at the hands of security forces in preceding crackdowns, this group of Brothers swore to counter violence with violence. Only in this way, they reasoned, could the torturers be checked. Deterrence with force was the only means left available to "confront [the regime's] tyranny and omnipotence."[107] Ali Ashmawi who was working concurrently but alongside other *Ikhwan* members relates a similar story. Upon organizing themselves into underground cells in Mit Ghamr and its environs, they began contemplating a retaliatory strike against the regime. Aiming in the beginning at punishing Nasser "for what he had done," they began training with firearms and grenades, if we are to believe the account of Ashmawi. Alongside Brothers such as Sayyid al-Bardini, who was responsible for storing the weapons, these rural Brothers had at their disposal a number of arms that had not been seized by the authorities. To fulfill this task of avenging their Brothers, they began erecting camps on the outskirts of the town, where noise from firearms could go relatively unnoticed.[108]

Corroborating such accounts, US reports from 1955 noted that *Ikhwan* members were being regularly arrested and brought to trial. Realizing that the *Ikhwan* had sustained its presence, the US diplomats observed that the Brotherhood was notably strong at universities, where it had had significant success in recruiting followers.[109] Adding further evidence to this claim, in late 1955 the CIA maintained that it seemed unlikely that the RCC could secure "spectacular gains in achieving organized support from important Egyptian political elements." Dissent against the regime appears to have remained strong well into 1955. This opposition, the CIA noted, "remains strong among urban intellectual and professional elements" and "other politically alert civilian elements."[110] Arising from the regime's exclusionary policies, defiance against the regime was expected to remain intact. As might be expected, these estimates conceived it as quite likely that the Brotherhood would continue their defiance of the regime, working for "its downfall."[111] In accordance with this, British assessments unequivocally pointed to the *Ikhwan* as a force to be reckoned with in society and in Egyptian politics. By way of illustration, a British report maintained that the Brotherhood possessed a large cadre of well-trained members, including "some two thousand unmarried men who were prepared to give their lives in order to ensure the success of any assignments given to them."[112] Implying the perceived danger of the *Ikhwan,* the report claimed that "it seems unlikely that recoveries [of arms] have accounted for anything like a major part of the stocks."[113] Certainly, the British still perceived the Brotherhood as a potent and destructive force, which would for the time being represent a dangerous threat to the regime. Alongside the emphasis on the "danger" of the Brotherhood as perceived by the British, the diplomats pointed to the *Ikhwan*'s experience as an underground organization in previous periods of "proscription." This important, if dearly attained, experience would undoubtedly enhance the Brotherhood's ability to survive persecution. Adding further evidence to the *Ikhwan*'s perceived continuation in society, the report noted that the Brotherhood remain the "main pre-occupation of the police" in various Egyptian cities.[114]

Taken together, these contemporary accounts, matched with accounts from Brotherhood members, buttress the impression that a tug-of-war had continued between the warring, if unequal, parties. British and American data juxtaposed with the historical accounts of Brotherhood activists paint a picture of the Brotherhood's ongoing but clandestine opposition to the regime. The CIA even contemplated the possibility of a Brotherhood alliance with a "military-Wafdist group in the overthrow of the regime."[115] As we know, this partnership did not materialize, but the very assessment is vital in understanding the contemporary views on the circumstances in Egypt and the role of the Brotherhood at that time. During the summer of 1955, a Brotherhood source informed US officials that the organization was preoccupied with restructuring itself into "a completely underground movement." This source stated that the *Ikhwan* were laying the groundwork for a propaganda campaign against the regime. This campaign, like those mentioned before, was intended to unmask the "brutal and undemocratic" face of the regime.[116] On account of these Brotherhood activities, the Egyptian authorities told US diplomats that the *Ikhwan* had *not* been eradicated but had remained "bodily intact."[117]

Exchanging views on the reasons for the Brotherhood's ability to survive, American diplomats highlighted its transnational character as a major source of strength and vitality. Pointing to the provision of finances for *Ikhwan* activities and the support of Brotherhood families, a US report maintained that much of the money emanated from abroad. These resources, which were lifegiving under such circumstances, were transferred to Egypt on a weekly basis, thus bolstering the organization's vigor.[118] The US Department of State remarked on this account that on two occasions King Saud of Saudi Arabia had donated large sums of money to the Brotherhood, channeled through Said Ramadan, the exiled senior Brother.[119] Lamenting this fact and seeming unable to curb it, Nasser condemned it during talks with Selwyn Lloyd in March 1955. Nasser, who was aware of the Saudi support of the *Ikhwan*, castigated the king's "unwise" use of money. Nasser was according to the telegram "annoyed by Saudi gift of money to Moslem Brotherhood."[120]

Being a direct outcome of the Brotherhood's previous structured work to establish a transnational scope for the organization, this assistance was sorely needed by the *Ikhwan* at this point. By dint of its establishment of sister branches in a number of Arab countries, the Brotherhood had built relationships and a relatively strong presence outside Egypt (see Chapter 2). This outreach was reinforced and expanded in this second *miḥna*, when prominent Brothers, such as Said Ramadan, Kamil al-Sharif, Hasan al-Ashmawi, Abdel Hakim Abdin, Abdel Mun'im Abd al-Rauf, and many others, fled Egypt to continue activities from abroad. In so doing, these Brothers became a vital source of material support for their peers in Egypt and an important voice of the *Ikhwan* beyond the reach of Nasser's repressive arm.[121] Thus, the space for expressing the ideas and viewpoints of the organization this transnational aspect offered was important in sustaining its ability to make its voice heard. Even when the political situation seemed to be at its bleakest, this dimension helped the *Ikhwan* sustain an oppositional voice. Consequently, this presence outside Egypt's borders furnished the Brothers with an ability to keep their propaganda alive without risking the relentless persecution of the Nasserite regime.

As discussed thus far, the activities of the Brothers had been characterized by endeavors to form Brotherhood collectivities as a way to preserve the *Ikhwan* organization. These sub-organizations, like those of 1955, had been formed heedless of the time's restrictive political atmosphere. Coming together, those generally young *Ikhwan* directed their attention primarily at charitable and religious endeavors. However, when state-authorized repression began to take more violent forms, some of those young men began to consider violence against the authorities as a legitimized response.

My account now proceeds to the Brotherhood's history in the years of 1956 and 1957. During these years, I contend, we observe a liberalization on the political scene in Egypt due to domestic and regional developments. Albeit limited, this observable change offered the *Ikhwan* some extended space, which they utilized without delay to increase their activities. In other words, when room for organizational maneuvering became slightly more open, the Brotherhood operated more actively, albeit still as a clandestine organization.

Welcome news was forthcoming for the Brotherhood during the summer of 1956. In light of the regime's rising confidence, the authorities began releasing large numbers of Brothers, usually young activists and of junior rank in the Brotherhood, who had been either sentenced to short terms in prison or held in detention without facing legal proceedings. This development, which undoubtedly received a warm reception by the Brothers, came against the backdrop of a number of political successes for Egypt on the international scene. By way of illustration, in March 1955, Nasser participated in the highly promoted Afro-Asian Bandung Conference in Indonesia. Here, he joined nonaligned leaders such as Yugoslavia's Tito, India's Nehru, and Chou En-lai of China in dismissing superpower hegemony. Egypt, until just prior to this under direct British control, had now become a stronghold of Third-Worldism. Nasser's participation in the conference and his reception as an influential statesman won him great prestige on the international scene and bolstered his image as the unchallenged leader of Egypt.[122] Nasser added to this eminence of his by concluding the "Czech" arms deal in September of the same year. This deal was a coup on the international scene, as he became the first leader of a noncommunist country to obtain arms from the Soviet Bloc.[123] Boosting its popularity and raising its self-confidence through these international successes notwithstanding their actual value, the regime felt confident enough to go ahead with liberalizing steps of sorts. The international achievements, which were greatly acclaimed, were utilized by the government domestically to normalize the political scene. This "normalization" occurred subsequent to a two-year period of rather tough authoritarianism and exclusionary policies.[124] On June 25, 1956, this (rather limited) attempt to liberalize the political system was manifested in the abolition of the RCC, the announcement of a constitution, and the installment of Nasser as president. Furthermore, Nasser declared that the regime had released "all detainees, without exceptions."[125] These steps were intended to symbolize the restoration of democracy in Egypt, after a period of revolutionary/military rule.[126]

Mahmoud Abdel Halim, who was released in June 1956 in light of this development, describes it as a tour de force. This "symbolic liberalization," as Abdel Halim describes it, was utilized by the regime to "present itself as democratic." Abdel Halim maintains, however, that these changes remained a scratch on the surface of despotism.[127] This refurbishing of the political system, notwithstanding its real underlying causes, entailed changes that many Brothers and other political detainees had yearned for. As an increasing number of members found themselves at large, the activities of the *Ikhwan* were boosted in society.

Release, however, did not mean complete unshackling, as those who left confinement would learn very soon. Directly upon release, Brothers were strongly urged to refrain from Brotherhood activities. Summoned by local intelligence forces, the activists were forewarned that recommencing political activities, in any form, would entail grave risk of re-arrest or repression. The Brothers were lastly apprised that they would remain under rigorous surveillance. Abbas al-Sisi, a middle-ranking member of the Brotherhood, offers such an account.

Abbas al-Sisi remembers receiving word of his release with surprise and great wariness one Friday in 1956. In prison, he had found a sheltered and routinized day-to-day life, and he feared that news of his release might be based on a mistake or bear within it an unwelcome trick. Al-Sisi soon learned that his fears were unfounded. Following two years of incarceration, al-Sisi was transferred from the Damanhur General Prison to his hometown Rashid (Rosetta) in the Beheira Governate, where he rejoined his family. As al-Sisi would quickly learn, however, release did not necessarily mean end of persecution. A few days after his release, al-Sisi was summoned to meet the head of the General Intelligence office in Damanhur, the capital city of his home governate. At this meeting, which the 38-year-old Brother attended with utmost unease, al-Sisi was exhorted to "stay away from the Muslim Brotherhood and to avoid taking part in political endeavors." Al-Sisi, who had just left prison, was asked to write a declaration pledging not to "take part in any activities." Instilling fear in al-Sisi, the intelligence officer informed him of the repercussions of violating his compact, warning him that he would remain under constant surveillance. If anything, this working procedure seems to have been the key measure taken by the authorities against released Brothers. Upon releasing them, the regime did not intend to let them resume their work within the ranks of the *Ikhwan* or to compromise a group of discontented opponents.[128] These warnings and the danger of being re-arrested or otherwise repressed, with what that entailed in the minds of the *Ikhwan*, undoubtedly left its mark on some Brothers.

> "Those who visited me following my release were less than ten. Talking to us caused people grave apprehension. The media campaign was still uncompromising, smearing both the mission and the missionaries. Add to this that the security forces were still pursuing our movements and terrorizing people from contacting us."

Such were al-Sisi's feelings upon leaving prison, as he sketched them in his memoirs. On account of this, al-Sisi, who had been dismissed from his job in the armed forces and deprived of the right to work in the public sector, went ahead with seeking employment and looking for a proper dwelling to accommodate him and his little family. Life after release was not smooth, as al-Sisi's account clearly illustrates. Having left one child at the age of two and another yet unborn when arrested, al-Sisi recalls that his children did not respond emotionally to him at first. This reserved reception no doubt troubled the newly released father. His bewilderment was therefore exacerbated when he felt isolated in local society as well. "Some people met me coolly and in a wary way without entering into conversations with me. Others were ogling me, while scarcely any would pay me a visit," al-Sisi downheartedly recalls.[129]

Mahmoud Abdel Halim described life after release in an equally gloomy vein. Abdel Halim, who was released around the same time, looked back at this period with mixed and conflicting sentiments. Release, no doubt, was warmly welcomed. This happiness which release gave rise to was, however, limited by apprehensions about what kind of society the released Brothers would face when leaving prison. "As much as I had loved and held Cairo dear to me [before imprisonment], just as much had I come to abhor it after what had happened," he recollects. Being released from prison was not equivalent to being free in Nasser's Egypt, according to Abdel Halim. "Those who left prison were let out to another prison … chains inside prison were replaced by other chains in society." A general and widespread "atmosphere of terror and trepidation" was surrounding the Egyptian people, was the impression Abdel Halim had of society at the time. Feeling that his movements were constrained by "heavy shackles," he felt he was being "monitored, constantly and everywhere."[130]

Consequently, being released was not necessarily synonymous with being unconstrained, as many Brothers learned in due time. Being released, simply put, represented a new journey of challenges and hardships, as revealed by the Brothers' narratives. This impression of being monitored, pursued, and isolated undoubtedly aggravated the *Ikhwan*'s ability to continue activism. No doubt the forewarnings by intelligence officers for *Ikhwan* to steer clear of political engagement and to avoid Brotherhood activities was a clear strategy pursued by the authorities. In view of this, Brothers who were released found themselves in a precarious position, especially if they considered resuming *Ikhwan* activities. Identified as *Ikhwan* by the authorities, their freedom of maneuvering was naturally more limited than Brothers whose affiliation had remained cloaked in secrecy. However, as we shall see in the following, such dilemmas had varying outcomes among the recently released Brothers. While some *Ikhwan* opted for the safe path, complying with the admonishments, others rejected it, continuing their activities in spite of the risks this entailed.

Turning once again to Abdel Halim's detailed memoirs, we find such a story that illustrates in clear terms the dilemmas with which released Brothers were confronted. Abdel Halim was released on June 26, 1956. Before long, a group of mostly young men came to see him and discuss with him the existing conditions and to vent their anger. Having remained at liberty following the repression, those young men bemoaned what they perceived as widespread corruption in society, deviation from religious regulations, and an official sanctioning of obscenity in all parts of life. And while these vices were allowed free rein in their beloved Egypt, they observed with great dismay the "unrightful" persecution leveled at the religious segment in society. Worse still was the apparent passivity of most segments in society, as they decried it. They had therefore decided to work in society to reform these despicable conditions, as they understood them. However, young and inexperienced in organizational work, these Brothers were "walking in a psychological revolution looking for a leader to guide them in the right direction."[131] Against this backdrop, they solicited Abdel Halim to join them "in a positive action" to change what they saw as society's calamitous condition. Commending their enthusiasm and sharing their sentiments, Abdel Halim had to turn down their bid. Abdel Halim, who felt he was being watched everywhere, told the young *Ikhwan* that he was still restrained by "invisible chains around arms and legs, and if you do not see the walls surrounding us, we nonetheless see them." These young members, longing for an organized reaction to repression and deviation from what they perceived as religious norms, lamented Abdel Halim's refusal and perceived it as cowardice.[132]

Such accounts illustrate with clarity the complex and clashing sentiments bothering those in opposition to the Nasserite regime at this juncture. Eager to shape Egypt in a specifically Islamic way, these young men who fervently implored Abdel Halim to join them were lacking the opportunities to do so overtly. In resuming the activities of the Brotherhood, even if in a depoliticized form, they were considered as opponents to the hegemonic regime of Nasser and thus subject to persecution. Therefore, they turned their attention to covert activities to continue working while avoiding repression. It was in this context that they challenged what they understood as Abdel Halim's defeatist attitude. In lamenting the reprehensible status of the Egyptian people, these young *Ikhwan* painted a picture of a battle between good and evil in their analysis of society.[133] Yet, lacking an established leader to guide them in the right direction, they were strongly disheartened by Abdel Halim's decision to stay on the sidelines.

However, not all released Brothers preferred the safe journey as in the above case. Abbas al-Sisi offers a similar account but with a different outcome. Sometime after his release, and at a time he portrays as wrapped in "complete darkness," he was frequently visited by groups of young "faithful men." These young men had resumed activities following the crackdown on the Brotherhood by continuing low-key meetings and discussions on different subjects in small circles. Al-Sisi, who does not hide his contentment in his memoirs, described such groups of Brothers as those who "awaken hope and bolster our ability to carry on and endure."[134] Praising them for their belief in the cause, al-Sisi characterizes them as "the vanguard." The young members who had already initiated a multiplicity of activities asked al-Sisi to join them in their efforts to fulfill "our obligations." Abbas al-Sisi acceded to their wish and joined them in their endeavors. However, despite the benign nature of their activities, such as apprising the local population about the *Ikhwan*, meeting to study religious subjects, and collecting funds to support Brotherhood families, they were subject to harassment. "Walls had ears," and this exposed any discussions or activities to retribution.[135]

Mostly students, this group of *Ikhwan* included young men in their teens. One illustrative example is Ahmad Farid Mustafa, a young Brother from Alexandria, born in 1939. Growing up in a well-to-do family, Farid Mustafa became acquainted with the Muslim Brotherhood while attending secondary school. He recalls being impressed by the Brotherhood's young activists, who embodied to him "the model of righteous Muslim, patriotic youth." In 1954, Farid Mustafa watched sorrowfully as his fellow Brothers were persecuted and put behind bars, but this did not prevent him from continuing to pursue his goals. The determined young man took up his university studies at the engineering faculty in 1955, and he remembers the "atmosphere of horror, persecution and restraints" that engulfed the faculty and those attending it.[136] This young engineering student was among the students who frequented al-Sisi to urge his support and whom the latter described as "the vanguard of a new generation."

Such examples, which were common in this period, clearly illustrate that the activities of the Brotherhood took the form of low-key endeavors organized by Brotherhood rank and file. And importantly, the activities were more often than not launched by young members without the direction of older and more established Brothers.

Yusuf Nada was among the students whose arrest deeply saddened Farid Mustafa, as narrated above. A close friend of Farid Mustafa, Nada's background and development resemble those of his younger friend to a great extent. Born in 1931 in Alexandria to a well-regarded family, the young Yusuf joined the Brotherhood in 1948.[137] In 1954, Yusuf Nada was arrested upon being identified as a member of the Brotherhood. While Nada's social background did not suffice to keep him out of prison, it saved him from the torture and mistreatment others were subjected to. Arrested after an attempted escape, he was brought to military prison, where he recalls witnessing cruelties in abundance. Nada spent two difficult but instructive years in prison, where he developed his ideas and gained new acquaintances.[138] Upon his release, the young Nada went back to Alexandria to recommence his studies. At the faculty, Nada came in contact with a group of like-minded young Brothers and sympathizers from Alexandria and its environs.[139] Looking for a way to support Brotherhood families and continue low-key activism, Nada and his peers began frequenting regular meetings to study the ideas of the Muslim Brotherhood. Lamenting the deplorable conditions of bereaved Brotherhood families, they also initiated charity campaigns to support these families. This group of *Ikhwan* who took it upon their shoulders to continue the work of the Brotherhood was among the young men who frequented al-Sisi's home and discussed with him the proper ways of continuing the *da'wa* of the Brotherhood.[140] According to Nada, these activities entailed high risks and could lead to accusations of conspiracy. He maintains in his biography that "[w]hen the Brothers were being herded into jails, others tried to help their families with food and money."[141] The motivating force, as we find it described in numerous accounts, was an unwavering aspiration to sustain the Islamic *da'wa* and to work for the betterment of society. As formulated by Nada, "The Muslim Brotherhood is not a club, it is an organisation based on the ethics of the Islamic religion. It's about trying to help people comply with the ethics in their life."[142] A similar account can be found in Ahmad Adel Kamal's memoirs. Kamal, whom we met earlier on account of his role in the Special Apparatus, formed a clandestine suborganization at this point to continue working in society. Pointing to the risks such work entailed, he remembers, "I conceived it most fitting to continue our bonds without a hierarchy. We meet and adhere to our relationships and we support each other in religious matters, but without mentioning it to any outsider."[143]

Accordingly, the primary stimulus at work at this point was the socio-religious aspect of the Brotherhood's reform idea, although this was impossible to distinguish from the political goals, as these were intrinsically linked. In the story of Ahmad Abdel Majid, we clearly observe this entanglement of socio-religious aims with the political dimension. Abdel Majid, who gained a BA in law and was hired as an official at the War Ministry's department of military secrets during the prison years, describes his activities to sustain the Brotherhood's presence.[144] Not identified by the authorities as a Muslim Brother, Abdel Majid could venture to resume activities with relatively lower risk. In view of this, he began, alongside like-minded young Brothers, establishing a small network to support the Brotherhood and to keep the Islamic identity alive among themselves and in society. Reminiscent of other networks and groups of Brothers, Abdel Majid and his peers bemoaned what they perceived as corruption encircling Egypt. "Our intention," he recalls, "was to do our outmost to rescue the country from falling into oblivion."[145] To this end, as shown in this chapter, small-scale networks were established throughout Egypt under local leadership.[146]

However, as restrictions began to decrease beginning from the summer of 1956, we observe a turn toward semi-centralized organizing, especially in the larger cities. A case in point was Farid Abdel Khaleq's assumption of responsibility for the Brotherhood in Cairo upon his release from prison in 1957. In conferring this task on him, the Brotherhood was attempting to reestablish a leadership structure to command and lead the activities inside Egypt, and to concentrate it under a senior leader. Assuming the leadership of Cairo in 1957, Abdel Khaleq recalls that he became responsible for the contact between Brotherhood members (both domestic and exiled Brothers) and Hasan al-Hudaybi. Al-Hudaybi, whose death sentence had been commuted to life imprisonment, had been transferred to house arrest due to his advanced age (mid-sixties) and bad health. Farid Abdel Khaleq's assumption of leadership in Cairo involved a wide array of responsibilities. Cairo's newly appointed leader was tasked, inter alia, with receiving funds from Brotherhood exiles in Saudi Arabia and other Arab countries to finance the Brotherhood's activities. This support, I need hardly say, was imperative for the *Ikhwan*'s viability.[147]

A similar example we find in Alexandria. In this Mediterranean port city, a hierarchical leadership was established in 1958, tasked with running the activities of the Brotherhood and linking local members with Brothers from other areas. Abbas al-Sisi became head of a command structure in Alexandria consisting of four Brothers. The main job of this leadership, in the words of al-Sisi, was to form a new generation of Brothers. To fulfill this task, al-Sisi tells us, they were occupied with educating the members and shaping them according to the principles of the *Ikhwan*. In this way, they were seeking to create a cadre of active Brothers who were able to continue the work of the Brotherhood.[148]

Thus, appointing prominent Brothers to head the Brotherhood networks in given areas constituted a blueprint at this time. By way of illustration, Muhammad Hilal was assigned the responsibility of heading the *Ikhwan* in the Dakahlia Governate, lying northeast of Cairo. Working as a counselor in Mansoura, the capital city of Dakahlia, Hilal had escaped arrest, which was why he was able to continue leading the Brotherhood in his home governate.[149] We observe similar developments in different parts of Egypt, such as Beheira and Damietta.[150] Accordingly, a turn toward a more centralized structuring, or at least an attempt to create such a centralization in these years of repression, can be seen in this period that followed the release of a large group of Brothers.

Definitely containing a certain degree of eulogy, the accounts presented above do, however, present a narrative of how the *Ikhwan* continued (and continues) its activities when forced underground. And when juxtaposed with contemporary British and American sources, we find ample data pointing to this continuing presence of the *Ikhwan*. Assessing political and social conditions in Egypt through their units on the ground, the British gained the distinct impression that the *Ikhwan* was beginning to stir. In December 1956, by way of illustration, a British report stated expressly that the Muslim Brotherhood "appear to have gained some ground." The *Ikhwan*, it was rumored at the time, might be in a position to "succeed Nasser" if "revived." The reports were not promising for any side hoping for the disappearance of the *Ikhwan*. If "Nasser fell now," according to the assessment, "he would probably be replaced by a still more extreme form of government and there has been talk of the Brotherhood in this connexion."[151]

While it goes without saying that such viewpoints were exaggerated, they clearly indicate the contemporary appraisals of the Brotherhood's prospects of survival. During the early months of 1957, and along the same lines, the British described the position of Nasser's regime as being subject to heavy and widespread criticism. The report, which cited the American and Ethiopian ambassadors as eyewitnesses, pointed to evidence implying "that Nasser is still worried by the Moslem Brotherhood."[152] Commenting on the then-current landscape of opposition to the Nasserite regime, the CIA remarked that the *Ikhwan* "retains a large number of sympathizers," suggesting why a propaganda offensive might achieve a degree of resonance in society.[153] Substantiating such impressions of an increasing Brotherhood opposition, a British diplomat recorded in July 1957 that the *Ikhwan* were "active against Nasser both inside and outside Egypt."[154] The British underlined that these activities were especially strong in Jordan, where the *Ikhwan* were reported to have waged a "vigorous campaign of propaganda." Against this backdrop, this report stressed that the regime's "main pre-occupation" is with the July elections, for which the Brotherhood "seem[ed] to be causing the régime some anxiety."[155]

Penned by contemporary British and American diplomats, these accounts clearly demonstrate that the Brotherhood continued to be a group to reckon with. While its activities certainly did not form an existential threat to the regime, they symbolized the *Ikhwan*'s continuing appeal at least among a segment of society.[156]

Conclusions

Mahmoud Abdel Latif's eight gunshots missed their intended target but came to change the history of the Muslim Brotherhood. As seen in this chapter, the botched assassination attempt on Nasser, notwithstanding the veracity of the official version, marked the starting signal for a hideous repression of the Brotherhood. This chapter began by contending that this virulent repression, despite its cruelty, did not terminate the Brotherhood's existence or its activities, thus critically assessing the argument presented by scholars such as Mitchell and Harris. Regarding the Brotherhood as defeated, these scholars interpreted the *Ikhwan*'s invisibility at this time as a sign of its termination.

Yet, as depicted in this chapter, this obscurity of the Brotherhood was more a result of the *Ikhwan*'s turning to covert activities rather than symbolizing its ending. When repressed and subjected to severe restraints, the Brothers cloaked their activities in secrecy so as to continue an "invisible" existence. On account of *Ikhwan* memoirs and recollections, we noted that while Brotherhood activities had by no means ended, their volume fluctuated according to political circumstances. Thus, while repression, torture, trials, executions, and prisons overshadowed any other feature in the early period that followed the Manshiyya incident, we clearly see a continuing stirring of opposition by the Brothers. Being disbanded, persecuted, and subjected to extensive smear campaigns, the Brotherhood suffered damage, no doubt. However, intended to uproot the *Ikhwan* and end its appeal in society, these punitive measures succeeded in weakening the Brotherhood but failed in ending their presence in society.

As outlined in this chapter, we can observe the sustained re-emergence of organized Brotherhood endeavors throughout Egypt, beginning from early 1955. Taking the form of low-key networks cropping up all over Egypt, these networks engaged mainly young members who had escaped arrest. In Nasser's policies and social system they observed a deviation from Islam which resulted in a deplorable corruption of society at large. Against this background, their accounts show that they took it upon their shoulders to forestall this undesired departure from Islamic principles.

Repression, as the Brothers came to learn, does not sustain the same degree of intensity for long periods. Accordingly, during 1956, when the domestic and regional situation became more favorable for the Nasserite regime, a concurrent easing of despotism took place, offering the Brotherhood greater leeway. In light of this, we observed a recovery of Brotherhood presence in society, albeit still covert. This development, which is depicted at length in the Brothers' accounts, is expressly corroborated by contemporaneous British and American reports. British and American officials alike pointed to the Brotherhood as sustaining its activities in societies, and they warned their respective governments that the Brotherhood would remain a force to be reckoned with.

On June 1, 1957, a hideous incident took place, reminding all parties that this tug-of-war had not yet reached its conclusion. What was coined as "the slaughter in Tura" by Brotherhood members was by all accounts a vicious act of violence that resulted in the killing of more than twenty Brothers, with around the same number wounded. The details of this event are beyond the scope of this study. Yet, as the next chapter argues, the violence meted out to the *Ikhwan* in the Liman Tura prison led a faction of younger members to rethink their strategies toward the regime. Arriving at the conclusion that the Nasserite state had reached unexpected levels of tyranny, they began reflecting upon ways to confront it.

6

Reorganization and the Role of Sayyid Qutb (1957–70)

At daybreak on August 29, 1966, Sayyid Qutb was brought to the gallows alongside two of his Brothers. He and his two companions, Abdel Fattah Ismail and Muhammad Yusuf Hawwash,[1] had been condemned for conspiring against the regime and were hanged. For the Brotherhood, this symbolized another link in the bloodstained chain of barbaric atrocities inflicted on them by the Nasserite regime. The "martyrs," Qutb, Ismail, and Hawwash, had paid the highest price for defying the authorities.[2] Their only "crime," according to the explanation of the *Ikhwan*, was that they had adhered to their sincere Islamic principles. By dint of these principles, they had taken an oppositional stance to Nasser's despotic regime, and for that, they were condemned to die.[3]

The aim of this chapter is to shed light on the events that ended up with Qutb and his Brothers walking toward their final fate. What preceded the unearthing of "Organization 65," as I contend, were eventful years that witnessed an increase in organizational activities in the Brotherhood. These organizing activities were a continuation of former attempts to sustain the Brotherhood's presence in society, which began in late 1954 and continued throughout 1955 and 1956. I argue, however, that the massacre in Liman Tura on June 1, 1957, changed the worldview of a group of Brothers, moving them toward greater acceptance of militancy. What occurred on that day convinced these Brothers that confronting the authorities militarily was the only way to settle the score with the regime. This horrifying massacre, seen by these young Brothers as proof of the regime's malicious intent, represented a landmark for many of them. What followed the first of June 1957 was a greater readiness to confront the Nasserite regime, as becomes clear in the following.

Thus, rather than understanding this new organization as a "*phoenix from the ashes*," as proposed by Zollner,[4] I claim that this *tanẓīm* epitomizes a continuation of the Brotherhood activities that had been ongoing since late

1954. This organization did not suddenly emerge in 1957/8 as a phoenix from the ashes. *Tanẓīm-65* was living proof, if not the earliest, of the Brotherhood's continuing work underground in society.

What role did Sayyid Qutb play in this organization? While Qutb is perceived today as the architect of modern *jihad*,[5] my intention in the following is to put the role of Qutb into its historical frame when studying the history of the Brotherhood. As I illustrate, Organization 65, of which he became commander, had already been established before he joined it. Qutb, as I argue, acquired a pivotal role when he offered this organization a powerful and compelling ideological framework. Through this framework, presented eloquently in his well-known "Milestones," the young members could define their position toward society and regime in more explicit terms. Offering a vigorous and bleak interpretation of society, Qutb set about educating these young men who were looking for direction. Qutb's role was, thus, in his provision of a powerful manifesto to this organization rather than in being its actual architect. Thus, while not its founder, Qutb became its theoretician and eventually its "martyr."

From Decentralized Organizing toward Unification

On June 1, 1957, in what came to be the single bloodiest day in the struggle between Nasser and the Brotherhood, a massacre took place in Liman Tura. Echoing with the terrifying and alarming noise of automatic weapons and the anguished cries for help, this massacre left twenty-one *Ikhwan* inmates killed. This event was particularly disturbing and bewildering for many Brothers. While previous cases, such as the hanging of six leading Brothers or the deaths of others under torture, were perceived as terrible and monstrous, these incidents had occurred at the height of a struggle between the Nasserite regime and the *Ikhwan*. However, this incident, which surpassed in cruelty anything before it, was perceived as taking place without warning. It was understood, furthermore, as an extralegal massacre, committed by compatriot soldiers and prison guards against unarmed and thus vulnerable prisoners. Dismissing the official account describing what had happened as a "suppression of a prison riot,"[6] Brotherhood accounts classified it unequivocally as outright manslaughter.[7] These accounts are not chary when it comes to describing the inhumanity of this act. It was, according to the accounts of Brothers who survived the incident, a truly villainous crime. Injured Brothers were subjected to severe beatings when removed from the dormitories, and some of them died of their injuries or under torture after being shot. The massacre itself took place, according to these *Ikhwan* accounts, while the Brothers were still in their cells, adding to its cruelty. The "martyrs" were shot point-blank, leading to the large number of dead and injured.[8]

Be that as it may, we can say with certainty that the incident in Liman Tura came to stir the blood of segments of the Brothers. From late 1954, the repression of the *Ikhwan* had taken various forms, including the imprisonment of the Brotherhood's upper echelons, the harsh treatment of *Ikhwan* inmates which regularly involved torture and humiliation, and the hanging of leading members. The exclusion of Brotherhood members from the political scene and from the public sector, which was primarily carried out through the regime's law of "political dismissal," exacerbated the Brothers' predicaments. This law, being directed against the regime's opponents, authorized it to discharge individuals from their jobs and obstruct their way to state employment.[9] Preventing them from acquiring employment in the public sector or returning to their former jobs, this law made life after imprisonment complicated for many Brothers who depended on these jobs. In other words, notwithstanding that repression of the *Ikhwan* had been persistent since late 1954, the Liman Tura incident seems to have been received with greater anxiety and fury.

What happened on that day in June 1957 rubbed salt into the wounds, provoking a reaction from the Brotherhood. As we see in the following, this particular incident stands out as key in stirring a large number of especially younger Brotherhood members. As a direct outcome of this incident, we observe a substantial increase in the number of clandestine structures outside prisons. This increase, which should be understood as part and parcel of the above-depicted covert activities, was inextricably linked to events in Liman Tura. Perceiving this incident as an awful wrongdoing committed by the regime against their fellow Brothers, a group of *Ikhwan* resolved to reorganize themselves in society. Only by reviving their Brotherhood activities, these members reasoned, could they ward off such incidents in the future.

Abbas al-Sisi, the Brother who had recommenced his activities following his release in 1956, discusses this incident and its reverberations at length in his memoirs. Narrating events, al-Sisi recalls the fury and awe with which he and many other Brothers received the news of the massacre. "Why were my Brothers killed?" and "What will our fate be after this?" were some of the questions that troubled al-Sisi when he understood the magnitude of what had taken place. More than anything else, this feeling of being subjected to an outrageous iniquity came to agitate feelings and to galvanize the increasing clandestine activities of Brothers. Not only did it horrify him and hundreds of his fellow *Ikhwan* but al-Sisi recalls that "this appalling incident awakened the Brothers' zeal and mustered their ranks." The incident, as al-Sisi puts it in his memoirs, had the effect of "awakening the Brothers." Sensing an imminent danger against themselves and against their organization, many young members of the Brotherhood began to "contemplate ways of working" subsequent to this incident. Hence, the unprecedented number of victims in one single day, and the young age of most victims, caused great despondency among the Brothers and turned bewilderment and anguish into a desire to "revive the *jihad*."[10]

As evident in the story of al-Sisi, these feelings of despair and anxiety were turned into a driving force for many Brothers. Abdel Majid, twenty-four years of age at the time, describes these sentiments that followed the Liman Tura incident. "In this cloudy and loaded atmosphere and in this pitch darkness, we began pondering how to rescue ourselves and our Brothers from falling into oblivion … the religious man was persecuted everywhere [in Egypt]." It was against this background of feeling at risk that Ahmad Abdel Majid began working underground alongside like-minded young men to change such conditions. Reacting to these feelings and conceiving it as obligatory to "rescue Egypt from what it had fallen prey to in terms of deviation and corruption," Abdel Majid and a small group of young *Ikhwan* set up a covert suborganization. This network, which at this point was limited to a tiny group of members, would become one of the nuclei of Organization 65.[11]

From its modest beginnings in an apartment in the el-Zeitoun district in Cairo, where young men met to discuss political and religious issues, this newly established organizational structure soon transformed into a hierarchical group of like-minded and active young Brothers. Its social fabric was predominated by young middle-class men and students who had met in this apartment on a regular basis to resume *Ikhwani* bonds. These meetings, involving young men from Cairo, were augmented during 1957, when a feeling of danger was combined with a desire to do something. The questions these Brothers asked themselves and each other at that point were: "Is there a way out? What will follow this frightening silence? Will there be a rescuer?" Ahmad Abdel Majid, who was a frequent visitor to this apartment inhabited by Brotherhood students, remembers the apartment as a rallying point for many Brothers. They would meet on an almost daily basis to socialize and to discuss issues that occupied them. Resuming secret, albeit unorganized bonds with each other, these Brothers looked for a way to continue Brotherhood activities in a more structured fashion. It was against this background that they set up a suborganization to prevent the Brotherhood from "disappearing in society."[12] Their aspiration, as Ahmad Abdel

Majid remembers it, was to bring together Brothers from all parts of Egypt and renew the vitality of the *Ikhwan*. The first step, as they conceived their path, was to establish a small network that would enable them to reach out to other clusters of *Ikhwan* in other parts of Egypt.[13]

To achieve these objectives, the young men agreed on a stratified order and a set of codes. Ali Ashmawi, the young man from Mit Ghamr whom we encountered in the previous chapter, became the *amir* (commander) of this organizational structure. Ali had been active in organizing Brotherhood activities in his home province, but he found in Cairo greater opportunities to achieve what he strove for. By joining this network, Ali Ashmawi could get the chance to merge the Mit Ghamr organizational structures with those developing in Cairo, thus expanding the links of Brothers working underground. Amin Shahin, a close friend of Ali Ashmawi and student at the faculty of engineering, was put in charge of its financial aspects, while Abdel Majid, who after graduating in law had secured employment at the ministry of war, became responsible for intelligence. The commanders of this nascent suborganization embarked on a study program to streamline the education of its members.

Taking the political framework into account and the risks involved in participating in such activities, the network was grounded on an idea of "complete secrecy and great caution in movement and contacts." Rather than being confined to one geographical area, the leaders decided to "reach out to all we knew in any place in Egypt."[14] However, and in the environment of anxiety engulfing their motions, this burgeoning organizational structure restricted entry to its ranks to Brothers already known for their commitment. Abdel Majid, one of the founding fathers of this organization, relates that only Brothers who were convinced 100 percent could be a part of their network. By necessitating the members' total conviction, Abdel Majid and his co-activists were trying to preclude the possibility of betrayal and infiltration.

Against this background of caution and confidence, the suborganization soon began recruiting members to its ranks. Although not confined to a specific geographical area, it had most success in in Cairo, al-Giza (southwest of central Cairo), and al-Daqahliya (northeast of Cairo).[15] This was no coincidence. The leaders of this organization, Ashmawi, Shahin, and Abdel Majid, hailed from these areas, which made the likelihood of success in them higher. A case in point is the influence of Amin Shahin, who hailed from Mit Ghamr, a center located in al-Daqahliya. Having escaped arrest in 1954, Shahin had since that time ventured to assemble those local Brothers he knew and who, like him, had stayed at large. Resulting from his attempts was the establishment of small circles of Brotherhood members in his hometown and its environs. When the young Shahin moved to Cairo to pursue a degree in the faculty of engineering in the late 1950s, he linked the networks he had established in his hometown with those Brothers he became acquainted with in the capital city and at campus. In so doing, Amin Shahin managed to link the suborganization of Ahmad Abdel Majid with those Brothers he had worked with in Mit Ghamr and its surroundings.[16]

At approximately the same time, and for roughly the same reasons, a similar organizational structure was underway, established by another group of young, like-minded Brothers. In contrast to the aforementioned, however, this structure was mainly comprised of former detainees who had been either sentenced to short terms in prison or placed under indefinite detention. Released after long and arduous months in confinement, these Brothers had had plenty of time during their prison terms to contemplate their next step when at large. The months that preceded release had occupied the *Ikhwan* with a number of thorny and decisive discussions and wonderings about what to do once outside prison: "Should I leave the Brotherhood?" "Can I return to working within an organization, risking the same degree inhuman repression and torture again?" "Should I leave both the idea and the organization behind, or should I leave the organization behind and carry on with the idea?" "Can the idea subsist without an organization?" "Does Nasser's flourishing popularity indicate that he is on the right path?" "Should the Special Apparatus be established once again?" "And what about Nasser? Should we avenge our martyr Brothers by killing him?"[17]

With these questions in mind and as a result of the long and laborious discussions, a group of Brothers resolved to form an organizational structure upon release. Restricting their network to Brothers with a "firm determination and an unquestionable desire to continue in the ranks of the Brotherhood," this leading group, which had emerged in prison, embarked on a screening exercise among *Ikhwani* inmates.[18] The core of this organizational structure comprised three middle-ranking Brothers: Muhammad Abdel Fattah Rizq Sharif, Abdel Fattah Ismail, and Awwad Abdel ʿAl Awwad. Sharif, the oldest of the three, was an engineer in his late forties hailing from Itay el Barud, a center in the governate of Beheira in Lower Egypt. A smiling and sympathetic man, older than most of his peers, he was revered as a diligent and pious man who "prayed far into the night."[19] Having been arrested in 1954 alongside the two other leading members in this organization, Sharif was admired as unwavering and dynamic by his Brothers due to his dedication to the Brotherhood.

Abdel Fattah Ismail is a name that looms large in our story from now on. The young man who bore this name hailed from Kaft al-Batikh in northern Egypt. Brought up in a religious but impoverished house, Ismail did not grow up with many educational options. Following a brief term at the Azhar preparational institute, the ambitious young man left school to make ends meet by working as a merchant. Despite his early lack of opportunity to pursue education, Ismail is described by his fellows as a knowledgeable, smart, and inspiring man. He joined the Muslim Brotherhood at an early age to become a close associate of Hasan al-Banna. Strongly convinced by the ideas of the late al-Banna, Ismail became an untiring preacher of the Brotherhood prior to his arrest in late 1954. Through his profession as a merchant, Ismail roamed Egypt inviting people to join the *Ikhwan*. By those who knew him, he is described as a man of a high diligence and unceasing activity. It was, however, in connection with his post-prison activities that Abdel Fattah would become the center of attention.[20]

The third Brother, Abdel ʿAl Awwad, was a charming young man in his early twenties known in the midst of the *Ikhwan* as *el-Khawaga* (the foreigner/Westerner) due to his light skin and auburn hair. *El-Khawaga* had joined the Brotherhood at a tender age when he became acquainted at school with local members of the organization. Taking part in one of the organizations that were unearthed in 1955 (see Chapter 5), Abdel ʿAl Awwad spent eight months in detention, accused of attempts to revive the Brotherhood.[21]

From the efforts and resolve of this disparate group emerged a covert and tightknit organizational structure. Coming into being in 1957 when these Brothers were released from prison, this organizational structure represented a pattern at this time.[22] Manned largely by newly released Brothers or others who had escaped arrest, these networks provided young men with structured and hierarchical formations through which they could resume their activities. Considering the current regime as unjust and brutal, their eagerness to oppose the authorities seems to have been buttressed by the Liman Tura incident. To Abdel Fattah Ismail and his Brothers, the possibility of using force as a way of defying the regime was not completely ruled out, as their deliberations when still in prison lucidly illustrated.[23]

Organizational structures emerged along similar lines in areas such as Damietta, el-Beheira, Tanta, el-Mansura, el-Mahalla el-Kubra, and el-Daqahliya, inter alia, evidencing a development at this time.[24] Often emanating from the burdensome and risky efforts of few Brothers, as the examples of Ashmawi's and Ismail's suborganizations demonstrated, these networks of Brothers seem to have been multiplying at this point.

The modus operandi of these organizations shared important traits: On the one hand, *Ikhwan* who were engaged in building such networks began their efforts by reaching out to Brothers with whom they were already familiar. This could be Brothers from the same geographical area, friends, participants in their former *usra*, or close associates from before the crackdown. In this way, the recruiters attempted to engage more Brothers in their activities while avoiding risks of exposure and consequently crackdowns. This period was more about involving Brothers already in the Brotherhood than recruiting new members to the organization. A case in point is the story of Muhammad Fathi Rifaʿi from el-Mahalla el-Kubra. An Arabic teacher who had joined the Brotherhood at an early age, he was released in 1956 after two years in military prison. Returning to his hometown after his release, Rifaʿi took upon his shoulders the precarious task of regathering the Brothers in his hometown and its environs. After some initial success in convincing a group of locals, such as Shaykh Abdel Wahhab al-Shaʿir, a mosque inspector, and Ahmad Muhammad Salam, a local merchant, Rifaʿi, and his fellows embarked on a push to invite more Brothers to join their activities. Through toilsome work and by utilizing already existing relational bonds and channels of communication, these Brothers in el-Mahalla el-Kubra managed to enlist more than forty members to their network. Predominantly composed of workers, those who joined this network were described as "resolute and diligent" activists who were devoted to the Brotherhood. Rifaʿi, so the account continues, "instilled in them the affection for sacrifice and struggle on the path of championing Islam."[25] Hagiographic to a certain extent, these accounts do, nevertheless, provide us with a view into the inner workings of the *Ikhwan* at this point.

On the other hand, there was the decentralization and secrecy of the Brotherhood's work at this point. These networks, as explained above, were cropping up in different parts of Egypt, by and large as a result of the eager efforts of disparate groups of *Ikhwan* to reorganize their local organizational structures. These efforts had to be kept under wraps in view of the inhospitable domestic situation. Abbas al-Sisi, the organizer who was working in areas close to Alexandria, presents such a story. During 1957, he met with fellow Brothers, including Muhammad Abdel Fattah Rizq Sharif, the Brother who, while in prison, had decided to revive the activities of the Brotherhood as soon as he left incarceration. Bewildered by the authorities' treatment of their fellow Brothers and especially by the brutality in Liman Tura, the two men agreed to work hand in hand to regroup the *Ikhwan* and revive its ideas in society. Agreeing to educate young Brotherhood members in the ideas of their organization as a first step to "form[ing] a new generation," their venture was not unencumbered by problems. Known to be a prominent *Ikhwan* member, al-Sisi was at this point closely shadowed by the Egyptian intelligence apparatus, which impeded his movements and ability to stay in touch with Brotherhood affiliates. Feeling that he was being watched and followed wherever he went, al-Sisi at times had to restrict and limit his meetings with fellow Brothers out of fear of persecution and crackdown. Such conditions, which many Brothers had to put up with, compelled them to find new and clandestine ways to resume their contacts unseen.[26]

Such was the landscape of Brotherhood activities and organizational structures until well into 1957. Characterized by a concurrency of low-keyed work, decentralization, secrecy, and often restricted to tight bonds of relations, these activities were on the rise despite a domestic situation that was unfavorable in many ways. A meeting took place at this point and under these conditions foreshadowing significant changes in the Brotherhood's organizational makeup. This meeting, which we turn to now, set in motion a development that would lead to the unification of the networks discussed above, hence preparing the ground for Organization 65.

At the port in Suez and subsequently on a ferry transporting them to Saudi Arabia, Abdel Fattah Ismail made the acquaintance of Zainab al-Ghazali.[27] The "dynamo of the Brotherhood," as Ismail was dubbed by fellow Brothers, commanded the respect of those who met him and such was the case when al-Ghazali met him the first time. A respectful and sincere young man, as he is described by those who knew him, Ismail appeared "imposing" and with an ability to persuade those who listened to him. Upon a short conversation aboard the ferry, the two activists agreed to meet in Mecca to discuss issues related to the Brotherhood. This first meeting took place in June 1957, shortly after the Liman incident, when they were heading to Islam's sacred city to perform the obligatory *hajj* (pilgrimage).[28] This meeting, which would pave the way for Organization 65, marks a turning point in my account. I therefore now turn to the meeting and its outcomes.

The Route toward Organization 65

"We swore our allegiance to fight and die for the sake of His [God's] *Da'wah* (mission)," thus narrates al-Ghazali about her agreement with Ismail reached during the summer days of 1957. Entered into by al-Ghazali and Ismail in Mecca, this covenant, as they describe it, marked the beginning of an effort to work hand in hand for the sake of Islam. In a concurring opinion, the two activists perceived the dissolution of the Muslim Brotherhood as "Islamically illegal" and took upon their shoulders the task of "reorganizing the group and re-starting its activities." Despite anticipating the path ahead of them to be arduous and risky, the two peers agreed to continue regardless. "[W]e will fight for His [God's] sake and won't languor until we unite the ranks of the Ikhwan and isolate those who do not want to work for Him [God], no matter what their position or weight [is in the Brotherhood]." With this end in mind, they embarked on a venture that eventually would prepare the ground for Organization 65.[29]

Zainab al-Ghazali was no stranger to the Brotherhood's activities nor to its leadership.[30] Al-Ghazali's brother Muhammad and some of her nephews had been members of the Brotherhood prior to the second *miḥna*, drawing her close to Brotherhood circles.[31] In 1955, in her late thirties, the activist had joined a group of female members in putting into action an organized venture to support the bereaved families of imprisoned or dead Brothers. These undertakings had allowed her to make the acquaintance of prominent members of the organization, most significantly al-Hudaybi, the *Murshid*, and his family. The *Murshid*'s wife and daughters were alongside other female members of the Brotherhood such as Amal al-Ashmawi,[32] head of the Muslim Sister's section, and Aminah al-Jawhari, working to collect and distribute funds to Brotherhood families throughout Egypt.[33] Mirroring the activities of male members of the organization and beginning at approximately the same time, these activities performed by the female branch enabled the Brotherhood to maintain vital lines of communication. Women, as was the case at this time, were subjected to little surveillance compared to the male activists, and this made them an alternative line of support and a means of tying the organization together.[34]

Al-Ghazali's and Ismail's agreement, in their own words, was to unite the scattered Brotherhood networks and activists, putting their work into a collective and united venture. However, taking the domestic situation into consideration, this was an audacious road to take. Keeping activities low-key and decentralized, as had been the case so far, was markedly different from establishing a nationwide and more hierarchical organizational structure, as these two were contemplating. Therefore, by dint of this venture's magnitude and risks, the two activists sought and received the consent of Hasan al-Hudaybi to shape a countrywide organizational structure, at least according to their own account. "Now we required Hasan al-Hudaibi's permission to start our new works and after several meetings with him we were allowed to do so."[35] Contrary to al-Ghazali's account, however, Farid Abdel Khaleq insists that the *Murshid* had at no time consented to this arrangement. Abdel Khaleq, at this time head of the Brotherhood in Cairo and a close associate of al-Hudaybi, emphasizes that the *Murshid* asked him to uproot any such nationwide network, thus demonstrating his disapproval of al-Ghazali's and Ismail's attempts. What al-Hudaybi authorized was a continuation of low-key activities and decentralized networks, according to the narrative of Abdel Khaleq.[36] Be that as it may, what can be ascertained is that the *Murshid* knew of these attempts from the very outset. And in the event that he had actually tried to halt them, as Abdel Khaleq maintains, the following account illustrates that he failed in doing so.

The covert endeavors of the Brotherhood went on uninterrupted and picked up pace from late 1957. Upon their return from Mecca, al-Ghazali and Ismail continued where they had left off before their journey to perform the pilgrimage. Hand in hand, they began reaching out to Brotherhood members throughout Egyptian governates, cities, and villages, inviting them to take part in the emerging organizational structure. These journeys went on during the subsequent months, leading to a growth in numbers and an expansion of organization.[37] Subsequent to his release from incarceration, Abdel Fattah Ismail had worked to form an underground suborganization, as shown above, and this was the work he continued with at this point upon returning from pilgrimage. I now offer a few examples of the recruitment in this period before I move on to discuss the rise of Organization 65 as a nationwide establishment.

In general, feelings among the Brothers were a mixture of apprehension and hope: apprehension due to the continuing constraints put on their movements and hope by virtue of the sustenance of their organization and bonds. Following the Liman Tura massacre, as seen above, an increasing number of organizational structures had cropped up throughout Egypt, all working to continue the ideas and organization of the Brotherhood. These endeavors had simultaneously resulted in activating Brothers at large but also in recruiting new members to the Brotherhood's ranks. Taking place in the provinces of Upper Egypt, the delta, Lower Egypt, Alexandria, Cairo, and its environs, inter alia, this recruitment was imperative in injecting new blood into the organization.

Muhamad Badiʿs entry into the Brotherhood in 1959 offers an illustrative example. Born in el-Mahalla el-Kubra in 1943, he attended the preparatory school for the faculty of science at a young age. At the faculty, where he eventually would graduate as a veterinarian, Badiʿ, the current *Murshid*, was approached by a Syrian member of the Brotherhood. Noticing Badiʿ's religiosity on campus, the Syrian Brother from Hama identified in the young man the potential to become a member of the *Ikhwan*. Following a short period of socializing, and before being told about the Brotherhood, the student Badiʿ was unknowingly put through a period of vetting and education by the Syrian Brother from Hama. Only when Badiʿ had proved himself trustworthy and sincere did his recruiter introduce him to the Brotherhood, invite him to join the organization, and eventually enlist him in an *usra*.[38] This enrollment marked the beginning of a long journey within the ranks of the Brotherhood. During these long and troublesome years, Badiʿ would witness various periods of repression and imprisonment, the most recent of which was the repression that began in 2013, when he was arrested alongside thousands of his fellows.[39]

The way Badiʿ was approached and eventually recruited in 1959 exhibits a working pattern of this time. In view of the risks associated with admitting new members into an organization working clandestinely, new recruits had to undergo a host of measures before being allowed in. Such measures entailed that recruits would undergo a period of scrutinizing and testing before actually being told about the Muslim Brotherhood. This was a way of minimizing the risks and keeping out potential infiltrators. Accordingly, on account of the "probability of betrayal," to borrow Simmel's words,[40] the recruitment of new members was restricted to men "who exhibited religiosity," like for example praying in the university prayer halls or attending a mosque regularly. Only when the recruiter had confirmed that the potential member had Islamic leanings and exhibited religiosity would he take the first steps toward establishing links to him. This was the case with Badiʿ, too.

Another way of infusing fresh blood into the organization was by utilizing already existing personal links, such as reaching out to men from one's own neighborhood, family members, friends, or colleagues. In so doing, the Brotherhood member could scrutinize potential Brothers before taking the risk of inviting them to the organization. As the following examples demonstrate, universities, mosques, and local neighborhoods, inter alia, were important sites for the Brotherhood's recruitment at this point.[41] This point is illustrated by Muhammad al-Sarwi's story. Born in April 1943 and growing up in a religious home, the young boy from Mit Yaʿish, a small village in the Sharqiyya governorate, recalls praying frequently in the village mosque with his father. At a tender age, al-Sarwi found great amusement in reading different genres. But it was the newspapers that especially caught the young boy's attention. Combining his early religiosity with an interest in politics, al-Sarwi found in the Muslim Brotherhood a natural avenue for him to develop these personal interests. Upon moving to Cairo to study at the faculty of engineering, al-Sarwi found a strong representation of Brotherhood students on campus. This group of students, who had met and established strong ties at the faculty prior to al-Sarwi's move to Cairo, were less strictly organized, but they were all engaged in a variation of Brotherhood activities. Headed by Farouq al-Minshawi, these students had joined the Brotherhood upon becoming acquainted with Mubarak Abdel Azim, eventually one of the leaders of *Tanẓīm 65*. Al-Sarwi, the young man who had known and admired the Muslim Brotherhood since his adolescence without joining the organization, was drawn into this circle of *Ikhwani* students sometime after enrolling at the faculty. In the lecture hall where he attended a class on physical sciences, this connection was commenced when by coincidence al-Sarwi came to sit right behind Farouq al-Minshawi. Born in 1943, just like al-Sarwi himself, Al-Minshawi was a tall young man, characterized by an aura of seriousness and serenity, and described by his peers as a man of few words. Alongside Mubarak Abdel Azim, he had invited a number of young men to the Brotherhood's ranks, thus establishing a network of *Ikhwan* at the faculty of engineering. Getting to know al-Sarwi better, al-Minshawi began to talk to him in the initial phase about religion in general and the importance of living in accordance with Islamic precepts. These conversations about religion blended with discussions about history and culture, and a general friendship emerged between the two students. Al-Minshawi, as al-Sarwi recalls, was always interested in asking questions and keen to tell his new friend about the importance of actively working for Islam. All this was, however, on a general level. Upon forging closer ties, al-Minshawi began introducing al-Sarwi to different books that were key publications of Islamist thinkers. These books included publications authored by, among others, Sayyid Qutb, Sayyid Abul-A'la Mawdudi, and Muhammad Qutb. Prior to this, the meetings and activities had been characterized by an informality and reservation: al-Sarwi had at no point yet been told about the Muslim Brotherhood and al-Minshawi's connection to them. Thus, before being openly introduced to the organization, al-Sarwi was put through a period of testing and vetting, where his personality and relationships were scrutinized to the smallest detail. This was to ensure that the newcomer was no infiltrator. At the end of this period of trial, he was finally asked to join the Brotherhood, which he did "without reservation, due to [his] former knowledge of the Brotherhood."[42]

Al-Sarwi's and al-Minshawi's stories were linked when the two men found common ground in the ideas of the Muslim Brotherhood from which they could pursue their goal. This goal, as they both perceived it, was among other things to live a religious life and to shape society according to Islamic principles. On a general level, such stories illustrate that the Brothers at this time were still able to recruit new members and to engage actively in society. The new recruits were mainly young university students who yearned to take an active role in society and to shape it Islamically.

That the Brotherhood had some degree of success in recruiting new members on university campuses was no coincidence. These sites, where literate and conscious young men in large numbers could meet and discuss religious and political issues largely unimpeded, provided the organization with a pool of potential recruits. Those disgruntled with the political situation or seeking an alternative path to that offered by the Nasserite regime could find this in the Muslim Brotherhood's ideas. Such was the case with Mahmoud Izzat, who is currently serving a life sentence for charges of "terrorism." Born in 1944 in Misr el-Jadida, northeast of Cairo, Izzat had been familiar with the Muslim Brotherhood since his early childhood. In the early 1960s he enrolled at the Faculty of Medicine, where he came in contact with Brotherhood students at the university. Being familiar with the organization and its ideas since his childhood and feeling discontent toward the general conditions in Egypt, Izzat joined the Brotherhood in 1962 to become a member of Organization 65.[43] Similar stories are manifold, and they often follow a pattern comparable to Izzat's.[44]

These networks of the Brotherhood discussed at length above continued to follow a hierarchical and structured mode. New members who were introduced to the organization were grouped in close-knit cells (*usar*) consisting of approximately three members in each *usra*. Cloaked in high secrecy and governed by strict discipline, these cells were kept under the radar and closed off for all outsiders. In a further attempt to maximize security and limit the liability to infiltration, a member of an *usra* would only know the members of his own *usra*.[45]

Ibrahim Ghusheh, a Palestinian member of the Brotherhood's Jerusalem branch, who studied in Cairo in the second half of the 1950s, substantiates these accounts. Landing in Cairo in 1955, Ghusheh witnessed the repressive climate toward the Brotherhood firsthand. When he first arrived, the Palestinian student was strongly urged by *Ikhwan* members to conceal his Brotherhood affiliation so as to avoid persecution and restrictions. Heeding this advice for some time, he soon realized that the Brotherhood was still organized in society. But the members were, as he describes it, "on the highest level of alert, and [had] to have a sense of security, control and discretion."[46] Pointing to the organization of the *Ikhwan*, he recalled that Brotherhood students from various Arab countries studying in Egypt had organized themselves hierarchically on various campuses, with a person in charge of Brotherhood students from the respective country.[47]

In this way, these Brothers could work as a unified group and offer some support to the Egyptian Brotherhood in withstanding the repressive climate they were enduring.

As illustrated so far, this period was characterized by a vibrant *Ikhwani* activism which attempted to recruit new members and increase the activities of the Brotherhood on the ground. Resulting from the various ventures to recruit new Brothers and to form Brotherhood networks in all parts of Egypt was the emergence of the nationwide Organization 65. As illustrated above, these undertakings had been ongoing since the beginning of the Brotherhood's dissolution, however, increasing numerically from the summer of 1956 when a substantial number of *Ikhwan* detainees began to leave prison. During the late 1950s, this had resulted in a considerable number of Brotherhood organizational structures and smaller networks cropping up all over Egypt. Previously, these groupings had been working independently from each other, merging sometimes, but for the most part continuing to work as disparate groups. This would, however, change in 1962, when an effort was made to unite these networks into an organizational structure on a national scale. A discussion of this nationwide organizational structure, its founding members, its ideas, and its raison d'être forms the focus of the remaining pages of this book.

The first step in this organization's risky voyage took place in in 1962, when Ali Ashmawi and Awwad Abdel ʿAl Awwad met as representatives of their respective networks. Abdel ʿAl Awwad was representing the network that included, among others, Abdel Fattah Ismail and Zainab al-Ghazali, while Ali Ashmawi, as seen above, had established organizational structures first in his hometown Mit Ghamr and second in Cairo alongside Brothers operating in Cairo and its environs. These different structures, as illustrated above, had been built up in the late 1950s and had been working underground to revive the activities and propagate the ideas of the *Ikhwan*. Against this backdrop, they had managed to spread their presence to different parts of Egypt such as Alexandria, el-Giza, Daqahliya, and, most numerically, Cairo.[48] While working separately in the underground, members of the networks had learned of each other's existence and seen an opportunity in approaching each other. A first meeting was quickly followed by several meetings in which representatives from the networks discussed the prospects of amalgamation and deliberated the aims of the projected network. A decisive and final meeting, attended by Ali Ashmawi and Ahmad Abdel Majid as representatives of one organizational structure and Abdel Fattah Ismail and Muhammad Fathi Rifaʿi as representatives for the other, eventually took place in an apartment in Cairo. Following protracted discussions, the four men finally agreed on a merger.[49]

The main issue that had occupied them and made an amalgamation difficult in the beginning was the question of violence. Representatives of Abdel Fattah Ismail's faction, according to the account of Ahmad Abdel Majid and Ali Ashmawi, advocated the idea of assassinating Nasser in retaliation for what he had inflicted on the Brotherhood. This idea involved the assassination being carried out by twenty to thirty well-trained, fully equipped militants who were prepared to die to achieve this end. This scenario, however, lay far outside the thinking of Ashmawi and Abdel Majid, which is why they categorically rejected the idea. What they envisioned was an educational organizational structure that worked toward the intellectual preparation of Brotherhood members and toward gathering of the scattered Brothers together. Following long and animated discussions, the two groups agreed to abandon violence altogether, opting instead for reorganizing the Brotherhood and educating its members.[50]

Having agreed on the organization's aims, the four activists planned to resume discussions in Abdel Fattah Ismail's home in Damietta. In this attractive city, lying on the banks of the Nile and famous for its palm trees, the four men recommenced their meeting for three consecutive days, discussing what form the organizational structure should take and how to proceed with building it and its activities. The outcome was a hierarchical formation led by four commanders: Abdel Fattah Ismail, Muhammad Fahti Rifaʿi, Ali Ashmawi, and Ahmad Abdel Majid. This leading circle would subsequently be expanded to include Majdi Abdel Aziz, a graduate from the faculty of science. Abdel Majid was put in command of the organization in Alexandria and Beheira and became responsible for the *tanẓīm*'s "scientific and chemical experiments."[51]

"The Dynamo of the Brotherhood," Ismail, would be responsible, among other things, for the network in the Damietta and Kafr el-Sheikh governates, the areas lying in the East Delta, and in shaping closer ties to Brothers in Alexandria and Beheira. He would in addition be the network's liaison with the *Murshid* and with Brothers inside jails, besides overseeing its financial aspects. Prior to this amalgamation, Ismail had managed to establish contacts with Brothers abroad through his regular journeys to Saudi Arabia and collected a considerable amount of money from Brothers residing inside and outside Egypt. Said Ramadan, a senior Brother and the late Hasan al-Banna's son-in-law residing abroad, is mentioned as one of the prominent Brothers with whom Ismail had formed relations.[52] This offered the budding organizational structure a financial stability and vital lines of communication to Brothers overseas.

Fahti Rifaʿi would in turn take charge of the areas situated in the center of the Nile Delta, such as Daqahliya, el-Gharbiya, and el-Monufia, alongside being responsible for molding the network's syllabus and taking charge of the educational work. When Rifaʿi left for Algeria some months after the setup of this organization, he was succeeded by Sabri Arafa al-Kumi. Characterized as a meticulous, calm man, al-Kumi, who had been an officer in the army, was working as a teacher, and he assumed his predecessor's responsibilities.[53]

Assigned the task of heading the Cairo and el-Giza branches and tasked with maintaining contact with Brothers overseas was Ali Ashmawi, the young activist who had been active since the repression of the Brotherhood. Ashmawi would also take charge of the members' physical training, which would take place at camps and in private apartments. Lastly, Ahmad Abdel Majid, Ashmawi's brother-in-law, was assigned the task of leading the organization in Upper Egypt and heading its intelligence activities.[54]

Constructing a hierarchical and tightly knit formation, these young men exhibited a conscious desire to work collectively toward achieving their goals. The reorganization of the Brotherhood as well as the expansion of its presence was among their prime objectives, and toward this goal they commenced their ambitious work. Meeting once a week but in different locations so as to avoid unnecessary attention, the commanding circle soon began to direct the work of this nascent organizational structure. The network was based on a strict hierarchical basis, meaning that every Brother involved in this endeavor was organized in a *usra* consisting of three to five members, headed by an *amīr* (commander). Only the *amīr* of each of the *usra* would be in touch with ascending levels, thus ensuring that the information flow would continue uninterrupted and in a relatively safe way. Every *usra* was thus put under the command of the geographical branch it fell under. In this way, a streamlining of activities could be achieved while ensuring that all Brothers followed the same regulations.[55]

With the organizational aspects in place, the *tanẓīm*'s architects began drafting specific working patterns to move on with their activities. A case in point was the financial aspects of the organization. To establish the financial tenacity of the *tanẓīm* and to secure that its funds would not run out, it was required from every member of the organizational structure to contribute at least 5 percent of his monthly earnings to its coffers. Supplementing this was the funding they could collected from rich Brothers residing inside Egypt and the support they received from *Ikhwan* overseas. Abdel Fattah Ismail, just to offer one example, had collected 14,000 EGP through the two latter lines of support to sustain the organization. Such resources were collected to fund the *tanẓīm*'s different activities. Said Ramadan features yet again as being among the most active exile Brothers in supporting the organization.[56]

Moreover, those responsible for the cultural, religious, and political education of the *tanẓīm*'s members composed a distinct program of study that would be implemented in all cells. Comprising the study of books on Islamic jurisprudence, legal schools within the Islamic legal tradition, the Prophet's *sīra* (biography), Quran exegesis, organization, and politics, inter alia, these readings were intended to be used broadly among all members to augment their ideological sophistication.[57] Along these lines but aiming at improving the members' physical abilities, Ali Ashmawi and Majdi Abdel Aziz designed a training program to be followed by the Brothers. Along with drills that aimed at raising the members' stamina and physical strength, the program included instructions in martial arts in addition to long-distance marching and jogging. To structure these exercises, the organizers established a number of camps where a more comprehensive program of training was pursued. Established in distant areas, these camps could provide the instructors with greater freedom to oversee and direct these drills without fear of being exposed. The camps were accordingly regulated by strict rules of secrecy and were treated with great circumspection. Added to the physical exercises was the firearms training, coordinated by the two ex-officers Majdi Abdel Aziz and Sabri Arafa. Meant to prepare the members militarily, instruction in these skills was described by Ahmad Abdel Majid as an important precaution to take.[58] By the same token, and in order to gain entry to the vital officers' corps, the organization began enrolling a number of Brothers into the Military Academy. In this way, and by gaining a footing in the Egyptian armed forces, the organization was contemplating ways of changing the status quo in a society they perceived as governed by a despotic ruler.[59] Accordingly, despite the fact that leading members of this organization stressed that militancy was far beyond the scope of their planning and not among their aims, the above issues clearly illustrate that preparations for a showdown with the regime were at least being made.

Considering links and contacts to Brotherhood establishments outside Egypt as key in supporting their undertaking and raising funds on their behalf, the *tanẓīm* set up different ways of continuing this contact clandestinely. By way of illustration, the fact that many of Islam's holy sites are located in present-day Saudi Arabia provided Brotherhood members with occasion to frequently travel there under the pretext of performing the obligatory pilgrimage (*al-ḥajj*), occurring at a specific time once a year, or the minor pilgrimage (*al-* ʿ*umra*), conducted at any time of the year. Such journeys offered Egypt's Brothers with an opportunity to establish contacts with the large group of Brotherhood exiles residing there or visiting Islam's holy sites from other countries. This had, for instance, been the case with Abdel Fattah Ismail, who upon his release had traveled to Mecca each year to perform the pilgrimage. Making these journeys annually, Ismail had established close links with Brotherhood leaders outside Egypt such as Said Ramadan, Mustafa al-Alem, and many others.[60] To ensure uninterrupted contact with those *Ikhwan* outside Egypt, the *tanẓīm* dispatched a Brother to act as the permanent liaison between their organization and Brotherhood members abroad. Muhyi al-Din Hilal, the Brother entrusted with this task, was to stay in Saudi Arabia, from where he could make contact with *Ikhwan* residing in different parts of the Arabic-speaking world without fearing the pervasive security apparatus of the Nasserite regime. This could be done under the pretext of performing the pilgrimage.[61] Other methods, such as appointing Brotherhood pilots employed as aviators to send letters from outside Egypt in order to avoid the Nasserite security apparatus, were also utilized at this point.[62]

In continuing these lines of communication, bonding, and preparation with Brothers in the region, Ali Ashmawi made a journey to Saudi Arabia during this lively period of organizational activities. Traveling under the pretext of performing the pilgrimage and visiting Islam's sacred places, Ashmawi had in fact been summoned by leading Brothers abroad to meet and discuss the proper ways of continuing with the organizational structure in Egypt. Upon learning, through Muhyi al-Din Hilal, about the network's progress in Egypt, the exiled leaders had summoned Ashmawi to address its financial needs and to bolster their links to its members. What Ali had in mind, however, was to discuss the organization's armament and funding, in addition to establishing more direct lines of communication. The day following his arrival in Mecca, it was organized for the visitor to set out for Jeddah, a port city on the Red Sea, where he would attend meetings with Brotherhood leaders. Under a veil of secrecy and robed in a Saudi Arabian cloak to hide his real identity, Ashmawi, who for reasons of safety presented himself as Ismail Abd el-Tawwab, was brought to Jeddah. In this city, lying about sixty-five kilometers west of Mecca, Ashmawi held several meetings with Brotherhood leaders. Discussing the needs of his organization and the concrete ways of supporting him and his Brothers in Egypt, Ali Ashmawi informed those gathered that what the organizational structure really needed was arms. The young militant from Egypt informed his peers that the network was in dire need of assault weapons, sniper rifles, explosives, and grenades, "enough to arm a thousand-man force with arms and grenades," in addition to amounts of explosive devices. These arms, as Ali assured those attending the meeting in Jeddah, would be stockpiled centrally, kept hidden, and only used in the case of utmost necessity.[63] The Brotherhood exiles in Saudi Arabia arranged for Mustafa el-Alem, an exile Brother who had gained experience in weapons purchasing and smuggling during the Arab–Israeli war of 1948 and the Canal War in 1951, to purchase the requested arms in southern Sudan in order to send them to Egypt at a later time.

Abdel Majid corroborates this account but argues that Ashmawi took this initiative single-handedly against the consensus of the commanding group. "It was against the direction of our path [to ask for weapons] and we had not asked him to do so in advance" was how Abdel Majid described the reception of Ashmawi's venture. Contradicting this claim, however, Ashmawi maintains in his memoirs that this had been the agreement reached by all leaders of the organization before his journey to Saudi Arabia. He was merely acting on the wishes of the leading committee of the organization.[64] Be that as it may, due to his trip to Jeddah, Ali set the *tanẓīm* on the path of militancy. Notwithstanding whether he was acting on behalf of the leading committee or autonomously, by asking for weapons and setting in motion the armament of the organizational structure, he had begun a development that could not easily be reversed, as we see below. Taking place in 1962, two years before Qutb's assumption of the organization's leadership, this incident shows that militancy did not begin with Qutb.[65]

As the abovementioned discussions have illustrated, appearing in 1962 as a unified body, the *tanẓīm* developed as a hierarchical order. Gathering the dispersed networks of Brothers that had cropped up in most parts of Egypt, this suborganization aimed at reinvigorating the Brotherhood in society and spreading its ideas among like-minded young men. While some Brothers presumably thought of assassinating Nasser as revenge for the regime's treatment of the *Ikhwan*, others aimed at nonviolent activities in society, seeing that as the appropriate way of refreshing the *Ikhwan*'s appeal. I contend therefore that the attention given to Sayyid Qutb on account of his radicalizing influence of this organizational structure somehow distorts its history. Rather than pointing to Qutb as the main actor in reviving the Brotherhood, as has been claimed by Gerges,[66] I argue that Qutb's role should be put into its correct historical context. The nuclei of this organizational structure, aiming at continuing the Brotherhood's activities, began working long before Qutb was affiliated with them, and the main "dynamo" of this venture was Abdel Fattah Ismail.[67] Rather than beginning with Qutb, the reorganization of the Brotherhood occurred as an organic continuation of the previous attempts to resume the activities of the

Ikhwan since 1955.[68] Thus, seeing the light of the day long before Qutb left prison, this venture should be understood as a link in the chain of covert Brotherhood activities beginning shortly after the Manshiyya incident.

I now turn to the role of Qutb in the last phase of this *tanẓīm*, namely from his assumption of its leadership in 1964 until it was uncovered by the authorities in the summer of 1965. As I do so, I ask whether Qutb tried to remove the organization from the path of militancy on which Ali's arms' request in Jeddah had set it.

Qutb Leading the Organization

Once the *tanẓīm* was firmly in place along with clear recruiting techniques and it had established links to al-Hudaybi and Brothers in exile, the commanding members began looking for a senior Brother to head their endeavor, as the organizational structure was composed predominantly of younger and less-experienced Brothers and needed a senior member to direct their activities and guide them ideologically.[69] However, in view of the likelihood of repression associated with this endeavor, the search for a leader turned out to be trickier than first expected.

Perceiving the *tanẓīm* as putting the entire Brotherhood on a road paved with dangers and opening it up for the recommencement of persecution, a group of senior Brothers renounced the whole venture and began counteracting it. As seen in the preceding chapter, Brotherhood members who had experienced the rough Nasserite repression on their own bodies did not always agree on how to continue their *daʿwa* in society. While a group of Brothers had decided to continue clandestine activities no matter the costs, others had decided to keep a low profile in order to avoid persecution. This divide would become even more pronounced with the emergence of this nationwide suborganization.

As a case in point, when Abdel Khaleq, at that time the head of the Brotherhood in Cairo, learned of the *tanẓīm*'s existence, he strongly opposed it. Regarding the organizational structure as a militant endeavor to kill Nasser and execute a coup d'état, Abdel Khaleq saw in this venture a pretext for the repression of the whole *Ikhwan* organization. Seeing the assassination of Nasser and militancy as deviating from the Brotherhood's original ideas, the close associate of al-Hudaybi became a strong opponent of the entire idea. For this reason, Abdel Khaleq and Munir al-Dilla, two key members of a faction within the Brotherhood,[70] urged al-Hudaybi to censure the suborganization.[71] They perceived low-key activities without a nationwide reorganization at that point in time as the best way of enduring repression.[72] In addition, as historic leaders of the Brotherhood, the abovementioned leading group might have seen this organizational structure as a challenge to their own standing in the Brotherhood, which is why they reacted with ferocity. Pointing to this disagreement, Ahmad Abdel Majid recalls that this leading circle did all in its power to oppose his nascent network, warning members against joining it and waging "a war against us and persecuting us everywhere."[73] According to another account, Salah Shadi went so far as to ask his son-in-law, Murad al-Zayat, to turn in the organization if its leaders did not dismantle it.[74] Heeding their warnings, al-Hudaybi appointed Abdel Khaleq to dismantle the suborganization, according to the narrative of Abdel Khaleq himself.[75] However, the accounts of other Brothers close to *Tanẓīm* 65 contradict this narrative, stressing that al-Hudaybi had endorsed the network and its continuation.[76]

Despite this repugnance, the commanders of the suborganization continued their search for a senior member to lead their network and bestow it with legitimacy. Consequently, in about 1963, Abdel Aziz Ali, previously a minister in the first period of post-monarchical rule and a former member of al-Hizb al-Watani, was chosen to head the *tanẓīm*. Ali, who according to Ashmawi's account was appointed by al-Hudaybi to head the formation, was experienced in clandestine activism, having cofounded and participated in a covert anti-British organization during the 1919 revolution. Islamically minded and with a background in underground activities, Abdel Aziz Ali seemed the right candidate for the position. Meeting several times with the former minister under complete secrecy, the leading members made an attempt to introduce Ali to their venture. However, this association did not last long, as the members of the *tanẓīm* disliked his high-handed style of leadership and did not find him fit for the task. Once they had decided to part ways with Abdel Aziz Ali, the committee began looking for a new leader, and their choice fell this time on Sayyid Qutb, whose writings and viewpoints from prison had inspired them.[77] Qutb had, in fact, and presumably as an attempt to propagate his ideas outside prison, contacted leading members of Organization 65. Reaching out to Abdel Fattah Ismail through his younger sister, Hamida Qutb, the incarcerated writer had sent these young men a letter underlining the importance of Islamic education and suggesting for them a list of readings that would put them on the right path. It is, however, important to stress that Qutb at this point was oblivious to the existence of this organizational structure.[78] Having come to know Qutb through his writings, before actually meeting him, the young activists found in the thinker in his late fifties an ideologue who could take their endeavor a step further. This was the beginning of a journey that would see its concluding pages with Qutb and two of his Brothers walking firmly to the gallows.

Since 1957 and as a direct result of the Liman Tura massacre, Qutb had pondered on the right way to keep the Islamic movement alive. Perceiving this fierce massacre as a continuation of the onslaught on the Brotherhood that had begun in late 1954, Qutb suspected a predetermined plan to eradicate the Brotherhood.[79] The Brotherhood's survival was seen by Qutb as crucial, because it represented a truly religious discourse in Egypt. Should the Brotherhood be eradicated, it would, according to him, amount to a "heinous crime."[80]

In light of this, Qutb began to review the state of society and the position of the "Islamic movement" within it. Spending long and arduous hours discussing this issue with his closest associate in prison, Muhammad Yusuf Hawwash, Qutb arrived at the conclusion that "the Islamic movement today faces a situation that is reminiscent of the situation prevailing at the dawn of Islam." What characterizes society at this point, according to Qutb and Hawwash, his fellow who eventually would be "martyred" alongside him, is an ignorance of the truth of Islamic creeds and a deviation from the Islamic mores, in addition to the detachment from the Islamic system and from Sharia. Perceiving this decay as forcefully shrouding society, the two inmates deplored what they perceived as "Powerful Zionist, Crusader, and imperialist camps that oppose every attempt of the Islamic mission and work to destroy [the Islamic movement] through the local regimes and systems." Thus, with the community at large deviating from Islamic doctrines and with the regime doing its utmost to oppose the Islamic *da'wa*, the two inmates began elaborating a study program to educate society Islamically. With this ambitious plan in mind, Hawwash and Qutb agreed that

> the Islamic movements should start from the grassroots to bring the right understanding of the Islamic creed (*aqida*) to the hearts and minds of people .... The Islamic order cannot and should not be established through a seizure of power. Only when the Islamic base [*qā'ida*] in societies demands the implementation of the Islamic order can it become a reality.[81]

In 1962, as an attempt to distribute this idea among fellow Brothers, Qutb and Hawwash began disseminating it among Brotherhood inmates. Talking to *Ikhwan* cadres about the idea of educating society Islamically before endeavoring to establishing an Islamic system, the two peers tried to attract adherents to their ideas. By reaching out to *Ikhwan* who came from different prisons to the infirmary for healthcare and recommending for them books to read, Qutb had begun forming a network inside prisons that would adopt his ideas. Suggesting readings for them, instructing them to distribute these ideas among other inmates, and asking them to form cells inside the prisons, Qutb had begun shaping a group of young men who would bear forward his ideas and eventually form the nucleus that would educate society. However, isolated in the infirmary and without a leading status in the Brotherhood to bestow their ideas with authority, the two men faced many bumps on the road. While a small group enthusiastically endorsed those ideas presented to them by Qutb and Hawwash, others rebuffed them resolutely. Contending that the Brotherhood's official leadership had the exclusive mandate to chart a course for the *Ikhwan*, those refuting these ideas began vociferously opposing Qutb and Hawwash. Qutb's critics accused him and his fellows of conducting *takfīr* (excommunication of fellow Muslims) and began warning fellow Brothers and Brotherhood leaders about the dangers of Qutb's ideas. Confronted with this serious accusation, Qutb denied all charges. The understanding he had reached, as he explained to an inmate who inquired about those *takfīr* rumors, was that society had deviated from the correct Islamic path. This necessitated that the Muslim Brotherhood resume its activities from the bottom rather than from the top. Qutb explained to his fellow that his ideas were related to the Brotherhood's methods and not to the beliefs of society. In deliberately refusing *takfīr*, Qutb told his inquirer, "We have not excommunicated people, and this is a distorted conveyance [of our ideas]." At a later date, Qutb discussed these ideas with Umar al-Tilmisani and Abdel Aziz Attiya, two members of the Brotherhood's executive office who had been transferred to the infirmary for medical care. Correcting their understanding and denying that he was performing *takfīr*, Qutb recalls that both Brotherhood leaders were appeased with what he told them.[82]

Such was the dynamism that had characterized the prison discourses before Qutb's release. Occupying Brotherhood cadres and leaders alike, these deliberations clearly exhibit that the *Ikhwan* at that point were discussing the proper ways to continue their activities in society once outside prison.

In May 1964, upon suffering a heart attack that severely weakened his health, Sayyid Qutb was released from prison after serving nine years. Qutb's release came after an intervention on his behalf from the Iraqi president Abdel Salam Aref, who had learned of the incarcerated thinker's illness from the Iraqi branch of the Brotherhood.[83]

Perceiving Qutb's ideas as close to their own and his personality as inspiring, the leading Brothers of the *tanẓīm* were eager to invite him to join their organizational structure and eventually to head them. Qutb's nine years in prison had undoubtedly boosted his reputation among many *Ikhwan*, who came to see him as an unwavering Brother who had held firmly to his beliefs.[84] Qutb was first approached by Abdel Fattah Ismail, the third Brother who would accompany him to the gallows. Visiting Qutb in his house in Helwan, a well-known suburb of Cairo, Ismail intimated to his host that he was "associated with a group of young men who aspire to fulfill Islamic work" and who were "looking for someone to direct them and guide them." Through this ambiguous presentation and without disclosing that these young men were part of a hierarchical suborganization that had already been founded, Ismail asked Qutb to meet some of those young men. Meeting Qutb for the first time in Ras el-Bar, a resort city in the Governorate of Damietta, during the summer days of 1964, the *tanẓīm*'s commanders found what they had yearned for. "[T]hrough an attractive way that is magnetic … we heard from him ideas that we were hearing for the first time … this first encounter left an enormous effect on us," such was the impression Ahmad Abdel Majid came away with after his first encounter with Qutb.[85] After a few meetings between Qutb and the leaders of the organizational structure in which they consulted him about different issues and discussed general ideas with him, they finally approached him with the request to lead their venture. Upon seeking and being granted the approval of the *Murshid*, Qutb agreed to become the *tanẓīm*'s lead figure.[86]

In other words, the formal association between Qutb and the suborganization began in 1964, when he joined the *tanẓım* as Ali's successor. This had taken place sometime after his release, when the network's leaders had approached him and eventually invited him to lead them. Corroborating this account, Qutb argues in his testimony written in prison between late 1965 and early 1966 that his association with the *tanẓīm* was limited to the period that followed his release and was restricted to six months in which he held about twelve meetings with its leading group.[87]

Now with a respected and revered leader, the suborganization continued its work in society, despite being unremittingly censured by other leading Brothers.[88] Sayyid Qutb handpicked for the *tanẓīm* a long list of books that would constitute its syllabus. This list would be distributed among its members, and they would individually and in groups discuss the ideas presented in these books so as to form a distinct understanding of their role in society. Containing books on faith (*īmān*), creed (*ʿaqīda*), Quran exegeses (*tafsīr*), and some of his own books such as *Milestones*, *In the Shades of the Quran*, *This Religion*, *The Islamic Concept and Its Characteristics*, and *The Basic Principles of the Islamic Worldview*, the list was intended to educate the young men in accordance with the worldview

Qutb and Hawwash had developed in prison. He set about studying with them "the history of the Islamic movement [tracing it back to the early days of Islam] and the position of the atheistic, Zionist and crusading powers towards Islam in ancient and modern times."[89] Qutb's main interest at this time, as it seems from the memoirs of those who were closest to him at this time and from his own testimony, was to point those young men in the right direction in terms of belief, as he understood it.[90] Impressed by their sincerity and dedication, Qutb committed himself to raising their awareness and refining their ideas. Meeting with the commanding five once a week or once every two or three weeks, Qutb worked at developing their minds so as to make of them the future leaders of this organizational structure. When he had first joined the network, the leaders had told him that the main task of their endeavor was to form a commando group that would carry out an attack to "remove the circumstances and persons who had suppressed the Muslim Brotherhood and stopped their *daʿwa*," and eventually to form an Islamic system. Qutb, who perceived this as a narrow goal "not worth the trouble,"[91] convinced them that their main aim should be to perform a bottom-up education of society in order to eventually reach the ultimate goal, namely the establishment of an Islamic system. Qutb perceived the *tanẓīm*'s task as a lengthy and laborious one. Working in society should, as Qutb explained to his young fellows, take place prior to the work in the state system. What should be the first step, before moving on with any other task, was to instill all members of the organizational structure with this correct methodology which Qutb had settled on in prison.[92] Paving the road for the *tanẓīm*, Qutb told its leaders that their first aim should be "to bring societies, rulers and ruled, to the correct Islamic concepts." Only when there is a popular base in society or a group of people who are able to "guide society towards the readiness to establish the Islamic *Niẓām*" can it become a reality.[93] In this way, Qutb labored to regulate the zeal of his followers by drawing a road map in which violent attempts to implement the Islamic order from the top were replaced by a bottom-up scheme, entailing an educational program to enlighten the masses on the "meanings of Islam and the substance of the Islamic creed."[94]

However, despite rejecting violence as the appropriate way of establishing the Islamic system, Qutb did not dismiss violence unconditionally. In what became the crux of the case against the organization, once it was uncovered, he relates that "we decided to apply force if any aggression against the *tanẓīm* occurred."[95] Seeing the repression of the Brotherhood since 1954 as a heinous crime committed against defenseless members of the Brotherhood, Qutb envisioned self-defense as a legitimate act, should any repression take place again.[96] Therefore, he allowed the group to maintain the paramilitary training which had been established before his assumption of leadership. He envisioned a paramilitary group of well-trained cadres that "does not start any aggression or attempt to execute a coup d'état, nor does it take part in the domestic political process." This group would stay passive as long as "the movement is safe and is able to educate society and as long as the *daʿwa* is possible without being repressed by force."[97] In so doing, Qutb maintained that he was implementing the Quranic commandment, "So whoever has assaulted you, then assault him in the same way that he has assaulted you."[98] In January 1965, Ali Ashmawi notified him that weapons to arm the group were on their way to Egypt from the Sudan, sent from Brothers in Saudi Arabia. These were the weapons Ashmawi had asked for when he visited Jeddah in 1962. Taken aback by this unexpected development, Qutb asked Ashmawi to hide the weapons to keep them out of the authorities' sight. However, by receiving and stockpiling the arms secretly, the organization had become an armed and secret organization with some members still considering the possibility of applying violence.[99]

Accordingly, while Qutb moved the group away from the intention to avenge "the aggression the Brotherhood had endured in 1954 and 1957 in the form of arrests, torture and the suppression of every human dignity through torture, killing and the destruction of homes and the dislocation of families," he was, like his followers, resolved not to surrender to a repetition of the vicious suppression it had been exposed to previously.[100] On this account, as the words of Sayyid Qutb clearly illustrate, the justification of violence as a defensive measure was firmly linked to what was perceived as an indiscriminate and unjust repression having befallen the Brotherhood in the past and fears of a recurrence. Qutb pointed to that explicitly when he explained that it was the violent repression of 1954 and its aftermath which shaped the idea of defensive violence as a countermeasure among the members of Organization 65.[101]

As a result, Qutb asked the *tanẓīm* to compile a plan for self-defense should any crackdown occur. In this regard, different suggestions were made by the leading committee on how to effectively limit the harm of such an assault. Knowing that the state would be too strong to stop, the plan was envisioned to be a "repelling strike which halts the aggression [by the state] for a while, thus securing as large a number of the young Muslims as possible."[102] Among the suggestions made was to strike hard by immediately assassinating President Nasser, Premier Ali Sabri, and others, and to attack critical infrastructural sites to paralyze the state structure. However, while the latter was dismissed as harming the Egyptian nation and society, the former was admitted as being too demanding for the group to put into effect, as the president and prime minister were too well protected, while the *tanẓīm* lacked the necessary number of men, armaments, and training. In the absence of the necessary means, they decided to accelerate the training "because there were signs of an imminent crackdown on the Brotherhood."[103]

All their fears came true during the blistering summer of 1965. On August 29, 1965, Gamal Abdel Nasser declared in a speech in Moscow that the authorities in Egypt had uncovered a plot organized by a nationwide Brotherhood organization to stage a coup against his government. In a follow-up, on September 7 and 8, the Egyptian press publicized "sensational revelations" about this alleged coup. According to these reports, the Brotherhood had prepared itself for an extensive violent campaign, which would have included the assassination of President Nasser, the demolition of key infrastructural installations, and the attack on cultural sites such as cinemas and theaters. Adding to this, the reports revealed the discovery of large quantities of firearms and explosives and disclosed that the organization allegedly had collaborated with the CENTO[104] through Said Ramadan.[105]

Subsequently, government-run newspapers launched a harsh attack on the Brotherhood, describing comprehensively the "horrors that would have been unleashed on the Egyptian public" had the *Ikhwan*'s plot succeeded. Interestingly, the propaganda campaign attached much importance to the religious violations the Brotherhood was committing by "conspiring against the government." In planning a coup and prepared for the killing of fellow Muslims, the Brotherhood had deviated from correct Islam—this was the charge raised against them.[106] Continuing this thread, in October 1965, merely two months after the first revelation, the authorities issued a book entitled "*Jarāʾim ʿIṣābat al-Ikhwan*" (the crimes of the Brotherhood gangs), in which it presented a detailed account of the Brotherhood's alleged plot and violent intentions. Interestingly, this book also placed a great deal of emphasis on the contention that the Brotherhood had "deviated from the right way of Islam, distorted religion and corrupted its brightness and light." The editor of the book continued the religion-based reproach of the *Ikhwan* by asking since when "did religion allow aggression, assassinations and rebellion."[107] Such statements were common at this time, portraying the government as the defender of true Islam against the wayward "demented fanatics" of the Brotherhood.[108] The application by the authorities of an Islamic discourse to strongly condemn the Brothers as "deviators from the true religion" may be a reflection of the Brotherhood's appeal in society, based on the politico-religious discourse which it applied in its opposition to the regime.

Consequently, the authorities seem to have felt compelled to apply a similar discourse to counterbalance the Brotherhood's outreach and growing appeal. For, as seen in the previous sections, the Brotherhood, through its application of an Islamic discourse, had succeeded in recruiting a number of young middle-class students to its ranks.[109] Pointing to this, a British mandarin highlighted that the magnitude of the repression and the media campaign against the *Ikhwan* at this time indicate that "their appeal was judged to be growing." It was further evaluated that the group had a wide appeal and "can attract religious zealots."[110]

The Brotherhood's success in appealing to segments of the population came at a time when the popularity of the regime was declining as a result of a number of political debacles. By way of illustration, the breakdown of the union between Egypt and Syria in 1961 and the costly war in Yemen into which the Egyptian army had been sent in 1962 may be cited.[111] Utilizing this popular discontent, the Brotherhood went on appealing to the young, educated and politically aware middle class by offering a diverging discourse, formulated in Islamic terms.

The very facts of this alleged plot are difficult to assess with certainty, as the stories presented by the Brotherhood and representatives of the regime vary to a great degree. While Brotherhood accounts emphasize that the plot was a fabrication invented by the security authorities to repress the organization, an account that was supported by Anwar al-Sadat,[112] regime narratives uphold that the Brotherhood was in fact plotting to kill Nasser and overthrow the regime.[113] However, some conclusions can be arrived at from the sources at hand. On the one hand, it is a known fact that the Egyptian regime was, at this point of time, facing considerable difficulties on both the domestic and international scene, which may have made the Brotherhood a convenient scapegoat for the authorities to move attention away from other challenges. With regard to the discontent in society, which was increasing at this time, a crackdown on the Brotherhood with harsh repression could be an opportune way of frightening other discontented groups.[114] The British Embassy in Cairo reckoned that popular resentment was increasing in Egypt at this time, which is why the regime was "faced with a choice between admitting a nationwide Moslem Brotherhood plot or admitting nationwide discontent," with the report concluding that the authorities had "chosen the former as the lesser evil."[115] On the other hand, however, as discussed in preceding sections, this *tanẓīm*, which represented a faction of the Brotherhood, had been working underground with members considering the idea of assassinating Nasser, which indicates that some degree of plotting had taken place, although the official account presented by the authorities was highly exaggerated and in many points self-contradictory.

Be that as it may, prior to Nasser's revelation from Moscow, the Military Security Service, headed by Shams Badran, and the General Intelligence, under the Ministry of Interior, had initiated an organized crackdown in which a large number of Brotherhood members were detained and subjected to cruel treatment. The roundup, which started on July 29, 1965, with the arrest of Muhammad Qutb, Sayyid Qutb's younger brother, was followed up with the arrest of Sayyid Qutb on August 9 together with a group of Brothers. On August 20, Abdel Fattah Ismail, Ali Ashmawi, and other senior members of the organization were arrested. When Ali Ashmawi was subjected to severe torture, he led the investigators to the entire organization, which was subsequently rounded up in all parts of Egypt.[116] Brotherhood accounts describe the torture meted out to the members as savage and merciless, "carried out by monsters."[117] In fact, a number of Brothers, including Rifʿat Baker, Sayyid Qutb's nephew, and Ismail al-Fayumi, a member of the Presidential Guard accused of being the would-be assassin of Nasser, died under torture, which points to its severity.[118]

According to British estimates, the Egyptian authorities were "surprised by the apparent strength of the Brotherhood" but maintained that "Egyptian security was easily able to crush its outbreak with rapid and widespread arrests."[119] Following this crackdown, which saw thousands of Brothers arrested,[120] a tribunal was set up to prosecute those involved in Organization 65 and in reorganizing the dissolved Brotherhood.

In all, 195 activists were convicted of felonies related to the *tanẓīm* and around the same number were convicted of "attempting to revive the Brotherhood,"[121] while thousands of detainees remained under arrest without trial. Altogether, seven cases were brought before a "state security court," four of them directly related to Organization 65, while three revolved around the resurgence of the Brotherhood. The trials lasted throughout the summer and autumn of 1966, with the first convictions being announced in August 1966.[122] The first seven convicts, accused of being the commanders of Organization 65 and for plotting to stage a coup d'état, were condemned to death; twenty-five others were sentenced to life imprisonment, while the remaining Brothers received varying prison terms. Al-Hudaybi, who did not play an active role in the *tanẓīm*, was sentenced to three years in prison in the resurgence case.[123] The British mission to Cairo interpreted the harsh sentences meted out to the Brotherhood as a reflection of "the Brotherhood's strength." A British mandarin established on account of these events that the Brotherhood was clearly "the main threat to the régime."[124]

On August 29, 1966, exactly one year after Nasser's decisive announcement from Moscow, three Brothers were hanged, convicted of leading a "terrorist organization," while the other four death sentences that had been handed out to the leading commanders of the organization were commuted to life imprisonment with hard labor.[125]

Late in the night of August 28, Sayyid Qutb, Muhammad Yusuf Hawwash, and Abdel Fattah Ismail were brought to the police headquarters in the old Cairene neighborhood of Bab el-Khalq, where the three men would meet their destiny. With the firm belief that they were being "martyred" because of their faith, the three men did not break until the end. Hanged at around 3 a.m., Qutb, Hawwash, and Ismail were added to the long list of "martyrs" that had fallen in the clash between the Brotherhood and the Nasserite regime.[126]

Qutb was of the firm belief that death did not interrupt the dissemination of ideas. Death for the sake of ideas was seen by Qutb as a vehicle through which ideas could be brought to life.[127] The diligent writer perceived death for one's ideas and beliefs as a distinguished and much-coveted death. He had written in his testimony:

> [T]he time has come that a Muslim man pays with his life for declaring the existence of an Islamic movement and a non-authorized organization that has been established as the foundation for the establishment of the Islamic system, no matter the methods it applies to arrive at this goal. And this according to the tradition of earthly laws is a crime for which one deserves a death sentence.[128]

Conclusions

In the United Arab Republic itself many [Brotherhood members] are still in concentrations camps, although a number were released towards the end of 1967 … It is clear, nevertheless, that the Brotherhood continues to be a force in United Arab Republic politics, and one against which the régime constantly shows signs of being on its guard. Its influence is widespread and extends not only to the country districts but in the Army, the Police, and the universities, and among the lower-class urban workers.[1]

By the end of the 1960s, the Brotherhood had evidenced a "great staying power in the face of official repression," according to the assessment provided in a CIA National intelligence estimate. Pointing to the *Ikhwan*'s endurance following almost fourteen years of dissolution and numerous waves of arrests and crackdowns, the report maintained that the Brotherhood's "reemergence" in 1965 has exhibited a strength that "surprised and shocked the government." Furthermore, the CIA seemed amazed by the fact that the Brotherhood "continues to have considerable appeal throughout the country."[2] Other US intelligence officers observing events at the time were in no doubt that the Brotherhood had a considerable appeal among "certain discontented and disillusioned elements [in Egypt]."[3] From the late 1960s, British intelligence officers likewise began to consider the Brotherhood as a potent organization with a remarkable degree of influence:

> A recent commentary has suggested that discontent in the United Arab Republic had chanelled itself into three main streams—Arab Socialist Union/left wing, United Arab Republic/nationalist, and right wing/Muslim Brotherhood. It is thought by many Egyptians (including Khalid Mohieddin [one of the Free Officers]) that the last of these would have the best chance of taking over if the régime were to collapse.[4]

Describing the Brotherhood's activities in society at the time, the same report maintained:

> [W]hile it seems unlikely that the Brotherhood itself would be capable of staging a revolt it is well placed to take advantage of any expression of discontent, and this appears to have been its role in the Helwan disturbances in February 1968. A protest against the leniency of the sentences in the Air Force trial ... got out of hand and exploded into violence when infiltrated and exploited by the Muslim Brotherhood.[5]

Looking into the history of the Brotherhood during two different periods of "ordeals," these assessments seem to mirror the perseverance of the Brotherhood. Such estimations, written contemporaneously with events in Egypt, clearly point to the main claim of this book, that is, that the Brotherhood was not obliterated during the different waves of restraints and repression it was subjected to. To highlight this continuity, I examined two decisive chapters of repression in the history of the *Ikhwan*, the first and second *miḥna* (ordeal), as the Brotherhood terms the periods of 1948–51 and 1954–70 respectively.

Secrecy in the ranks of the Brotherhood has a long history and is inextricably linked to the domestic and political circumstances surrounding the *Ikhwan*. Against the background of the restrictions and the growing repression witnessed by the Brotherhood during the Second World War years, as depicted in Chapter 1, the *Ikhwan* institutionalized secrecy and made it an elementary part of its organizational thinking. By establishing the *usra* formation in 1943, just as the restrictive policies adopted by the British and Egyptian authorities were reaching unprecedented proportions, the Brotherhood was moving toward protecting its ranks against infiltration. Built on an idea of confidentiality and mutual responsibility, the *usra* restricted its meetings to its own members, thus keeping outsiders at arm's length.

Constructing the *usra* as the central organizational component, the *Ikhwan* ensured, furthermore, that every member of the Brotherhood was placed in a hierarchical unit of about five members, with a *naqīb* (chief) overseeing each cell. Khalil al-Anani has correctly described this formation as the "basic unit" of the *Ikhwan*, embracing every member of the organization and requiring weekly meetings to be held by each cell.[6] I agree with al-Anani in perceiving this structure as instrumental in the Brotherhood's inner workings and as fundamental for the internal coherence of the organization. Established during the first half of the 1940s, a period described as formative in the Brotherhood's organizational development, this structure signified the substitution of the early dependence on al-Banna's charismatic leadership with institutionalized structures and lines of authority.[7]

In addition to perceiving the family structures as elemental in the Brotherhood's ability to continue clandestinely during periods of repression, I also made a concise excursion into the history of the Brotherhood's secret paramilitary organization, the Special Apparatus. In so doing, I argued that this structure came as a result of the *Ikhwan*'s deliberate intent to fight the British in Egypt and became another key aspect of the Brotherhood's underground activities in times of restrictions and repression.

These different clandestine structures accounted for a duality in the framework of the organization. Resting on the two elements of the *Ikhwan* being an overt mass organization on the one hand and having secrecy inherent in its organizational structures on the other, this duality would become instrumental to its survival in times of oppression.

With Hasan al-Banna's death in February 1949 and the concomitant crackdown on the Brotherhood, the organization underwent its hitherto severest challenge. The repression which had been triggered by the escalating violence on the Egyptian scene resulted in the incarceration of more than 4,000 Brotherhood adherents, the closure of its branches, and the suspension of its activities, rendering difficult the *Ikhwan*'s overt activities. Pointing to these obstacles, Barbara Zollner claimed that the Brotherhood was in "a deep crisis," adding that "the survival of the idea of this political-religious movement was at stake."[8] In line with this understanding of the *Ikhwan* as in a crisis, I concisely sketched the internal dynamics of the Brotherhood during this first "ordeal" to shed some light on this important but not exclusively studied period in the organization's history.

Via the life journeys of Brotherhood activists like Muhammad Mahdi Akef, Yusuf al-Qaradawi, Salah Shadi, Hasan Duh, Umar al-Tilmisani, Ali Sadiq, and Fathi Osman, we observed that neither the dissolution of the Brotherhood in December 1948 nor the subsequent death of Hasan al-Banna in February 1949 interrupted the workings of the organization. As the accounts of these figures and of many others clearly demonstrated, a degree of hierarchical structuring was upheld while low-key activities continued in most parts of Egypt. When a leader was apprehended or fled Egypt, for example, the next in line took over his responsibility, thus ensuring a hierarchical persistence. Furthermore, and pointing to what al-Anani has described as a "two-pronged decision-making mechanism"[9] inside the Brotherhood's structures, meetings on the cadre level were held on a weekly basis and organized in private homes or in other secluded locations where a degree of confidentiality could be assured. In this way, a decentralized implementation of the Brotherhood's activities was continued while such activities were kept invisible for the ubiquitous security agency. The *usra* formation contributed greatly to this ability, as meetings within its framework could continue largely uninterrupted in such periods of restriction due to its discreet methods. Cells of five members would meet in a public garden or in an apartment to continue their connections without being at risk of clampdowns or restraints. Inside prison walls, just as outside them, we observed a similar two-pronged decision-making that combined hierarchy with decentralization. Inside the overcrowded prisons, where large numbers of Brothers were huddled together, hierarchical and centralized leadership committees were established to direct Brotherhood detainees. Receiving their directions from those committees, Brotherhood inmates continued their everyday activities through the framework of a "jail" *usra* in which every Brother was placed. This made activities inside prisons possible and paved the way for a streamlining of such activities.

The Special Apparatus, according to some of its members, had been founded to combat "the British and their lackeys [in Egypt]"[10] and to "fight in Algiers, Tunis, Marrakesh or in any other Arab country, just as [it] had done in Palestine previously."[11] Taking such statements and the very history of the Apparatus into consideration, I argue that violence in the history of the Brotherhood should be understood and studied as part and parcel of a widespread and general struggle that encompassed almost every political group in Egypt at the time. This violence came as a result of a pervasive disgruntlement with the occupation of Egypt and its "sister countries," as the stories of Mustafa Mashhur, Muhammad Mahdi Akef, and Mustafa al-Sabbagh, among others, illustrated. Perceiving death on the battleground as "a much-coveted honor,"[12] this understanding of "*jihad*" was broadened to include, inter alia, armed confrontation with those of Egypt's rulers who opposed the Brotherhood and who were perceived as "lackeys" of the occupation. This was exemplified by the assassination of al-Khazindar and al-Nuqrashi in 1948. The militants interpreted these murders of high-ranking Egyptians as acts of *jihad* against enemies of Islam. Such ideas, as these militants professed, were further radicalized by the death of Hasan al-Banna and the intensive repression of the entire organization that followed the assassination of al-Nuqrashi. Here, the botched attempt on the life of Ibrahim Abdel Hadi, al-Nuqrashi's successor, gives us an illustrative example of how political assassinations had become an accepted method of those young men. Thus, when visions of anti-establishment violence reappeared during the Nasserite years, as illustrated in Chapters 4, 5, and 6, they did so as a link in the chain of former ideas held by almost every political organization in Egypt.[13]

When Hasan al-Hudaybi assumed leadership of the Brotherhood, many inside the Brotherhood harbored great hopes that the second Hasan would lead the Brotherhood away from secrecy and militancy. Having experienced the loss of their leader and suffered under the first *miḥna*, many Brothers wished for a new direction to be adopted, a direction in which political assassinations were not a part of the Brotherhood's repertoire. Thus, appointed as the second *Murshid* of the organization, al-Hudaybi was expected to fill the large shoes of his successor, settle the leadership crisis that had exhausted the Brotherhood, and refurbish the *Ikhwan*'s tarnished reputation. Embracing the challenge, the Brotherhood restructured its upper echelons in response to the second *Murshid* and declared openly that there was "no secrecy and militancy in Islam," thus pledging to rid the *Ikhwan* of both. However, by so doing, al-Hudaybi had placed himself at cross-purposes with a strong segment inside the Brotherhood, a segment that perceived armed *jihad* as an Islamic obligation that neither al-Hudaybi nor any other leader in the Brotherhood could discard. This faction, oftentimes members and leaders of the Special Apparatus, claimed that they had a sacred right to continue their *jihad*. This signaled the beginning of a protracted strife and disagreement inside the Brotherhood over ideas and methods. Hence, the question on how and when to use violence, as seen here, goes far back in the *Ikhwan*'s history, with dissenting opinions being loudly weighed against each other.

Interestingly, however, when al-Hudaybi's attempts to dismiss secrecy and militancy were frustrated by resistance by some Brothers and by events on the ground, we observe a greater inclination on his part to accept secrecy and even militancy. This is best illustrated by the Brotherhood's full-hearted participation in the Suez Canal war of 1951, as shown in Chapter 3, and al-Hudaybi's subsequent move to preserve the Special Apparatus and to control it, as described in Chapter 4.

Thus, from 1952, at the critical moment when Nasser's "blessed movement" was consolidating its hold on power to reshape the political and social landscape in Egypt, the Brotherhood was an organization exhausted by internal frictions and disagreements. Squabbling on what position the *Ikhwan* should take vis-à-vis the nascent regime, the Brotherhood was further divided at a momentous time in Egypt's and more particularly the Brotherhood's history. This led to fragmentation in the upper echelons of the organization and disarray among the *Ikhwan*'s rank and file.

During the crucial months of 1954, when the Brotherhood was heading toward an imminent showdown with the military regime, we observe a militarization of a group of the Brothers, as illustrated through the stories of, among others, Abdel Mun'im Abdel Rauf, Mahmoud Abdel Halim, Mahmoud Abdel Latif, Hasan Duh, and Hasan al-Ashmawi. Conceiving the Nasserite regime as despotic and un-Islamic, such Brothers came to justify a violent showdown with it. This was, according to those Brothers, an Islamic *jihad* against unrightful rulers who deviated from Islam. Having seen the unmasked and violent face of the regime in the early months of 1954, when the government dissolved the Brotherhood and arrested and tortured some of its leaders, those Brothers wanted to be ready to retaliate should another repression take place. In light of this, I demonstrated in Chapter 4 that, notwithstanding the veracity of the Manshiyya incident, which was dismissed by the Brothers as a staged act by the regime, we can clearly see a transition toward anti-establishment *jihad* appearing in this period of intensified conflict. In other words, even if this particular incident was orchestrated by the government to offer it a pretext to repress the Brotherhood, the course leading to this momentous incident definitely saw a militarization of a group of Brothers.

Mahmoud Abdel Latif's eight misplaced but fateful shots on October 26, 1954, put the entire Brotherhood on a collision course with Nasser's military regime and brought forth a brutal response from the Nasserite security apparatuses. Vowing to disband the *Ikhwan* and interrupt their activities, the Egyptian regime unleashed a relentless onslaught that left the Brotherhood severely wounded. Further unmasking its vengeful face, in early December 1954, the regime hanged six members of the Brotherhood organization and handed out heavy sentences to Brothers in large numbers. These sentences and the concurrent mistreatment of the *Ikhwan* were intended to break the Brotherhood's appeal in society and to curtail its ability to restore itself. Consequently, instead of killing Nasser and achieving a regime change, those eight shots seemed to have sealed the Brotherhood's fate.

Having challenged the nascent military regime and suffered a shattering defeat, the Muslim Brotherhood undoubtedly seemed a long-gone organization or at best an irrelevant one that had lost its presence in Egyptian society during those early days of postcolonial rule.[14] However, as the stories of many members of the Brotherhood clearly illustrated, the organization was not eliminated despite the agonizing wounds that had been inflicted on it. Tracing the *Ikhwan*'s journeys after imprisonment, Chapter 5 illustrated that, following an early period of harsh mistreatment, torture, humiliation, and a widespread feeling among the Brothers of defenselessness, a new reality soon developed both inside and outside the prison walls. Through the prison experiences of Mahdi Akef, Mustafa Mashhur, and Ahmad al-Bess, among others, we observed how jails were transformed into Brotherhood camps where activities continued and where a hierarchical and well-organized *Ikhwani* life went on. Prisons were also the scene of intense discussions among the Brothers on how to relate to the Nasserite state. While a group of inmates advocated a supportive course toward the Egyptian government, most probably due to pragmatic reasons, others held their ground, refusing to support the regime even if that meant prolonged terms of incarceration.

Beyond the prison walls as well, clandestine networks of Brothers began cropping up in large parts of Egypt from at least early 1955. Constructed as vehicles to sustain the Brotherhood's presence in society and to continue the bonds among Brothers, these networks started initially by virtue of the agency of young members in different geographical areas. Adopting different objectives, most of them were devoted to continuing the Brotherhood presence in society, meeting in *usar* to study religious matters, discussing political issues, and collecting funds to support bereaved *Ikhwan* families, others aimed at avenging what they perceived as the inhumane treatment of their leaders and fellow Brothers. Conceiving the Nasserite regime as despotic and un-Islamic, the latter Brothers promoted a violent path to counter the officially sanctioned violence against them. By repressing the Brotherhood and interrupting its activities in society, the regime was perceived to have become guilty of weakening Islam among the Egyptian masses. Holding the regime guilty of this "crime," these young men justified violence against it. This, I argue, was a continuation of previous ideas of violence that had existed among some of the Brothers since the 1940s.

Accordingly, rather than being obliterated at the hands of the Egyptian authorities, the Brotherhood evidenced a great staying power during those days of harsh repression. This endurance resulted in a nationwide clandestine organizational structure during the early 1960s, referred to by the local press as "*Tanẓīm 1965*." Consisting of young men, mostly middle-class students and white-collar, salaried workers, this *tanẓīm* emerged as the result of ceaseless efforts by young and lower-ranking Brotherhood members to revive the Brotherhood. Thus, *Tanẓīm 1965* was a link in the chain of former organizational structures and networks that had begun emerging since early 1955.

The two main aims of this *tanẓīm* were to revive the *Ikhwan*'s activities all over the country and to continue attracting new members to its ranks in order to create a large cadre that understood and adopted the ideas of the Brotherhood. However, considering the dissolution of the Brotherhood and the repression of its members as illegal, the question of violence arose once again to occupy this organization and its commanders. Should the organization's aspiration be to kill Nasser in retaliation for his repression of the *Ikhwan*? Would the killing of Nasser change anything in society? Should the organization adopt a long-term strategy to educate society in order to reach the ultimate goal of establishing an Islamic system? Such were the questions occupying the organization's commanders following its establishment in 1962. Thus, when Sayyid Qutb was invited to lead this organizational structure in 1964, following his release from prison that same year, he came to head a group of young men who had already considered the idea of assassinating Nasser on their way to establishing an Islamic government.[15]

There are therefore a number of subjects pertaining to Qutb's influence on the Brotherhood that could indicate new avenues for further research. First, it is vital to ask whether Qutb came to radicalize these young men, as has been indicated in a number of studies.[16] Having established their *tanẓīm* while Qutb was incarcerated, these young men had formed a worldview that incorporated violence, even before the detained thinker had known of their existence. The probability of violence had in fact been present since 1955, when small networks of Brothers considered violence as an appropriate response to the Nasserite regime. This study has therefore suggested that Qutb may even have attempted to deradicalize the young activists whose leadership he assumed in the summer of 1964. Qutb explained in his last written text that he had attempted to move the young men away from their intention to kill Nasser. He perceived such an act as insignificant and lacking a strategic dimension. By contrast, Qutb tells us that he envisioned bottom-up education of society as the best way of reforming the masses and establishing a truly Islamic society.[17] Importantly, he told his followers that such a system could not and should not be brought about through "violent methods." The only way to construct the right system of governance should be through grassroots education, he underlined.[18] In light of this, one may ask, did Qutb in fact adopt a gradualist approach, in many ways similar to that of Hasan al-Banna?

Furthermore, and in contrast to the viewpoint that Qutb was *the* radical ideologue of the *Ikhwan*, one may ask whether Qutb was as much influenced by the *Ikhwan* as he influenced them. Was Qutb radicalized by his interaction with the radical fringe of the *Ikhwan* and did he attempt to direct his young followers away from violence? For, as seen throughout this study, when Qutb joined the Brotherhood, there already existed in its ranks a radical and militant fringe that had fought the state and normatively justified this violence as an "Islamic *jihad*."

Summing up, we can argue that the Brotherhood continued its existence in society despite the unrestrained repression it was subjected to. Furthermore, regardless of how Qutb influenced this organization, he became its "martyr" together with al-Hawwash and Ismail. Walking to the gallows with firm steps, the three men paid with their lives the penalty for their involvement with the organization. Qutb had in his previous writings talked about death as a way of making ideas and words last permanently. Writing in 1953, the Islamist thinker declared:

> Writers can indeed contribute greatly—but on one condition: They must die so that their ideas can live. They must feed their words from their own flesh and blood. They must say what they believe is right and sacrifice their own blood as a price for the word of truth. Our ideas and words remain dead and silent corpses until [at the moment] we die for them or nurture them with our blood they rise up alive to live among the living. … The unaccompanied word—no matter how sincere and pure it is—cannot do anything until it is turned into a movement and becomes embodied [in a person]. Human beings are indeed the living words that can fully carry out its meanings.[19]

Notes

Introduction

1 NA 1954, I: 8; Abou El Zalaf 2022: 1.
2 NA 1954, I: 8.
3 The agreement is also known as "The Suez Canal Base Agreement", cf. Selak 1955.
4 NA 1954, I: 8–14.
5 The Muslim Brotherhood, *al-Ikhwan al-Muslimun*, *al-Ikhwan al-Muslimin*, the Brotherhood, the *Ikhwan*, and the organization will be applied interchangeably when referring to the Muslim Brotherhood.
6 For a contemporary report on the executions, see FO 371/108319, JE 1016/24, No. 226, (1012/126/54) Murray, British Embassy Cairo, December 11, 1954.
7 In the spelling of names and the transcription of Arabic terms, I follow the style manual of the International Journal of Middle East Studies (IJMES), but in a somewhat simplified way. Accordingly, I write names only using hamza (ʾ) in the middle of names and ayn (ʿ) also in the middle of names, as in Talʿat.
8 Those hanged were Mahmoud Abdel Latif (the would-be assassin), Yusuf Talʿat (head of the Special Apparatus), Ibrahim al-Tayyib (head of the Apparatus in Cairo), Hindawi Diwayr (head of the Apparatus in Imbaba), Abdel Qader Uda (a member of the guidance office), and Shaykh Muhammad Farghali (head of the Brotherhood in Ismailiyya).
9 Throughout the book, I apply the terms *the regime*, *the Nasserite regime*, *the military regime*, and *the Revolutionary regime* interchangeably, but all terms refer to the regime that assumed power in Egypt following the July revolution of 1952.
10 For contemporary accounts, see FO 371/108319, JE 1016/24, No. 226 (1012/126/54) Murray, British Embassy Cairo, December 11, 1954; FO 371/125415, JE 1015/135, 16821/2/57, British Embassy Washington DC, April 9, 1957. A record of Tyranny, Corruption and Mediocrity, Memorandum Submitted to the U.S. Government by the Committee for Free Egypt, Beirut, July 5, 1955.
11 Mitchell 1993: xxiii–xxiv.; for other early Western studies dealing with the Brotherhood organization, see Heyworth-Dunne, 1950; Husaini 1956; Harris 1964.
12 Kepel 2014: 23, 29–30.
13 Today there is prodigious and rich research dealing with the Brotherhood. The recent decades have seen a proliferation of studies on Islamism in general and more notably the *Ikhwan* organization. This discussion of historiography therefore

has its primary focus on studies dealing with the Brotherhood during periods of repression, and most significantly the Nasserite years. Thus, the historiographic discussion should not read as a comprehensive overview of all studies dealing with the Brotherhood. My discussion is rather a selective outline of studies dealing with issues closely related to this book. However, for studies dealing with different aspects of the *Ikhwan*'s ideas and history and more broadly with Islamism, see Lia 2010; Ayubi 1993; Aly and Wenner 1982; Davis 1983; Sattar 1995; Khatab 2001, 2002, 2009; Arjomand 2010; Commins 2008; Krämer 2010; El-Awaisi 2010. For a comparative analysis of the Brotherhood in Egypt and Sudan, see Zahid and Medley 2006. On the Muslim Brotherhood's role in the Palestine, see, e.g., Jankowski 1980; Gershoni 1986; El-Awaisi 1998. On the Muslim Brotherhood as a social movement, see Munson 2001; Wickham 2002; Hafez and Wiktorowicz 2004; Anani 2016. On the Muslim Brotherhood in Europe, see, for instance, Maréchal (2008); Vidino (2010); Rich (2010); Khosrokhavar (2010). This list of literature is limited to studies dealing primarily with the Egyptian Brotherhood, the main exception being the studies dealing with the Brotherhood in Europe.

14 Qutb penned a number of books during his prison time (1954–64, 1965–66), the most well known of these being Milestones (1964) and "In the shade of the Quran," a Quran exegesis of thirty volumes published in 1960 as a second and revised edition. The first edition had been published by a Brotherhood magazine in the early 1950s. As his bibliographer, al-Khalidi, puts it, this second edition of the "shade" was highly affected by Qutb's prison experience. Besides being a "Quran exegesis," it consists of Qutb's understandings of the role to be played by the Islamic movement (al-Khalidi 1994: 544–7).

15 Kepel 1985: 57. For similar accounts see Kepel 2014: 27; Calvert 2010: 4; Gerges 2018: 148; Pargeter 2016: 1, 89; Khatab 2001; Khatab 2002.

16 Khatab 2002: 163 (italics in original).

17 Gerges 2018: 17.

18 James Toth, in his influential book on Sayyid Qutb's life and legacy, has argued for a nuanced reading of Qutb's legacy. Challenging the monochromatic portrayals of Qutb as the "diabolical genius behind terrorism," Toth offers a reading in which he pays meticulous attention to the complexity of the circumstances in which Qutb's ideas and personality developed (2013).

19 Zollner 2011: 3–4. For similar accounts see also Zollner 2007; Ashour 2009; Wickham 2013; al-Arian 2014; Jung 2011.

20 Cf. Kepel 1985; Toth 2013; Calvert 2010; Moussalli 1992; Khatab 2001.

21 While a limited number of existing studies have examined the first *miḥna* as part and parcel of the Brotherhood's history, no study has yet delved into the historical development of the *Ikhwan* organization during this period. Most significantly we can mention Richard Mitchell's (1993) discussion of the first dissolution in late

1948 and Omar Ashour's (2009) discussion of al-Hudaybi's attempt to dissolve the Special Apparatus following his appointment as leader of the organization in 1951. Gerges (2018) offered an account of the struggle between the Nasserite regime and the Muslim Brotherhood in his study. Yet, Gerges' focus was predominantly on the clash of ideas, thus shedding light on the differences between Arab Nationalism and the ideas of Qutb. In his outstanding study of the Brotherhood's complex relation to the West, Martyn Frampton (2018) shed light on different aspects of the *Ikhwan*'s history during the two ordeals. In a recent book, Victor J. Willi studied the history of the *Ikhwan* following the Nasserite era. Thus, while Willi's book is of great importance, it traces a subsequent period to that of my study.

22 By shedding light on how the Brotherhood was able to endure the persecution of the Egyptian regimes during the two "ordeals," this examination is of current significance. The Brotherhood has yet again been forced underground as a result of exhaustive persecution that followed the coup d'état of July 3, 2013. Therefore, this book can contribute significant insights into the ways in which the Brotherhood has reacted historically to harsh persecution.

23 See, for example, Willi 2021: 9.

24 Members of the Brotherhood were gradually released from Egyptian prisons during the first half of the 1970s, and exiled Brothers were invited home. The Brotherhood began working overtly in society during the Sadat era (1970–81). Sadat aligned himself with the Islamists against the remnants of the ancient regime, known as the "power bases" (*marākez al-quwā*), to secure his hold on power. In 1976, as an example of the Brotherhood's return to overt activism, its magazine *al-da'wa* reappeared in Egypt and became the organization's mouthpiece.

25 Della Porta examines clandestine political violence committed by the extreme right, extreme left, ethnonationalists, and religious groups. In applying della Porta's framework, I do so heuristically. I do not state that the Brotherhood outright turned to political violence once persecuted. On the contrary, I treat the period of 1954–70 as a dynamic period in which the Brotherhood's stance toward political violence transformed and developed in different ways.

26 della Porta 2013: 26–7.

27 The ways in which the police and other security apparatus respond to protests and other forms of social and political activism.

28 della Porta 2013: 21.

29 The different levels of analysis are not organized in different segregated parts or sections of the analysis but are applied interchangeably throughout the analysis. Consequently, the analysis constantly moves between these levels to grasp the comprehensive development of the Brotherhood. Considering the chronological approach of this book, this seems to be the most fitting way of applying the different levels of analysis. For a discussion of recruitment processes in clandestine organizations, see della Porta 1998.

30 I am not, however, completely oblivious to the importance of the micro-level analysis, i.e., the psychological, affective, or motivational components of decision-making and reactions to repression. I believe, however, that these aspects have been sufficiently elucidated in other studies (cf. Calvert 2010; Kepel 1985, 2014; Sivan 1990; Toth 2013; Zollner 2007, 2011).

31 Kerr 1975. The two major antagonists in this Arab Cold War were Egypt (UAR) and Saudi Arabia. They represented two competing visions, i.e., Pan-Arabism, advocated by Nasser's Egypt and his allies on the one hand, and Pan-Islamism, on the other hand, advocated by Saudi Arabia and its allies, among them the Muslim Brotherhood.

32 Wiktorowicz 2004: 13–14.

33 Hasan al-Banna (1906–49) was born in al-Mahmudiyya in the governate of Buhayra. After completing his studies at the Dār al-ʿUlūm in Cairo from 1923 to 1927, he was assigned as a schoolteacher in al-Ismailiyya in 1927. Upon moving to al-Ismailiyya, which had a large presence of British soldiers and Westerners living in the city and working at the Canal Zone establishment, Hasan al-Banna found a city with a "peculiar inspiration." The concomitant British presence and the disparity between the extravagant neighborhood with big houses inhabited by foreigners and the small and humble houses inhabited by the Arabs were hurtful to the young Banna and to "every nationalist." These characteristics "inspired the missionary [al-Banna]" to establish the Brotherhood in March 1928 (al-Banna 2013: 94–5).

34 I demonstrate in Chapter 1 that the Brotherhood developed a clear-cut organization with clear traces of secrecy during the years of the Second World War. These secret structures were developed to enable the Brotherhood to combat the British and to secure its durability in the face of repression.

35 However, when the disadvantageous circumstances change, be it with a shift of regime or a shift in the policies toward the Brotherhood, the organization may opt for overt activities, as was the case with the Brotherhood following the regime shift in 1970.

36 I only use the English translation from 1906 by Albion W. Small in this study.

37 Society is here understood as a group of people who are involved in a persistent social or political interaction.

38 By being hierarchical, classified information can be restricted to top-tier members, thus keeping the "secrets" of the organization concealed when deemed necessary. Furthermore, according to Simmel, the hierarchical construction of secret societies secures an initiation period in which the newcomers can be initiated in the society, thereby keeping the secrets of the organization restricted to those who have proven their loyalty.

39 Simmel 1906: 463, 470, 478–9.

40 Simmel 1906: 477, 472.

41 P. Gist 1937: 349; Erickson 1981: 188–9.
42 Simmel 1906; P. Gist 1937: 350; Erickson 1981: 189.
43 Such aspects can include but are not limited to membership, structures, ideas, activities/operations, and finance.
44 Weber 1949: 90.
45 Ibid.
46 The Palgrave Macmillan Dictionary of Political Thought defines extremism as a "Vague term, which can mean: 1. Taking a political idea to its limits, regardless of 'unfortunate' repercussions, impracticalities, arguments, and feelings to the contrary, and with the intention not only to confront, but also to eliminate, opposition. 2. Intolerance towards all views other than one's own (for which, see *toleration). 3. Adoption of means to political ends which disregard accepted standards of conduct, in particular which show disregard for the life, liberty and human rights of others" (Scruton 2007: 237).
47 Scruton 2007: 237.
48 Neumann 2013: 876.
49 For studies on radicalization, cf. Sedgwick 2010; Ashour 2009; Borum 2011; Neumann 2013; Malthaner 2017; Cross and Snow 2012.
50 Cf. Ashour 2009; Sedgwick 2010.
51 Jordanova 2019: 199.
52 Since the 1970s and 1980s, there has been a prodigious output of memoirs and accounts by Brotherhood activists who witnessed its history firsthand. Many of these Brotherhood activists felt obliged to publish their own memoirs "to inform the public" and to enlighten future *Ikhwan* and Islamist generations, as they put it.
53 As a result of the so-called corrective revolution in 1971 to purge the state of Nasserite remnants and the concomitant political liberalization that took place under the auspices of the late Anwar al-Sadat (d.1981), a vast number of memoirs were published by Brotherhood activists and by activists from other political currents describing the political, social, and cultural life in Nasser's Egypt. What these accounts had in common was in large part a condemnation of the previous military regime. This freedom to write extensively on the Nasserite years and the harsh condemnations of the prison experiences present in many of these accounts written by a plethora of political activists continued after Sadat's death in 1981. Husni Mubarak, like al-Sadat, saw no threat in letting the political activists bemoan a harsh past in which they were persecuted. By demythologizing Nasser and his regime, his successors were able to portray themselves as a lesser evil.
54 al-Tilmisani (1985), Abul Nasr (1988) Shadi (1987, 1988), al-Ashmawi (1977, 1985), Abdel Khaleq (1987). They all played a very central role in the events that followed the coup in 1952. Al-Tilmisani and Abul Nasr went to the top of the Brotherhood as its third and fourth *Murshid* (leader) respectively. Of the less-known activists of the Brotherhood, see Al-Firmawi (1976), Rizq (1978, 1979,

1991), Raif (1986, 1990), Abdel Majid (1991), al-Sarwi (2004, 2006), Khafaji (2006), and al-Hajj (1977, 1987, 1995). See also Duh (1983 and 1989), Hammuda (1985), Qaud (1985), al-Bess (1987), Abdel Rauf (1988), al-Qaradawi (2000, 2002, 2004, 2006), al-Sisi (1981, 1987, 2003), Abdel Halim (2013, vol. I–III), al-Ghazi (2008). Among the most famous of these accounts is al-Ghazali's (1994, 2012) *Ayām min Ḥayātī* (Days of my Life), which was translated into English, French, Persian, and other languages. Al-Ghazali was one of the leading members of the Muslim Brotherhood organization, which emerged in the late 1950s. She describes the horrors she and other members of the Brotherhood were subjected to.

55 The ruling military Junta, which seized power in July 1952, came to be known as the Revolutionary Command Council (*Majles Qiyādat al-Thawra*) after January 1953.

56 Al-Baghdadi (vol. I and II, 1977), Muhyiddin (1992) Naguib (1984, 2011), al-Sadat (1957, 1978); for al-Shafiʿi, see Mansour (2004), Allam (1996), Sharaf (2015 vol. I–V).

57 It was not safe to seek contact with Brotherhood members in Egypt due to the political situation in the country since 2013.

58 Jordanova 2019: 206–7.

Chapter 1

1 Abdel Halim 2013, II: 79–85; Muhammad 1987: 511–17; Abou El Zalaf 2022: 8 9.

2 The events that took place from October 1951 till late January 1952 are known as the War in the Canal Zone. These events came against the background of the unilaterally Egyptian abrogation of the 1936 agreement. By abrogating the treaty, al-Nahhas made the presence of British troops in Egypt illegal, at least in Egyptian eyes. Resulting from the abrogation was a political crisis that ended up with guerilla attacks against British soldiers and installments. Of the groups that took lead in these attacks was the Brotherhood, being the most organized and best equipped organization in Egypt at that time. We turn to these events in the Chapter 3. For a detailed account of the war, see Thornhill 2006.

3 Cf. Harris 1964: 151; Sattar 1995: 10–12; al-Tilmisani 2003: 17.

4 By so contending, I agree with the line put forward by Brynjar Lia. Discussing the early history of the *Ikhwan*, Lia contended that the Brotherhood's success in becoming a major mass organization during the period of 1928–42 lay in its structures, ideology, and activities. By so doing, he challenged the arguments that conceived this success as being only a result of al-Banna's charismatic leadership. See Lia 2010, 120.

5 For this repressive experience, see Lia 2010: 261–5.

6 For example, Hasan al-Banna bemoaned the conditions of the "Eastern" societies as deprived of their integrity, dignity, and independence and dispossessed of their blood and money. These societies are "subdued by the Western yoke which has been forced on them. Therefore, these people are trying to get rid of this yoke by whatever power they can mobilize." However, and in contrast to the nationalistic approach, this anti-colonial approach was to be found in Islam, according to al-Banna (al-Banna 2004: 19–20). For an elaborate discussion of the Brotherhood's expansion and its ideas throughout the 1930s and early 1940s, see Lia 2010; Ghanem 2011.

7 Lia 2010: 256. This was a remarkable expansion considering the relative insignificance of the *Ikhwan* just prior to the war. Despite what is reported by the director-general of the Egyptian Public Security as a "particularly active" Muslim Brotherhood in 1938, it is argued that "as these societies were trivial and had no real background, their activities need not be taken seriously." However, the British were more anxious of "the scurrilous anti-British articles which have appeared in 'El Nazir', the organ of the Moslem Brethren's Association." Therefore, the activities of the Brotherhood were described as "undesirable" and "some action … to curtail these activities" was called for by the British. Anti-British policies in Egypt and Palestine were among the main activities conducted by the Brotherhood, according to the British complaints to the Egyptian Public Security director-general (FO. 371/21881, E 5898/10/10, Telegram No. 1077, (8/259, 38), Embassy in Alexandria to Halifax, September 26, 1938). In another report from October 1939, the Brotherhood was described as a "fanatical and subversive anti-British association of Moslems, led by one Hassan [*sic*] al-Banna." The *Ikhwan* was in touch with German agents in Egypt, states a report from late 1939 (WO 208/502, No. SD. P. 866, Note on Wilhelm Stellbogen, October 23, 1939). See also WO 208/502, Correspondence and notes of MP Wilhelm Stellbogen, n.d..

8 Cf., Abdel Khaleq 1987: 33; Zaki 1954: 107–8; Lia 2010: 190; Mitchell 1993: 168.

9 Dessouqi 2012: 17.

10 For a discussion of the battalions, see Lia 2010: 172–7; see also Abdel Aziz 2004: 36–43; Haydar 1989: 98; Mahmoud 1997: 101–2.

11 Following the beginning of the war, Ali Maher, suspected of possessing "fascist leanings," was dismissed and replaced by Hasan Sabry, and when Sabry died in November 1940, he was replaced by the independent Hussein Sirri Pasha. Sirri Pasha stayed in office until February 1942, when the disreputable "February coup" took place. As a result, Sirri Pasha was dismissed and a Wafdist government was established (Rogan 2009: 210; Mansfield 1971: 273).

12 Rogan 2009: 209; Mansfield 1971: 274.

13 WO 208/1560, "Fifth Column Activities in Egypt," November 20, 1941; WO 208/1561, S.I.M.E. Cairo, Security Summary Middle East No. 20, February 12, 1942.

14 FO 371/27433, No. 900 (1/112/41) British Embassy Cairo, September 23, 1941; Marsot 2007: 118–20; Rogan 2009: 210.

15 FO 371/27434, J. 3601, No. 3570, From Cairo to Foreign Office, November 14, 1941. For a report on the conceived results of this arrest, see WO 208/1560, "Fifth Column Activities in Egypt," November 20, 1941; see also Mahmoud 1997: 120.

16 Ramadan 1993: 42.

17 Bayyoumi 2012: 105.

18 Lia 2010: 261–5, 268–9; Krämer 2010: 63–4; Abdel Aziz 2004: 236–8, 272–6.

19 FO 141/838, 15322, telegram No. (E)140/1 from R. J. Maunsell GHQ ME, Cairo to Walter Smart, the British Embassy in Cairo "with reference your OS/294/1 of 7th October 1942," October 10, 1942.

20 Consisting of about eighteen different offices in eighteen geographical areas.

21 Abdel Aziz 2004: 9; Mahmoud 1997: 124; Zaki 1954: 101.

22 Mahmoud 1997: 125–34.

23 Cf. Shalabi 1978: 408–27; Zaki 1954: 101–8; Lia 2010: 176.

24 Mitchell 1993: 198.

25 No exact date of its establishment has been offered by the Brotherhood; different actors have offered different dates. But the main figures of the Apparatus date its establishment to between 1938 and 1940. For some of the diverging accounts, see, for instance, Abdel Halim 2013, I: 288; al-Sabbagh 1989: 65.

26 For a detailed account of the Special Apparatus, its founders, raison d'être, and history, cf., Shadi 1987; Adel Kamal 1989; al-Sabbagh 1989, 1998; Ramadan 1993; Abou El Zalaf 2022.

27 *Farḍ ʿayn* (a legal obligation that must be performed by each individual Muslim).

28 Al-Sabbagh 1989: 62; see also Abdel Halim 2013, I: 290.

29 Al-Sabbagh (1918–2011) was born in a small village called Hariya Razna in the governate of al-Sharqiyya to a family occupied with cotton trade. His childhood is described as harmonious. He spent his time at school and his leisure time playing football and attending the mosque. He describes an early nationalism, recalling how he named his football club after the "great Egyptian hero Ahmed Urabi." Due to this early nationalism, he relates how he felt strongly embittered by what he perceived as an abandoning of the nationalist cause by the established parties. They had all, according to al-Sabbagh, seemed to accept the British presence in Egypt (al-Sabbagh 1989: 31–2). For al-Sabbagh, the nationalist cause and particularly the evacuation of the British army from Egypt could only be achieved by an armed struggle—a fulfillment of the *jihad* obligation, as he understood it (al-Sabbagh 1989: 49).

30 Mashhur (1921–2002) came from the village of al-Saadiyin in the governate of al-Sharqiyya. Born to a large family of six boys and four girls, Mustafa's upbringing is described as religious. His father, who was a pious man, endowed the young

Mustafa with religious learning and the desire to memorize the Quran and attend the mosque. During his time at secondary school, Mashhur moved to Cairo to spend the last years of his secondary education at the Fuad, the first secondary school where he became acquainted with the Muslim Brotherhood and became a member at the age of fifteen (Muhammad and Mashhur 2005: 13–15).

31 As Eppel has shown in his paper on the conceptual meaning of *Effendiyya*, the concept has had different meanings at different times and in different contexts, but in the Egyptian context, which interests us here, it referred to the "(primarily urban) middle class and the *bashawiyya*, the wealthy ruling elite" (Eppel 2009: 535).

32 Al-Sabbagh 1989: 32.

33 Fanon 2001: 97.

34 Al-Sabbagh 1989: 62–3.

35 Ibid.: 63.

36 Ibid.: 64. Such descriptions of al-Banna applying the Quran to present solutions for current problems are in abundance in the accounts of Brotherhood members (cf. al-Kilani 2006: 49; Shadi 1988: 20).

37 Abdel Halim offers a diverging account on the establishment of the Apparatus. According to him, the Apparatus was established in 1940 by a five-man leading body, of which he numbered third in the hierarchy. The remaining founding brothers were respectively Saleh Ashmawi, Kamal al-Din Hussein, Hamid Sharit, and Abdel Aziz Ahmad. However, once the Apparatus was established, he soon learned that he had become the actual leader of the Apparatus due to the lack of activity of the remaining heads. When sometime later Abdel Halim found employment as a white-collar worker in Damanhur, thus having to leave Cairo, he had to assign a deputy commander of the Apparatus. The choice fell on Abdel Rahman al-Sindi (Abdel Halim 2013, I: 288–91).

38 Al-Sabbagh 1989: 65–7.

39 The revolt (1936–9) broke out as a result of the death of Shaykh Izz al-Din al-Qassam, a Syrian-born cleric who had organized secret anti-British cells in Palestine to resist their colonization of the country. Al-Qassam was killed after a battle with British troops in November 1935. The following months witnessed scattered violent incidents, which from the spring of 1936 turned into a proper revolt lasting for three years.

40 Abdel Halim 2013, I: 288.

41 Al-Sabbagh 1989: 131; NA 1954, I: 33, Hindawi Duwayr's testimony (d. 1954). Hindawi, who in 1954 was head of the Apparatus in Imbaba, a popular neighborhood in the northern part of Giza, explained that the Apparatus fulfilled the Islamic obligation of fighting the British and liberating the Arab and Muslim countries from foreign colonization. But because the government forbade the organization to acquire arms, the Apparatus had to take a secret form. See also NA 1954 I: 40–1.

42 Akef (1928–2017), born in Kafr ʿAwaḍ al-Sinīṭa, a village in the province of Daqahliyya. The son of a wealthy landowning family, Akef was the middle of twelve children, and he describes his childhood in the village as harmonious and happy. Akef recalls how his father endowed him with a religious upbringing, instructing him in the Quran and the Islamic rules while life in the village presented him with the meanings of "manhood and responsibility." He moved with his family to Cairo to attend the upper secondary school in 1940. There in Cairo, he became familiar with the Muslim Brotherhood which had succeeded in mobilizing a number of students to its ranks. Akef joined the local Brotherhood branch in 1941 in al-Sakakini neighborhood, where he lived. He recalls how, during his university days, he studied the ideas of Sayyid Abu Aʿla al-Mawdudi alongside the ideas of al-Banna, Akef (2017–18) I–III, https://bit.ly/34fVEdf, https://bit.ly/2YIxDuo, and https://bit.ly/2PCjeM6 (accessed December 12, 2019).

43 Akef 2017 IV, https://bit.ly/2t3zwpt (accessed December 12, 2019); see also Al-Sabbagh 1989: 150, 162.

44 Abdel Halim 2013, I: 289; al-Sabbagh 1989: 134–8.

45 It seems that the British were gaining wind of the existence of this Apparatus at this point, although not knowing its exact nature and structure. British sources, beginning from about 1940–1, start pointing to the Brotherhood as holding subversive and dangerous ideas. To the British, the Brotherhood had acquired "a predominant position among subversive associations in Egypt," and this may indicate intelligence about the Brotherhood's militant development was reaching the British (see for example WO 208/1560, "Fifth Column Activities in Egypt," November 20, 1941). The apprehensions of the British authorities seemed only to increase the following year. A British report pointed out with apparent concern in May 1942 that the *Ikhwan* "had laid down the nuclei of sabotage organizations and it was believed that a number of the members had for some time been engaged in espionage on behalf of the enemy" (FO 141/838, telegram D.S. (E)/200/42 reporting "First fortnightly meeting with Amin Osman Pacha held at the Embassy on May 18, 1942"). It is of course difficult to say whether these "nuclei organizations" were the Special Apparatus. But taking the timing into consideration, this may very well be the case. In December of the same year, a British report buttressed the above-described apprehensions by voicing the alarm that the Brotherhood was establishing "suicide squads" and that the organization was seeking "to buy arms, and they could bring out shock-troops in a time of disturbance" (FO 141/838 "The Ikhwan al Muslimin Reconsidered" December 10, 1942).

46 Zaki (1924–?), a schoolteacher from Giza who joined the Special Apparatus in 1944 and became a leading member of it.

47 Hasanein (1919–2007), from the governate of Qalyubia, was born into a rural family. He joined the army in 1939 and moved to Cairo to take up his duties

in its ranks. He joined the Brotherhood in 1940 after meeting al-Banna at the Brotherhood's headquarters in Cairo; he recounts that he immediately understood that "this course [of the Brotherhood's] is obligatory" and that it required "self-sacrifice and struggle," Ikhwan-wiki (n.d.), https://bit.ly/2Peh6uT (accessed December 12, 2019).

48 In 1954, following rising tensions between the Brotherhood and the Revolutionary Regime of the Free Officers, the Brotherhood reconstructed the Apparatus, increasing the membership of each cell to seven members (NA 1954, I: 34).

49 Al-Sabbagh 1989: 87–95; NA 1954, I: 33; Abdel Halim 2013, I: 289.

50 While this description is from 1954, the Apparatus had previously been organized on similar lines, but prior to 1954, the cells contained five members in each, rather than seven. Another difference should be found in its personages. In 1953 Talʿat had become head of the Special Apparatus, thus replacing its first leader, Abdel Rahman al-Sindi.

51 NA 1954, I: 38–9.

52 Mansfield 1971: 276–8; Rogan 2009: 209–10.

53 It came to be known as the February Incident or the Abdin incident.

54 Al-Wafd, a liberal nationalist party, was founded in 1918 by Saad Zaghloul (1857–1927), a lawyer, journalist, and politician representing "the secular moderate generation of Egyptian nationalist leaders." Zaghloul's "moderation" stood in contrast to the extremist nationalists and Pan-Islamic groups also present at that time. The newly formed party, which came as a response to Egyptian aspirations for independence after the First World War, appealed to students, Copts, and intellectuals. Prior to the formal foundation of the Party in late November 1918, Zaghloul and his associates had set about forming a delegation to go to London to present Egyptian National demands. Among these demands was the abolition of martial law and the Protectorate, and that Egypt should be heard at the Paris Peace talks to be held shortly. This delegation became the formal "Wafd Party." In 1919, the newly formed Wafd had succeeded in rallying countrywide support for its position on the Egyptian case. From that time until the 1940s, the Wafd was Egypt's mass party (Vatikiotis 1985: 260–5).

55 Following the 4 February incident, the British noticed a widespread dissatisfaction with al-Wafd's assumption of power. "About 5000 students presented a petition at the Palace, in which they demanded that Ali Maher should form a government." The report furthermore recorded, "[i]f their demands were not accepted, they threatened [with] a general strike and widespread sabotage" (WO 208/1561, Security Summary Middle East No. 20, February 12, 1942).

56 Rogan 2009: 210; Mansfield 1971: 278.

57 Marsot 2007: 120.

58 El-Sadat 1978: 32.

59 *Maṣr al-Fatāt* (Young Egypt) was a radical nationalist party founded in 1933 by Ahmad Hussein. The movement merged extreme patriotism with a religious discourse.

60 El-Sadat 1978: 22–3.

61 Abdel Rauf 1988: 26. He noted in his memoirs that what he had in common with officers like Al-Sadat and others was their shared hatred for the British, whom they perceived as the main reason for the weakness of the Egyptian army. See also Vatikiotis 1978: 49.

62 Vatikiotis 1978: 47–8.

63 Abdel Mun'im Abdel Rauf (1914–85), known for his abortive attempt to help 'Aziz al-Misri to escape Egypt in May 1941 to participate in Rashid Ali al-Kilani's uprising against the British in Iraq.

64 Abdel Rauf 1988: 25, 41.

65 Labib was a retired major and a veteran of the Ottoman army who had joined the Sannusi campaign on Egypt in 1915 in an Ottoman attempt to seize the Suez Canal from the British during the First World War. When the campaign failed, Labib fled to Istanbul, where he stayed until 1924. Labib joined the Muslim Brotherhood in 1938—two years after he had retired from the army. He became deputy of the Brotherhood for military affairs in 1947 and a member of the General Guidance Office (Hammuda 1985: 29; Shadi 1987: 176; Abdel Rauf 1988: 43; Mitchell 1993: 97).

66 Abdel Rauf 1988: 41–2. The idea of having Brotherhood cells in the army went back to 1939, according to Abbas al-Sisi, who recalls that al-Banna encouraged him and other *Ikhwan* to join the army as early as 1939. Al-Sisi adds that he joined the army that year and at once began to proselytize in the army among the rank and file and invite them to the regular Brotherhood meetings every Thursday (al-Sisi 2003: 53–5).

67 Al-Sadat 1957: 80. These contacts between discontented officers and the Brotherhood did not go unnoticed to the British either. As early as October 1942, R. J. Maunsell, head of Security Intelligence Middle East (SIME), informed Sir Walter Smart, the oriental minister at the Embassy in Cairo, that "Hasan el Banna had had meetings with Egyptian Army Officers" (FO 141/838, 15322, telegram No. (E)140/1 from R.J. Maunsell GHQ ME, Cairo to Walter Smart, the British Embassy in Cairo "with reference your OS/294/1 of 7th October 1942," October 10, 1942). And again in December 1942, there were British reports pointing out that the Brotherhood had acquired "influence […] among all ranks of the Egyptian Army" (FO 141/838 "The Ikhwan al Muslimin Reconsidered," December 10, 1942).

68 Kamal al-Din Hussein was one of the Free Officers and a member of the RCC. His first public office following the coup d'état in 1952 was as minister of Social Affairs. From 1956 he served as secretary of general education.

69 Mansour 2004: 54.
70 Khaled Muhyiddin, a member of the RCC, recalls in his memoirs that he was introduced to Gamal Abdel Nasser by Abdel Rauf, who also introduced him to Mahmoud Labib (Muhyiddin 1992: 43).
71 Abdel Rauf 1988: 43. This account was verified in a series of articles from October 1952 believed to be presenting Nasser's own recollections. In these articles, it is narrated that Nasser met with Labib in the summer of 1944 on the Tea Island in Cairo Zoo. Discussing national issues with Labib, Nasser found himself "profoundly affected" by what he heard from Labib (Shadi 1987: 164; Mitchell 1993: 97).
72 Al-Sadat 1957: 79.
73 Hammuda 1985: 25–6, 31–2.
74 Ibid.
75 Ibid.
76 Muhyiddin 1992: 43.
77 Ibid.
78 Abdel Rauf, Hammuda, Salah Khalifa, and Maʿruf al-Hadri were among those who continued their loyalty and affiliation with the Brotherhood.
79 Muhyiddin 1992: 44. Muhyiddin, Nasser, and Abdel Hakim Amer were among the officers who at a particular point in their ideological upbringing joined the Brotherhood, but as stated by Muhyiddin, they were not unconditionally with the Brotherhood.
80 Cf. al-Sadat 1957: 80; Muhyiddin 1992: 45.
81 Hussein Kamal al-Din, cited in Jawhar 1976: 31–3; see also Muhyiddin 1992: 45; Hammuda 1985: 32–3.
82 This "unknown" figure was, according to different accounts, presumably Saleh Ashmawi, the deputy of the Brotherhood and a leading figure in the Special Apparatus. According to Mahmoud Abdel Halim, Ashmawi was chosen by Hasan al-Banna as the head of a five-man group to establish the Apparatus in 1940 (Abdel Halim 2013, I: 288).
83 Muhyiddin 1992: 45. For another account of this initiation ceremony, see al-Sadat 1957: 80. The phrase applied by the Brotherhood "in ease and hardship" has its roots in Islamic tradition. According to this tradition, the companions of the Prophet took an oath of allegiance in which they "pledged to the Messenger of Allah to hear and obey, in times of both ease and hardship […]" (Sunan an-Nasa'i 4149).
84 Hammuda 1985: 32–3.
85 This group consisted of Abdel Rauf, Abdel Nasser Kamal al-Din Hussein, Saʿd Hasan Tawfiq, Khaled Muhyiddin, Hammuda, and Salah al-Din Khalifa. Attending these meetings was Mahmoud Labib, the deputy for military activities in the Brotherhood. These meetings acquired a secret nature and were held in private homes as recollected by Khaled Muhyiddin and Hammuda (Hammuda 1985: 33; Muhyiddin 1992: 44).

86 Abdel Khaleq 1987: 82; Shadi 1987: 70.

87 For anti-British activities, see, for example, Shadi 1987: 71, 87–91; al-Sisi 2003: 133; Al-Sharif 1987: 40–1; Al-Bahi 2011: 31; FO 141/1342 "Arab Societies, Ikhwan el Muslimeen" 108/2/49G, Jenkins, Cairo to Head of SIME, GHQ MELF, DS (E) DS/P/62, January 6, 1949.

Chapter 2

1 Al-Sisi 2003: 229; Shadi 1987: 114–15; Abdel Halim 2013, II: 222; Abou El Zalaf 2022: 13.

2 Mahmoud 1997: 124.

3 For a discussion of this, see Abou El Zalaf 2022.

4 This mindset had already existed since the early 1940s, as put forward in the preceding chapter.

5 According to Ikhwan-Wiki, the Brotherhood's online database, Hasan al-Banna wrote his first article on the Palestine issue in 1929. Al-Ikhwan wal-Qaḍiya al-Filisṭīniya (The Brotherhood and the Palestine question) Ikhwan-Wiki (n.d.) https://bit.ly/2M5mvlY (accessed December 18, 2019).

6 Al-Banna in Abdel Aziz 2006c: 33–9.

7 Al-Banna in Majalat al-Fatḥ No. 255, sixth year, June 18, 1931, cited in Abdel Aziz 2006b: 33–4.

8 Ibid.

9 Al-Banna 2013: 268–9.

10 Al-Banna 2013: 278–85.

11 Al-Sharif 1987: 28, 56. Al-Sharif (1926–2008) was born in al-Arish in the Sinai Peninsula, where he was endowed with religious learning from his parents, both of whom had been Sufis. The young Kamil subsequently moved to Cairo to study journalism. In 1947 he moved to the coastal city of Jaffa in northern Palestine, where he met the local Muslim Brotherhood chapter and joined the organization. Al-Sharif took part in the Palestinian-Israeli struggle, and he fought alongside the Palestinian Brotherhood during the first Arab-Israeli war of 1948–49. He met Hasan al-Banna in Palestine and was appointed to lead the *Ikhwani* volunteers sent from Egypt to fight in Palestine (Al-Uqayl (n.d.), https://bit.ly/36mLvNn) (accessed December 12, 2019).

12 Al-Qassam (1882–1935). Born in Syria, al-Qassam took part in the Syrian anti-French resistance in 1921, which is what forced him to flee his native country and relocate in Haifa in the British mandate of Palestine. As a religious cleric, al-Qassam began using the mosques in Haifa to preach anti-British and anti-Zionist messages to the local inhabitants. By combining religious learning with

anti-colonial agitation, al-Qassam quickly came to acquire a mobilizing voice among disillusioned Palestinians. In 1930, al-Qassam began organizing small squads of armed men, named "*al-Kaf al-Aswad*" (the black hand), to resist his two main enemies, the British and the Zionists. His organization, which was limited in size, acquired a strong symbolic legacy as an early *jihad* group, combining religion with nationalism. After conducting a number of covert actions against the British and the Jews, together with his fellow "*al-Qassāmiyūn*" (the Qassamiyans), al-Qassam was killed by the British army after a manhunt and a gun battle. His fall made a martyr and a hero of him, and today he is still remembered as a symbol of anti-British resistance. As an example, Hamas' military branch, the Izz al-Din al-Qassam Brigades, are named after him.

13 Al-Sharif and al-Sibaʿi 1984: 46. This is of course difficult to confirm due to the lack of other reliable sources, but his statement does bear some significance, notwithstanding its accuracy. Such stories have become standard narratives among Brothers who underpin the *Ikhwan*'s long history of *Jihad* against injustice, as they portray it. See also Baqouri 1988: 45. Al-Baqouri mentions Ahmad Rifʿat as one of the Brothers who fought and died alongside al-Qassam. Hasan al-Baqouri, a senior Brother, went as far as stating that al-Qassam himself was a member of the Brotherhood (Al-Baqouri 1988: 45).

14 For such early British perceptions, see for example FO 371/21881, E-5898, No. 1077 (8/259/38), British Embassy, Alexandria, September 26, 1938. Here it is stated that Brotherhood members "volunteer their services in aid of the Palestinian Arabs in their fight against the British and the Jews." According to the report, the Brotherhood decided "to incite the young men to volunteer for the defence of El Aksa Mosque [*sic*]."

15 Frampton 2018: 40.

16 The Brotherhood tried to remain as discreet as possible throughout the war years (1939–45) while establishing its structures and building a mass membership; a low-key rhetoric about neighboring Palestine can consequently be observed during these years. However, as the war ended, bringing a decrease in war restrictions, the Brotherhood intensified its engagement regionally.

17 According to Brotherhood accounts, the first branches had already been established in Palestine as early as 1936–7, but probably as integrated branches of the Egyptian Brotherhood, and not as autonomous organizations. Ikhwan-Wiki (n.d.), *Tārīkh al-Ikhwan fī Filisṭīn* (The history of the Brotherhood in Palestine), https://bit.ly/3aqWTd1 (accessed March 4, 2020).

18 Within six months of its establishment, the Brotherhood in Palestine was estimated to have almost outgrown the two major Arab paramilitary groups in the country, i.e., the Najjadah and Futtuwah, which had estimated memberships of respectively 3,000 to 8,000 and 6,000 to 13,000.

19 Known as a dynamic and energetic member of the Brotherhood, Said Ramadan (d. 1995) was born in April 1925 in the city of Tanta, located between Cairo and Alexandria. In 1946, the twenty-one-year-old Said graduated from law school at Cairo University (at the time named Foud I University). While pursuing his law degree in Cairo, Ramadan joined the Muslim Brotherhood and became one of its most influential activists. In the 1940s, Ramadan seems to have acquired a leading role in expanding the Brotherhood beyond Egypt's borders; see Hathut 2000: 17–18; Ikhwan-Wiki (n.d.), *Said Ramadan*, https://bit.ly/3ARa713 (accessed February 2, 2022).

20 CIA-RDP82-00457R000100570002-0, Intelligence Report, Central Intelligence Group, "Arab Para-military Groups," Palestine, December 13, 1946. The report cites the British General Staff Intelligence's assessment.

21 For an in-depth discussion of the Muslim Brotherhood's expansion in the Arab and Muslim countries, see Frampton 2018: 125–34.

22 Dessouqi 2012: 129–31.

23 Abdel Aziz 2006a.

24 Ikhwan-Wiki (n.d.), *Tārīkh al-Ikhwan al-Muslimin fi Djibouti* (The history of the Muslim Brotherhood in Djibouti), https://bit.ly/34BKqQC (accessed December 19, 2019).

25 FO 371/45927 228/38/45, Dispatch no. 1441, British Embassy in Cairo to FO, October 27, 1945; see also FO 371/53286, XC15100, J 946, telegram no. 377, Lord Killearn to FO, March 3, 1946.

26 For accounts of events in this period, see al-Tal 1990: 1–10; Al-Sharif and al-Sibai 1984: 29–43.

27 The Egyptian, Syrian, Transjordanian, and Iraqi armies declared war on Israel.

28 Gelber 2001: 137.

29 Al-Banna, cited in Ghanem 2011: 178, 184–5, 188–9.

30 Ibid. For contemporary American estimates of the situation at the time and the possible role to be played by the *Ikhwan*, see CIA-RDP78-01617A003000050001-2, Country Report on Egypt, Report to the Special AD HOC Committee by the SWNC Subcommittee for the Near and Middle East, July 31, 1947; CIA-RDP78-01617A003000180001-8, Central Intelligence Agency "The Consequences of the Partition of Palestine," Ore 55, November 28, 1947; CIA-RDP78-04864A000100040003-2, "Arab States' Attitudes, Plans, and Activities Relative to possibility of Palestine Civil War," Central Intelligence Group, Information Report, Report no. oo-F-31, November 6, 1947.

31 Mayer 1982: 109–11.

32 Ibid.

33 Ronald Campbell, the British ambassador to Cairo, estimated in March 1949 that 2,000 Moslem Brotherhood members had "volunteered for active service in Palestine" (FO 371/73464, No. 170, 17/4/49G, British Embassy Cairo, March 21, 1949).

34 Abdel Rauf 1988: 51–3.

35 The Huckstep camp east of Cairo had been a major base for the allied forces during the Second World War.

36 Abdel Aziz (1907–48) retired from the Egyptian army to command the volunteers in the war. He was killed in Gaza in August 1948.

37 Cf. Al-Jamal 2000: 22–3; Hathut 2000: 53–4; Sadiq 1987: 13–15.

38 Shadi 1987: 102.

39 Gelber 2001: 28, 57; Gerges 2007: 153.

40 Cf. Gelber 2001: 147, 200, 205; Gerges 2007: 153.

41 CIA-RDP82-00457R002500210003-2, Information Report, CIA "Activities of the Ikhwan al-Muslimin (Moslem Brotherhood), Lebanon, March 22, 1949. According to this report, ten members of the Brotherhood had arrived in Lebanon to urge the "Moslem Organizations [there] … to demand that the Lebanese Government resume fighting in Palestine."

42 CIA-RDP82-00457R002500210003-2, Information Report, CIA "Activities of the Ikhwan al-Muslimin (Moslem Brotherhood)," Lebanon, March 22, 1949.

43 Cited in al-Sisi 1981: 278–9.

44 Azb and Khalifa 2011: 330.

45 For an account of the violent incidents, cf. Ramadan 1993: 74–8; Azb and Khalifa 2011: 327–31; Abou El Zalaf 2022.

46 Muhammad 1987: 411.

47 Mitchell 1993: 72.

48 Adel Kamal 1989: 263.

49 Adel Kamal 1989: 277–9; see also Abou El Zalaf 2022: 12.

50 FO 371/69212, J 8308/68/16G, Foreign Office to Ambassador in Cairo, December 29, 1948.

51 Muhammad 1987: 511–12.

52 Al-Harani 2014: 44; Al-Sabbagh 1989: 450; Adel Kamal 1989: 277.

53 Yusuf al-Qaradawi (1926–) was born in Ṣafṭ al-Turāb, a small, traditional village located twenty-one kilometers from Tanta, the capital town of the Sharqiyya governate. Al-Qaradawi's upbringing was religious: he attended a kutāb in his village where he memorized the Quran at the age of nine and had his first schooling. The young Yusuf also attended a modern school, and as such he recalls that he "collected the good of both institutions." In his memoirs, he recounts the obvious inequalities in his little village, which had an impact on him, because he came from a family that did not own any land. The young al-Qaradawi listened to al-Banna for the first time in 1940, when the latter was visiting Tanta. Two years later, in 1942, he officially joined the Brotherhood. Al-Qaradawi graduated from al-Azhar in the early 1950s (Al-Qaradawi 2002: 15, 44, 61, 126, 159, 178).

54 Al-Qaradawi 2002: 324. According to this account, diplomats from the British, French, and American embassies had collectively urged al-Nuqrashi Pasha to

disband the organization. This was, according to al-Qaradawi, a natural request from colonizing countries, as they conceived the Brotherhood as the major barrier to their greed in the region. Whether the Western governments had urged al-Nuqrashi to dissolve the *Ikhwan* or not is beyond the scope of this study and cannot be assured due to the lack of official documents, but the reactions of British diplomats expose an explicit support on the British side for this measure. The British maintained following the Brotherhood's dissolution that the Egyptian government had at last "agreed on the necessity of pursuing the recently adopted out-and-out policy against the Moslem Brethren" (FO 371/73462, J304/1015/16, No. 14, British Embassy Cairo, January 5, 1949).

55 Al-Qaradawi 2002: 335, 337. See also Abdel Halim 2013, II: 37; he claims that al-Nuqrashi's death was a result of his "malice and narrowness of sight and his tyranny with regard to his opinion and his surrender to the usurping colonizers"; see also Sadiq 1987: 45.

56 della Porta 2013: 38–9; della Porta points out that "escalating policing has been an important causal mechanism at the onset of clandestine political violence" and "produces martyrs and myths; this process justifies violence and pushes militant groups underground."

57 Zollner 2011: 16; for a similar account, see Soage and Franganillo 2010: 41.

58 Hafez 2004: 46–7.

59 Erickson 1981: 188, 191.

60 By continuation, I mean the persistence of organizational forms and structures, persons, leadership, and ideas.

61 Al-Baqouri 1988: 81–2. According to British reports, al-Banna had shortly before his death decided "to retire to the country and to continue to supervise the activities of his followers from there," and thus he chose a successor to take over in Cairo; see FO 371/73463, No. DS (E) P. 997, J. G. Tomlinson, British Embassy, Cairo, February 14, 1949. This was not an accidental or novel tactic applied at a moment of crisis, but was a manifested aspect of the Brotherhood's organizational thinking going far back in its history. As early as 1942, a British report stated that "al-Banna is believed to have chosen a series of substitute leaders in case the present leaders of the movement in Cairo and the provinces were simultaneously arrested"; see FO 141/838, General HQ Middle East, "The Ikhwan al Muslimin Reconsidered" (Appendix A to Security Summary Middle East, No. 103, December 10, 1942); see also FO 371/41334, J 3812/16/44, "PIC Paper No. 49 (Revised): Ikhwan el Muslimeen," July 25, 1944.

62 Erickson 1981: 188.

63 Abdel Halim 2013, II: 439. Mahmoud Abdel Halim recalls that such meetings were held, among other places, in mosques, where security measures are limited.

64 Al-Anani 2016: 111.

65 Al-Qaradawi 2002: 68–9, 358.

66 Al-Qaradawi 2002: 359. This term is derived from a prophetic tradition which had it that "When three are on a journey, they should appoint one of them as their commander [*amīr*]" (Sunan Abi Dawud 2608, https://bit.ly/3aAjq8f) (accessed January 23, 2020).

67 FO 371/73464, No. 170, 17/4/49G, British Embassy Cairo, March 21, 1949.

68 Munir al-Dilla (1921–74) was born to a rich landowning family in Upper Egypt. He moved to Cairo at some point to study law at Cairo University. While in Cairo, the young al-Dilla befriended a fellow law student, Hasan al-Ashmawi, son of Muhammad al-Ashmawi, Minister of Education during different periods. When he graduated from law school, al-Dilla became councilor of state, and soon after, he married Hasan al-Ashmawi's sister, Amal al-Ashmawi. It was about this time that he also joined the Brotherhood. That was, according to Richard Mitchell, in 1947; his joining was described as "the introduction into the movement of 'Cadillacs and aristocracy'" (Mitchell 1993: 85). Devout followers of Hasan al-Banna and the principles of the Brotherhood, al-Dilla and his wife contributed immensely to the Brotherhood.

69 Cited in Rizq 1991: 23.

70 Baqouri 1988: 82. Muhammad Hamed Abul Nasr, a senior Brother, recounts in his memoirs that an office had been formed in Cairo where senior Brothers such as Munir al-Dilla, Hasan al-Ashmawi, Fahmy Abu Ghadir, and Taher al-Khashab met to study the situation of the Brotherhood, to collect funds for the organization, and to consider the situation of its members (Abul Nasr 1988: 52).

71 Al-Sisi 2003: 258–9.

72 Aminzade and Perry 2001: 159.

73 Vatikiotis 1985: 366.

74 Ikhwan-Wiki (n.d.), *Amal al-Ashmawi*, https://bit.ly/3awFCAf (accessed January 20, 2020).

75 Khayal and al-Jawhari 1993: 239.

76 See, for example, FO 371/69212, J 8096, 172/65/48, British Embassy, Cairo, to African Department, Foreign Office, December 13, 1948: FO 371/73463, No. DS (E) P. 997, J.G. Tomlinson, British Embassy, Cairo, February 14, 1949;

77 FO 141/1342, "Arab Societies, Ikhwan el Muslimeen," 108/2/49G, Jenkins, Cairo to Head of SIME, GHQ MELF, DS (E) DS/P/62, January 6, 1949.

78 Italics in original.

79 FO 371/73464, J2528, 517/4/49G, No. 170, British Embassy Cairo, March 21, 1949.

80 Ibid.

81 CIA-RDP82-00457R002200760006-2, "Activity of the Ikhwan al-Muslimin: Information Report, Central Intelligence Agency," Egypt, January 14, 1949.

82 Ibid.

83 Al-Qaradawi 2002: 68–9, 358–9; see also Akef 2017–18, VI: https://bit.ly/3tMiqZX (accessed February 11, 2019).

84 Duh 1983: 51.

85 Al-Tilmisani (1904–86) was born in Cairo to a cotton-trading family. His grandfather was a diligent reader of Wahabism, and he published a number of Ibn Abdel Wahab's books. The young Umar was therefore brought up in a religious atmosphere in this home by his middle-class parents. In 1933, he graduated from law school and established a law office in Cairo. In the same year, he joined the Brotherhood to become the first lawyer in its ranks. In 1973, he was appointed the third leader of the *Ikhwan*, a position he held until his death in 1986 (al-Uqayl 2008: 657–8, see also Qaud 1985; al-Ghazi 2008).

86 Al-Tilmisani 1985: 42.

87 Osman (1928–2010) was born in al-Minya, a town 150 miles south of Cairo. He was exposed to political discussions during his early adolescence when he accompanied his father to the coffee shops; this endowed him with an interest in politics, which at this time meant interest in the national cause. Attending a speech by Hasan al-Banna in his hometown, al-Minya, Fathi Osman was attracted by the way in which al-Banna presented Islam as relevant for success in this life and not only in the hereafter, in contrast to the traditional preachers he had been used to hearing. He joined the Brotherhood in 1942. In 1948, at twenty years old, he graduated from the history department at Cairo University (Osman 2011: 1–5, 30–3, 69).

88 Osman 2011: 81–2.

89 Shadi 1987: 113; Al-Sisi 2003: 225–7, 254.

90 Yavuz 2004: 270: Yavuz describes opportunity spaces as including "independent newspapers, TV stations, magazines, financial institutions, and private educational facilities, all of which provided autonomous networks of association for the production and dissemination of religious values and ways of life." We can similarly argue that the Brotherhood had enjoyed such spaces of opportunity in nonrepressive periods prior to the 1948 dissolution.

91 Ikhwan-Wiki (n.d.), *Al-Amr al-ʿAskarī bi-Ḥal al-Ikhwan al-Muslimin li-Sanat 1948* (The military commandment for dissolving the Muslim Brotherhood, for the year 1948) https://bit.ly/2O2RAYJ (accessed January 27, 2020).

92 Al-Sisi 2003: 223. The Senussis were a well-known sufi order, clan, and politico-religious movement. Idris al-Senussi, a grandson of the clan founder, became king of Libya in 1951. He was toppled by a coup d'état in 1969 by army officer Muammar al-Gaddafi.

93 865.014/3–2149, Telegram, "The Consul at Tripoli (Taft) to the Secretary of State," Tripoli, March 21, 1949.

94 Al-Sisi 2003: 223, 256. One of those Brothers who reached London at this early stage was Izz al-Din Ibrahim. Ibrahim received his PhD from Cambridge in 1963, after which he continued his work in the Gulf (al-Qaradawi 2004: 472–3).

95 FO 141/1342, 108/3/49 G, DS (E) DS/P/62, "Arab Societies, Ikhwan El Muslimeen," G. J. Jenkins, British Embassy, Cairo, January 20, 1949; for a similar account but relating to Brotherhood activities in Yemen, see FO 141/1342, 108/4/49 G, DS (E) DS/P/62, G. J. Jenkins, British Embassy, Cairo, January 28, 1949.

96 CIA-RDP82-00457R002500210003-2, Information Report, Central Intelligence Agency "Activities of the Ikhwan al-Muslimin" Lebanon, March 22, 1949; for earlier reports indicating that this had been a pattern since 1947, see CIA-RDP82-00457R000400630001-1, Intelligence Report, Central Intelligence group, "Egyptian Attempts to strengthen Moslem Brotherhood in Lebanon and Syria," Lebanon/Egypt, April 2, 1947.

97 FO 141/1342, 108/2/49G, DS (E) DS/P/62 "Arab Societies, Ikhwan el Muslimeen," Jenkins, Cairo to Head of SIME, GHQ MELF, January 6, 1949.

98 Simmel 1906: 472.

99 Vatikiotis 1985: 366.

100 Mitchell 1993: 72.

101 Hopwood 1993: 29. The dismissal of Abdel Hadi's cabinet was understood as the king's "Bairam [Eid] gift to the nation," indicating how unpopular the Prime Minister had become in his last days (FO 371/80347, JE 1016/23, 1011/9/50, No. 49, British Embassy, Cairo, January 25, 1950). The same celebration of the dismissal as an "Eid-gift" is also to be found in the Brotherhood accounts; see, for instance, al-Tilmisani 1985: 26; al-Banna n.d.; https://bit.ly/35ZIIsR (accessed January 16, 2020).

102 Four main cases were raised against the Brotherhood: (1) the Jeep case, (2) the case regarding the assassination of al-Nuqrashi, (3) the *awkār* (nests/cells) case, and (4) the Hamid Juda case.

103 For a detailed outline of the court case, see Mitchell 1993: 73–9.

104 Mitchell 1993: 78; Abdel Halim 2013, II: 302.

105 Abdel Halim 2013, II: 303.

Chapter 3

1 FO 371/96870, JE 1018/1, No. 1, 1012/1/52, British Embassy, Cairo, January 1, 1952.

2 Ashour 2009: 64.

3 Abul Nasr 1988: 53. Abul Nasr (1913–96) is a descendant of Ali Ahmad Abul Nasr, a respected Azhari who took part in the Urabi uprising in the late nineteenth century. Hamed Abul Nasr was born in Manfalut, a city located on the west bank of the Nile in the Asyut Governorate, about 360 kilometers south of Cairo. The young Abul Nasr began participating in socio-religious movements before his association with the Brotherhood. In the early 1930s, he was a member of the YMMA before he eventually joined the *Ikhwan* in 1934. He quickly climbed the

ladder inside the Brotherhood, becoming a member of its general assembly and subsequently its general guidance office before he was appointed as its fourth General Guide in 1986 (Al-Uqayl 2008: 834–5).

4 FO 371/80343, JE 1013/18, No. 82, "From Cairo to Foreign Office," April 3, 1950. The British embassy seems to have followed the developments inside the Brotherhood closely. In this report, penned by Sir. R. Campbell, it is argued that al-Baqouri had been elected as al-Banna's successor. Although mistaken, this assessment was probably based on discussions inside the Brotherhood, where al-Baqouri was indeed one of the nominees for the position. This may also be a result of al-Baqouri's role as caretaker of the Brotherhood during al-Banna's last days.

5 I will not go into depth describing these events that occurred when the *Ikhwan* was looking for a new leader. These events have already been described by Mitchell 1993: 84–7.

6 Abdel Rahman changed his surname to Al-Banna after Hasan al-Banna's death in 1949; he had previously been known as "al-Sa'ati" (the watchmaker, which was his father's occupation). This alteration was presumably an attempt to consolidate his position in the Brotherhood as a senior member and as the rightful inheritor of its leadership.

7 Abdel Halim 2013, II: 445; Shadi 1987: 122.

8 Abul Nasr 1988: 51; Abdel Khaleq 1987: 61; Shadi 1987: 122.

9 Abdel Rahim 1989: 23; Shadi 1987: 122.

10 Shadi 1987: 122; Abul Nasr 1988: 52.

11 Mitchell 1993: 85; Shadi 1987: 122. Rumors about this conflict had also reached British diplomats in Cairo in April 1950: FO 371/80343, JE 1013/18, No. 82, "From Cairo to Foreign Office," April 3, 1950.

12 Rizq 1991: 23; Mitchell 1993: 85; see also Al-Antabli (n.d.) https://bit.ly/2u7KMl6 (accessed November 26, 2018).

13 According to the recollection of Abdel Qader Hilmi, who attended the meeting in Al-Dilla's home, which was organized to find an heir to the vacant post, al-Dilla asked the four contenders to choose one of them to lead the Brotherhood, but no agreement was reached. Munir al-Dilla therefore outlined the potential dangers a crisis would trigger if they did not come to an agreement. The impression from the meeting was one of total disagreement. Against this background, al-Dilla mentioned Hasan al-Hudaybi as a candidate for the position of General Guide. As we learn from Abdel Qader Hilmi, the reaction to this idea was not one of rejection. Cited in Shadi 1987: 124.

14 Abdel Khaleq 1987: 64; Abul Nasr 1988: 54; Abdel Halim 2013, II: 469.

15 Abdel Khaleq 1987: 64.

16 The British Embassy in Cairo points to May 1950 as the date for al-Hudaybi's appointment as leader of the *Ikhwan* (FO 371/96870, JE 1018/1, No. 1, 1012/1/52, British Embassy, Cairo, January 1, 1952).

17 On the one hand, the Brotherhood had not yet regained its legality. On the other, al-Hudaybi was still a functioning judge, who according to Egyptian law was not allowed to be a member of a political party or organization, hence the reason his appointment as *Murshid* had to remain unofficial until he retired as a judge in October 1951.

18 Lia 2010: 118; Tilmisani 1985: 107.

19 The chief of the royal household was al-Hudaybi's brother-in-law (Mitchell 1993: 85; Ramadan 1993: 92).

20 Shadi, cited in Rizq 1991: 45; see also Ahmad 1977: 5; Abdel Halim 2013: II: 491.

21 Jung and Abou El Zalaf 2019: 7.

22 FO 371/90115, JE 10110/18, 1011/16/51G, British Embassy, Cairo, May 17, 1951.

23 In March 1951, less than a year after al-Hudaybi's de facto appointment as leader, the British and Americans were still considering the possibility of "reemergence of the assassination-type of politics of the Moslem Brotherhood"; see for example CIA-RDP79T01146A000100200001-9, Daily Digest of Significant Traffic, Office of Current Intelligence, March 23, 1951.

24 Shadi cited in Rizq 1991: 47.

25 As I highlight in the coming sections, al-Hudaybi was strongly supported by the upper-class Brothers who at first had suggested his appointment; among these Brothers were al-Dilla, Ashmawi, Farid Abdel Khaleq, Salah Shadi, and Abdel Qader Hilmi. This group of Brothers had the social background in common: most of them had upper-class backgrounds, while they also had family connections. A number of them had matrimonial alliances.

26 Al-Hudaybi made it his demand that Abdel Qader Uda be appointed his deputy (*wakil)* (Ahmad al-Bess, cited in Rizq 1991: 100; Abdel Khaleq 1987: 67; Abul Nasr 1988: 56).

27 Saleh Ashmawi was, according to some accounts, the founder of the Apparatus. When al-Sindi acquired the leadership of the Apparatus sometime after its establishment, al-Ashmawi stayed in close contact with him, and a strong relationship seems to have continued throughout the years (Shadi 1987: 128; Abdel Halim 2013, I: 289).

28 The organization's top executive authority.

29 Abul Nasr 1988: 55–7. Tariq al-Bishri stated that al-Hudaybi, upon his appointment, purged the leadership of opponents while he chose associates from judiciary posts and members known for their moderate stances (al-Bishri 2002: 455).

30 I say at this particular stage because, as we will see later, al-Hudaybi seems to have changed his mind at a later point in time, restructuring the Apparatus instead of dissolving it.

31 For this line of argument, see, for example, Adel Kamal 1989: 318.

32 Abdel Khaleq 2004, VII: https://bit.ly/31jRVvk (accessed March 3, 2020).

33 Jamal Salem (1918–68) was a member of the Revolutionary Command Council and a military judge in the court martial established to prosecute the Brotherhood for the assassination attempt on Nasser's life in October 1954.
34 NA 1954, III: 557–9.
35 NA 1954, III: 559.
36 Saleh Ashmawi is described by the British as "fanatical and, in many ways, irresponsible in his actions" (FO 371/90115, JE 10110/18, 1011/16/51G, British Embassy, Cairo, May 17, 1951).
37 CIA-RDP82-00457R007100070004-6, Information Report, "Fu'ad Siraj al-Din and the Ikhwan," Egypt, February 28, 1951. See also FO 371/90115, JE 10110/18, 1011/16/51G, British Embassy, Cairo, May 17, 1951, in which the British describe al-Hudaybi as a "mere figurehead" and as not having anywhere near Hasan al-Banna's strength of personality.
38 Mitchell 1993: 88.
39 Adel Kamal 1989: 327.
40 Ibid.: 318.
41 See for example Hamida's statement in court in 1954 (NA 1954, III: 559).
42 Mitchell 1993: 88.
43 FO 371/90115, JE 10110/15, 1019/27/51, No. 167, British Embassy, Cairo, May 2, 1951 (underline in original).
44 Vatikiotis 1985: 368.
45 FO 371/90115, JE 10110/4, "Protest March in Cairo, Student Demands," January 15, 1951.
46 FO 371/90115, JE 1011/7/51G, British Embassy, Cairo, February 23, 1951.
47 Louis 1985: 691.
48 Ibid.: 720.
49 FO 371/90115, JE 10110/19, 1011/42/51, No. 191, British Embassy, Cairo, May 23, 1951.
50 FO 371/134, JE 1051/131, No. 458, Alexandria to Foreign Office, July 6, 1951.
51 Thornhill 2006: 34.
52 FO 371/90117, JE 10110/71, 1657/2/51, British Embassy, Alexandria, September 26, 1951.
53 Ibid.
54 FO 371/90115, JE 10110/26, 1011/4/13/51, No. 307, British Embassy, Alexandria, September 5, 1951.
55 Louis 1985: 732.
56 Vatikiotis 1985: 368.
57 WO 236/15, Narrative of Events in the Canal Zone, October 1951 – April 1952.
58 CIA-RDP79T00975A000400250001-9, Central Intelligence Bulletin, Copy No. 47, October 20, 1951.

59 CIA-RDP79T00975A000400320001-1, Central Intelligence Bulletin, Copy no. 47. Office of Current Intelligence, CIA, October 28, 1951.

60 Ibid.

61 FO 371/90117, JE 10110/60, No. 276, British Embassy, Alexandria, October 16, 1951.

62 Ibid.

63 Ibid.

64 Mitchell 1993: 89.

65 FO 371/90116, JE 10110/49, 32524 G (0) A, From G.H.Q, Middle East Land Forces to War Office, October 20, 1951.

66 FO 371/90116, JE 10110/49, 32336 G (0) A, From G.H.Q, Middle East Land Forces to War Office, October 19, 1951.

67 FO 371/90116, JE 10110/49, Recd: 2353, October 19, 1951.

68 FO 371/90118, JE 10110/77, from G.H.Q. Middle East Land Forces to Ministry of Defence, London, October 29, 1951.

69 FO 371/90116, JE 10110/49, Recd: 2227, October 23, 1951.

70 FO 141/1433, 1011/35/51G, W. Morris, November 6, 1951.

71 It changed its name to the Social Party after the Second World War.

72 FO 371/90117, JE 10110/73, from G.H.Q Middle East Land Forces to Ministry of Defence, London, October 27, 1951.

73 Ibid.

74 Ibid.

75 FO 371/90117, JE 10110/74, Memorandum by Bowker, October 30, 1951.

76 FO 371/90118, JE 10110/75, From G.H.Q. Middle East Land Forces to War Office, October 18, 1951; FO 371/90118, JE 10110/87, no. 284, 1011/4/42/51, Stevenson, Cairo, to Mohamad Salah El Dine Pasha, Minister of Foreign Affairs, October 31, 1951; for Brotherhood accounts, see Al-Sharif 1987: 46–8; see also Duh 1989: 55; Al-Jamal 2000: 114.

77 FO 141/1433, 1011/41/51G, Record of Conversation, November 28, 1951.

78 Al-Sharif 1987: 43.

79 Duh 1983: 52–5.

80 Talʿat (1914–54) was born to a poor family in al-Ismailiyya, the city in which al-Banna placed the foundation stone for the Brotherhood when the young Yusuf was fourteen years of age. After finishing primary school, the poor Yusuf became a carpenter to earn a living for his family. Soon after the establishment of the Brotherhood in 1928, he became an early attendee of its meetings and was introduced to the Brotherhood's first excursion troop at a young age. Through this early engagement with the Brotherhood and directly with its founder al-Banna, Talʿat became a respected and appreciated member of the Brotherhood. When the Special Apparatus was founded sometime between 1939 and 1940, he became the leader of this paramilitary foundation in his hometown al-Ismailiyya, a center for anti-British activities. There, Talʿat became renowned for his engagement against

the British and his participation in the first Arab–Israeli war, earning himself the nickname "*Asad al-Canāl*," "The lion of the Canal [Zone]." He was hanged by the military regime in 1954 (al-Uqayl 2008: 1234–51; al-Bahi 2011).

81 Duh 1983: 54.

82 Shadi 1987: 193.

83 Akef 2017/18, V: https://bit.ly/3uHOyPq (accessed February 11, 2019).

84 Akef 2017/18, VIII: https://bit.ly/3h3luKb (accessed February 11, 2019); Sadiq 1987: 56.

85 Duh 1983: 54–6.

86 FO 371/90119, JE 10110/112, No. 54, from British Middle East Office (Fayid) to Foreign Office, Sir T. Rapp, November 16, 1951.

87 FO 371/90118, JE 10110/91, No. 15, from British Middle East Office (Fayid) to Foreign Office, November 6, 1951; FO 371/90119, JE 10110/109, 1041/2/362/51G, Ralph Stevenson to Ibrahim Farag Pasha, Acting Minister for Foreign Affairs, Cairo, November 30, 1951.

88 See, for example: FO 371/90119, JE 10110/115, No. 304, 1041/2/295/51G, November 14, 1951; FO 371/90119, JE 10110/112, No. 54, from British Middle East Office (Fayid) to Foreign Office, Sir T. Rapp, November 16, 1951; FO 371/90119, JE 10110/113, No. 1018, from Cairo to Foreign Office, November 17, 1951; FO 371/90119, JE 10110/118, No. 62, from British Middle East Office, Fayid, to Foreign Office, November 19, 1951; for a report on the death of British officers, see FO 371/90120, JE 10110/143, No. 86, T. Trapp to Foreign Office, December 1, 1951; for accounts on Brotherhood actions, see FO 371/96870, JE 1018/1, No. 1, 1012/1/52, British Embassy, Cairo, January 1, 1952.

89 Kamil al-Sharif notes in his book that al-Hudaybi endured a lot of criticism as "the one who thwarts the Brotherhood in participating in an armed struggle" (1987: 42). One such example came on January 1, 1952, when the prominent Egyptian author and activist Sayyid Qutb, at that time not yet a member of the Brotherhood, asked for an unambiguous position from al-Hudaybi regarding the Canal Zone battles (Abdel Halim 2013, II: 504).

90 FO 141/1433, 1011/39/51G, Record of Conversation, November 24, 1951.

91 FO 141/1433, 1011/41/51G, Record of Conversation, November 28, 1951.

92 FO 141/1433, 1011/44/51G, Cecil Campbell, December 16, 1951.

93 FO 141/1450, 1011/3/51G, "Arab Societies: Ikhwan el Muslimeen," D. L. Stewart, December 4, 1951.

94 CIA-RDP79S01060A000100260001-6, Current Intelligence Review, December 19, 1951, vol. I, no. 19; The Anglo–Egyptian Crisis.

95 CIA-RDP82-00457R007100070004-6, Information Report, "Fu'ad Siraj al-Din and the Ikhwan," Egypt, February 28, 1951.

96 For such accounts, see: Sadiq 1987: 59; Duh 1983: 55–6; al-Qaradawi 2002: 448–9.

97 Al-Jamal 2000: 109.

98 FO 141/1433, 1011/44/51G, Cecil Campbell, December 16, 1951.

99 CIA-RDP82-00457R007100070004-6, Information Report, "Fu'ad Siraj al-Din and the Ikhwan," Egypt, February 28, 1951.

100 Abdel Khaleq 1987: 73.

101 Al-Sharif 1987: 42.

102 See, for example, FO 141/1450, 10112/4/51G, "Arab Societies, Ikhwan el Muslimeen, II," December 11, 1951.

103 FO 141/1433, 1011/44/51G, Cecil Campbell, December 16, 1951.

104 FO 371/96870, JE 1018/1, No. 1, 1012/1/52, British Embassy, Cairo, January 1, 1952.

105 Ibid.

106 Ibid.

107 Ibid.

108 Ibid.

109 Husaini 1956: 122–3.

110 Ibrahim al-Tayyib, a senior member of the Special Apparatus and head of the Apparatus in Cairo from February 1954, explained before court in November 1954 that the task of the Apparatus and of the Brotherhood was to prepare a generation of well-trained and armed men who could fight an obligatory *jihad* against occupying forces in "Tunis, Algiers or Egypt" (NA 1954, II: 431–2).

111 Ashour 2009: 64–5.

112 See Chapter 1.

113 Shadi 1987: 192, 207.

Chapter 4

1 Gerges 2018: 186.

2 Kepel 1985: 27.

3 Sharaf 2015, IV: 964–5; Allam 1996: 54, 99.

4 Gerges 2018: x.

5 FO 371/108319/ JE 1016/12, "The Moslem Brotherhood under the Naguib Regime," February 1954.

6 Frampton 2018: 205.

7 Shadi 1987: 391–4; FO 371/96879, JE 1018/292, No. 1162, Sir R. Stevenson to Foreign Office, August 2, 1952.

8 Gordon 1992: 57–8; Mansour 2004: 78: Shafiʿi explains that decisions taken at this early point of time were not a part of a preconceived plan but were taken as the issues occurred. He also points to the fact that the officers did not wish to acquire state power but intended to be guardians of the revolutionary course on which they had put Egypt (2004: 114).

9 Abdel Khaleq 1987: 84–5.
10 Ibid.: 84; al-Ashmawi 1977: 23; Shadi 1987: 213.
11 FO 371/96879, JE 1018/289, "Statement on Egypt for Nato," August 1, 1952.
12 Ali Maher refused to let the officers push the law through. He therefore resigned in protest when they tried to get the law through without his consent.
13 774.00/9–852: Telegram No. 1006 The Ambassador in Egypt (Caffery) to the Department of State, Cairo, September 8, 1952; for a corresponding account, see FO 371/96881, JE 1018/362, No. 1333, September 13, 1952.
14 For an in-depth discussion of this issue, cf. Mitchell 1993: 107.
15 Al-Baqouri 1988: 118.
16 Abul Nasr 1988: 71.
17 Mitchell 1993: 108; for the RCC's lack of popular support, see, e.g., FO 371/108319/ JE 1016/12, "The Moslem Brotherhood under the Naguib Regime," February 1954.
18 Mitchell 1993: 108.
19 Cf. Abdel Khaleq 1987: 85; Shadi 1987: 226; Abdel Halim 2013, III: 165; al-Tilmisani, cited in Qaud 1985: 95.
20 Ibid.
21 Frampton 2018: 215.
22 This consolidation of power had been underway for some time. In October 1952, the CIA pointed to "evidence that the army is steadily consolidating its position." Adding to this, the report maintained that the junta was trying to "to curb the Brotherhood's influence," CIA-RDP79T00975A000900050001-6, Current Intelligence Bulletin, October 16, 1952.
23 Gordon 1992: 77.
24 CIA-RDP79R01012A002500040001-1, National Intelligence Estimate, "Probable Developments in Egypt," March 25, 1953.
25 Ibid.; for a British estimate of the Rally's purported role, see FO 371/108319/ JE 1016/12, "The Moslem Brotherhood under the Naguib Regime," February 1954.
26 Gordon 1992: 80–1.
27 Abdel Khaleq 1987: 86, see also al-Tilmisani's view; Qaud 1985: 101. The British support this reading. A British report claims, for instance, that al-Hudaybi perceived the rally as "a threat to the Brotherhood." It was argued that if the Rally succeeded, "the Army would be less inclined to rely on his [Hudaybi's] support"; FO 371/108319/ JE 1016/12, "The Moslem Brotherhood under the Naguib Regime," February 1954.
28 Qaud 1985: 94.
29 Shadi, cited in Jawhar 1976: 44.
30 El-Sadat 1978: 124; for a corresponding account by Hussein al-Shafiʿi, another leading member of the junta, see Mansour 2004: 138–9.
31 Mitchell 1993: 111; al-Sisi 2003: 312.

32 Abdel Halim 2013, III: 165.
33 Gordon 1992: 103.
34 FO 371/ 102704, JE 1015/51, No. 67, Ralph Stevenson, from Cairo to Foreign Office, March 17, 1953.
35 Ibid. See also Frampton 2018: 227. This view was also shared by British diplomats. Understanding the conflict between al-Hudaybi's faction and the regime as a root of discontent within the Brotherhood, according to British estimates it had divided the *Ikhwan* into at least two different opposed groups (FO 371/102706, "The long-term prospects of the Army Movement," British Embassy, Cairo, September 1953). On September 10, 1953, Nasser had informed Trefor Evans in person that he was personally on "bad terms" with al-Hudaybi "and his immediate supporters, including Munir Dallah [*sic*], Abu Rouqak [*sic*] and Sayed [*sic*] Ramadan" (FO 371/102706, JE 1015/129, 1012/22/53, British Embassy Cairo, September 17, 1953).
36 Al-Sabbagh 1998: 89; NA 1954, V: 1028–9.
37 Al-Sabbagh 1998: 91.
38 NA 1954, IV: 789–90.
39 Adel Kamal 1989: 330.
40 See, e.g., FO 371/108319/ JE 1016/12, "The Moslem Brotherhood under the Naguib Regime," February 1954.
41 Abdel Halim 2013, III: 229; see also Shadi 1987: 144–5.
42 Adel Kamal 1989: 144–5.
43 FO 371/108319, JE 1016/1, 1012/5/53G, British Embassy Cairo, December 30, 1953.
44 Mitchell 1993: 122; for a contemporary account, see FO 371/108319, JE 1016/1, 1012/5/53G, British Embassy Cairo, December 30, 1953.
45 Abdel Halim 2013, III: 231.
46 For detailed accounts, see Mitchell 1993: 122–4; Shadi 1987: 147–54; Adel Kamal 1989: 354–60; Abdel Halim 2013, II: 235–46.
47 Shadi 1987:154; Abul Nasr 1988: 92.
48 Adel Kamal 1989: 360; Abdel Halim 2013, II: 471.
49 Mitchell 1993: 126.
50 FO 371/108319, JE 1016/1, 1012/5/53G, British Embassy Cairo, December 30, 1953.
51 FO 371/108319/ JE 1016/12, "The Moslem Brotherhood under the Naguib Regime," February 1954.
52 FO 371/108319, JE 1016/2, No. 54, Sir R. Stevenson, From Cairo to Foreign Office, January 13, 1954; see also, Mitchell 1993: 127; al-Sisi 2003: 370; Abdel Halim 2013, III: 285. According to official announcements, following the dissolution, 450 members were arrested, while 20 were immediately released.
53 Qaud 1985: 105. Among the arrested Brotherhood leaders was Abdel Qader Uda (until then a strong voice in the pro-Nasser faction of the Brotherhood, but who had played a major role in directing the pro-democracy demonstrations which

requested the dissolution of the RCC and the army's return to its barracks on February 28, 1954) and Umar al-Tilmisani.

54 Shadi 1987: 350; Abdel Rauf 1988: 107–9. Among the arrested and court-martialed officers were Colonel Abdel Mun'im Abdel Rauf, Major Ma'ruf al-Hadri, Lieutenant Colonel Abu al-Makaram Abd al-Hayy, and Major Hussein Hammuda.

55 Kepel 1985: 26–8; Bergesen 2008: 4; Calvert 2010: 203.

56 Kepel 1985: 27.

57 FO 371-108319, JE 1016/4, No. 61, Sir Stevenson addressed to Foreign Office, January 15, 1954; for the full communique, see Shadi 1987: 401–10.

58 Ibid.

59 The Brotherhood would continually insist that these accusations, and in particular those regarding the weapons discovered on al-Ashmawi's estate, were fabricated by the regime to defame the organization and to acquire the necessary evidence to dissolve it. Al-Ashmawi continued to claim that he had helped Nasser move and hide these illegally held weapons in January 1952 following the notorious Cairo Fire on January 26, 1952 (Al-Ashmawi 1985: 30; al-Ashmawi 1977: 19–22: 53; Shadi 1987: 207).

60 FO 371-108319, JE 1016/9, No. 13, Stevenson from Cairo to Foreign Office, January 19, 1954.

61 FO 371-108319, JE 1016/7, No. 11, Stevenson addressed to Foreign Office, January 18, 1954.

62 Most Brothers, including al-Hudaybi, were released on March 25 (Moussalli 1992: 34).

63 Abdel Halim 2013, III: 298, 322–4.

64 Al-Qaradwi 2004: 55.

65 Abdel Rauf 1988: 91, 99.

66 Ibid.: 103; Shadi recalls likewise that he together with more than fifty officers in the police had retired before the January arrests (1987: 350).

67 Abdel Rauf 1988: 103–5.

68 Ibid.: 103–5, 145, 148–9, 156.

69 Ibid.: 163–5.

70 Not all Brothers, however, adopted such an approach. Farid Abdel Khaleq, a close associate of al-Hudaybi, claims that the *Murshid* had instructed the Brothers "not to apply violence against the existing regime." Al-Hudaybi, Abdel Khaleq contends, envisioned a mass demonstration to protest against the autocratic nature of the regime, echoing the pro-democracy demonstrations of February 1954. Abdel Khaleq 1987: 106; Abdel Khaleq 2004, XII https://bit.ly/3ePTqGW (accessed July 22, 2020); Shadi 1987: 337.

71 For a similar version, see Duh 1989: 69, 78, 83.

72 Abdel Rauf 1988: 182–4.

73 NA 1954, I: 34, 40–2.

74 Adel Kamal 1989: 360–1.
75 al-Hudaybi, cited in Ahmad 1977: 178–9.
76 Mitchell 1993: 135.
77 Frampton 2018: 242.
78 Abul Nasr 1988: 125–6.
79 NA 1954, III: 622–30; Mitchell 1993: 135.
80 NA 1954, III: 627.
81 Abul Nasr 1988: 108.
82 NA 1954, III: 668.
83 These pamphlets were issued as a reaction to the restrictions imposed by the government on the Brotherhood's weekly newspaper (NA 1954, IV: 726).
84 Mitchell 1993: 136.
85 Al-Khalidi 1994: 323; NA 1954, III: 629; Toth 2013: 79.
86 Abul Nasr 1988: 127–9. For Brotherhood criticism of Nasser from Damascus, see also FO 371/110840, V1781/7, 17806/8/54, British Embassy Damascus, September 15, 1954.
87 Frampton 2018: 244.
88 FO 371/108319, JE 1016/13, No. 187, Ralph Stevenson, from Cairo to Foreign Office, August 30, 1954; for Duh's account on the incident, see Duh 1983: 71.
89 FO 371/108319, JE 1016/14, No. 198, R. Stevenson, from Cairo to Foreign Office, September 14, 1954.
90 Al-Ashmawi 1977: 60.
91 Ibid.: 63.
92 FO 371/108319, JE 1016/14, No. 198, Ralph Stevenson, from Cairo to Foreign Office, September 14, 1954.
93 Mitchell 1993: 142.
94 Al-Ashmawi 1977: 66.
95 NA 1954, VI: 1302.
96 Cf. Al-Hajj 1993: 116–17; Abdel Rauf 1988: 193–4; al-Sisi 1987: 76.
97 Cf. Gerges 2018; Kepel 2014.
98 FO 371/108319, JE 1016/14, No. 198, R. Stevenson, from Cairo to Foreign Office, September 14, 1954.

Chapter 5

1 WO 208/3965, Canal Zone Local Intelligence Committee, ISUM 11/54, covering the period October 28 to November 10, 1954.
2 Among these authors were, for example, Taha Hussain and Ali Amin.
3 Taha Hussain cited in Mesbar 2014: 15–16.

4 Ali Amin cited in Mesbar 2014: 30–1.

5 Mitchell 1993: 152.

6 Ali Amin cited in Mesbar 2014: 34.

7 Cf. Taha Hussain, cited in Mesbar 2014: 23; Mitchell 1993: 152.

8 NA 1954, I-VI; Gordon 1992: 179–82; Frampton 2018: 248.

9 NA 1954, I: 154, II: 461.

10 As an example, upon encouraging the audience to give its judgment of Ibrahim al-Tayyib, one of the attendees asked the court to "blow him up with a mine" (NA 1954, II: 467).

11 Mitchell 1993: 156.

12 FO 371/108319, JE 1016/24, No. 226, (1012/126/54) Murray, British Embassy Cairo, December 11, 1954; other authors offer conflicting dates for the execution; Mitchell and John Calvert date it to December 9 (1993: 161, 2010: 194), while James Toth puts it on December 4 (2013: 79).

13 Those hanged were Mahmoud Abdel Latif (the would-be assassin), Yusuf Talʿat (head of the Special Apparatus), Ibrahim al-Tayyib (head of the Apparatus in Cairo), Hindawi Diwayr (head of the Apparatus in Imbaba), Abdel Qader Uda (a member of the guidance office), and Shaykh Muhammad Farghali (head of the Brotherhood in Ismailiyya).

14 Harris 1964: 222; Mitchell 1993: 160–2.

15 Harris 1964: 235.

16 Ibid.: 235, 224.

17 Mitchell 1993: 331, xxiv, xxv.

18 Kepel 2014: 30.

19 FCO 39/970, File no. NA U 1/11, British Embassy Tel Aviv, May 25, 1971. It is important to note that Sadat was never officially a member of the *Ikhwan*.

20 Ibid.

21 FCO 39/970, File no. NA U 1/11, 1/1, "Muslim Brotherhood," R. A Beaumont, British Embassy Cairo, June 11, 1971.

22 Ibid.

23 FCO 39/970, File no. NA U 1/11, (1/8) P. Joy, "Release of Muslim Brethren in U.A.R.," June 24, 1971. The A.S.U. was the official political party founded in 1962 by Nasser as the country's single party; it remained functioning until 1978.

24 Weismann 2017: 42.

25 FO 371/108319, JE 1016/24, No. 226, (1012/126/54) Murray, British Embassy Cairo, December 11, 1954; for the last words of the Brotherhood members, see Mitchell 1993: 161; Abu al-Fadl 2012: 89; al-Qaradawi 2004: 122.

26 Mitchell 1993: 161.

27 The Syrian Brotherhood mobilized for example popular protests against the repression (Sharaf 2015, IV: 998).

28 Mitchell 1993: 161.

29 The fragmentation of the Brotherhood was discussed in Chapters 3 and 4.

30 Toth 2013: 79; Zollner 2011: 38; in July 1955, the "Free Egypt Committee" announced that 50,000 political prisoners were in jail in Egypt; FO 371/125415, JE 1015/135, 16821/2/57, British Embassy Washington DC, April 9, 1957. Pamphlet title "A record of Tyranny, Corruption and Mediocrity, Memorandum Submitted to the U.S. Government by the Committee for Free Egypt, Beirut, July 5, 1955."

31 Al-Sarwi 2006: 72; Duh 1989: 85; al-Sisi 2003: 499; see also in a pamphlet directed to President Dwight D. Eisenhower in July 1955, mentioning that the incarcerated members of the Brotherhood were 20,000 (FO 371/125415, JE 1015/135, 16821/2/57, British Embassy Washington DC, April 9, 1957).

32 Al-Sisi 2003: 484.

33 Abul Nasr 1988: 144–8.

34 Cf. Duh 1983: 76; Abu al-Fadl 2012: 71; al-Tilmisani 1985: 133; Abdel Halim 2013, III: 441; Ahmad al-Assal cited in Rizq 1991: 109; Saleh and Dessouqi 2009: 254; al-Sisi 2003: 472; al-Sarwi 2006: 72.

35 FO 371/125415, JE 1015/135, 16821/2/57, British Embassy Washington DC, April 9, 1957. Pamphlet title "A record of Tyranny, Corruption and Mediocrity, Memorandum Submitted to the U.S. Government by the Committee for Free Egypt, Beirut, July 5, 1955." See also Rizq 1978: 29; Duh 1989: 82–5; Abul Nasr 1988: 149; al-Sarwi 2006: 71–2; al-Sisi 2003: 572. WO 208/3965, Canal Zone Local Intelligence Committee, ISUM [Intelligence Summary] No. 7/54—1454, vol. IX, ISUM 12/54, "Covering the Period 11th November to 24 November 1954."

36 Abdel Khaleq 1987: 107; Al-Qaradawi 2004: 115–17; Abu al-Fadl 2012: 85; al-Sisi 2003: 484; Al-Sarwi argues that the number was as high as nearer to 100 (2006: 71).

37 It is important here to highlight that prisoners with diverging political convictions witnessed similar treatment. For an account from non-Brotherhood prisoners, see FO 371/125423, JE 1019/1 Middle East Mirror "US Plot against Nasser Regime," August 18, 1957.

38 Al-Qaradawi 2004: 111; al-Tilmisani 1985: 112; al-Sisi 2003: 507; Abdel Halim 2013, III: 445. This song was composed following the Manshiyya incident and performed on various occasions by Um Kalthoum, Egypt's most celebrated female singer.

39 Al-Sisi 2003: 484–5.

40 Duh 1989: 84; Abdel Halim 2013, III: 445; Abul Nasr 1988: 150–4; al-Sisi 2003: 485; for the picture see https://bit.ly/34RQYMM.

41 Akef 2008 III: https://bit.ly/3bvmsup (accessed April 22, 2020); al-Tilmisani 1985: 141, 143.

42 Al-Qaradawi 2004: 111.

43 Al-Sisi 2003: 485.

44 FO 371/125423, JE 1019/1 Middle East Mirror "US Plot against Nasser Regime," August 18, 1957.
45 WO 208/3965, Canal Zone Local Intelligence Committee, ISUM [Intelligence Summary] No. 7/54—1454, vol. IX, ISUM 12/54, "Covering the Period 11th November to 24 November 1954."
46 Built by the British in 1886 in the Tura district just south of Cairo.
47 Al-Sarwi 2006: 81–3; WO 208/3965, Canal Zone Local Intelligence Committee, ISUM [Intelligence Summary] No. 7/54—1454, vol. IX, ISUM 12/54, "Covering the Period 11th November to 24 November 1954."
48 Al-Sisi 2003: 577; Al-Sarwi 2006: 81.
49 Al-Shawi 1998: 200.
50 Abul Nasr 1988: 160; Al-Sarwi 2006: 83.
51 For his account of life in prison, see Akef 2008; Akef (2018) XIX: https://bit.ly/2Un3b7W (accessed June 9, 2020). For Akef's sentence, see FO 371/108319, JE 1016/23, No. 263, Mr. Murray, addressed to Foreign Office, December 15, 1954.
52 Destiny would have it that the "prisoner of all eras" would die in confinement during Abdel Fattah al-Sisi's reign in 2017. At the age of eighty-nine, Akef had been behind bars since 2013 upon al-Sisi's military coup of 2013.
53 See Akef 2008 II: https://bit.ly/3eJVT6C (accessed April 22, 2020); III: https://bit.ly/3bvmsup (accessed April 22, 2020).
54 Akef 2018 XVII: https://bit.ly/2XLPZf6 (accessed June 9, 2020).
55 Akef 2008 III: https://bit.ly/3bvmsup (accessed April 22, 2020).
56 Ibid; see also Hammuda 1985: 115; also al-Sisi 2003: 568–9.
57 Akef 2018 XVII: https://bit.ly/2XLPZf6 (accessed June 9, 2020).
58 Khafaji 2006: 191.
59 Saleh and Dessouqi 2009: 254–6.
60 For similar accounts, see al-Sisi 2003: 580; Duh 1983: 84–6; Abdel Halim 2013, III: 489.
61 Akef 2008 II: https://bit.ly/3eJVT6C and III: https://bit.ly/3bvmsup (accessed April 22, 2020).
62 Al-Khalidi 1994: 369.
63 Al-Khalidi 1994: 361. For a list of his prison-authored books, see al-Khalidi 1994: 367.
64 Khafaji 2006: 203; al-Khalidi 1994: 365–7.
65 Al-Bess 1987: 54.
66 Ibid.: 54–5.
67 Ibid.; al-Sisi 2003: 570; Abul Nasr 1988: 159–60.
68 Akef (2018) XIX: https://bit.ly/2Un3b7W (accessed June 9, 2020); see also Sadiq 1987: 96.
69 Muhammad and Mashhur 2005: 34–5.

70 Ibid.: 49.
71 Al-Qaradawi 2004: 111.
72 Saleh and Dessouqi 2009: 250, 254; Abu al-Fadl 2012: 72–4.
73 Zollner 2011: 39.
74 Abu al-Fadl 2012: 74.
75 Al-Sisi 2003: 536.
76 Al-Tilmisani 1985: 112.
77 Hammuda 1985: 114–15.
78 Raif 1990: 39.
79 Eisenhower 1965: 33.
80 Cf. Rogan 2009; Mansfield 1971.
81 Cf. Hammuda 1985: 118–22; al-Bess 1987: 82–3.
82 Duh 1989: 96.
83 Al-Bess 1987: 83–5.
84 Akef 2008 III: https://bit.ly/3bvmsup (accessed April 22, 2020); Muhammad and Mashhur 2005: 37.
85 These groups should not be understood as static, as we observe a high degree of flexibility in moving one way or the other under different circumstances. As an example, Umar al-Tilmisani, who was a strong proponent of accommodation prior to the October repression, subsequently came to strongly reject any recognition of the regime and remained in prison for more than twenty years.
86 Husaini 1956: 153.
87 Frampton 2018: 260.
88 Abul Nasr 1988: 161–2.
89 Sharaf 2015, IV: 999.
90 Hammuda 1985: 121.
91 Gordon 1992: 197.
92 Al-Tilmisani, cited in Qaud 19875: 133; Rizq 1979: 51.
93 Adel Kamal 1989: 435; Abul Fadl 2012: 89–91.
94 Cf. Kedourie 1980: 58.
95 Rodinson 1968: 108.
96 For contemporary reports on the Brotherhood's continuing activities cf., CIA-RDP91T01172R000300170001-1, "Nasr Regime Alienating Egyptian Masses," December 16, 1954; FO 371/113579, JE 1015/27, "Mr. Shuckburgh's Conversation with Nuri el Said on June 11," T. E. Bromley, June 16, 1955.
97 Al-Sarwi 2004: 90.
98 These different organizational structures and groups that I discuss in this section were all part of the Brotherhood organization. However, established by young men in different parts of Egypt, they were not always aware of each other's existence, due to the restraints under which they were operating. Having as their main goal

to revive their *Ikhwani* bonds, resuming the Brotherhood organization, supporting Brothers in need, and opposing the regime, these different organizational structures were all established under the banner of the Muslim Brotherhood.

99 Khafaji 2006: 133.

100 CIA-RDP91T01172R000300170001-1, "Nasr Regime Alienating Egyptian Masses," December 16, 1954.

101 Khafaji 2006: 133; Al-Sisi 2003: 587; Frampton 2018: 258.

102 Al-Sarwi 2004: 89; al-Sisi 2003: 587; Khafaji 2006: 132, 147.

103 Al-Sarwi 2004: 92–6 (see list of those arrested with names, ages, and professions).

104 Ashmawi 1993: 35–40.

105 Abul Fadl 2012: 99.

106 Ibid.: 96.

107 Khafaji 2006: 145–6; al-Sarwi 2004: 97–9.

108 Ashmawi 1993: 40–1.

109 Cited in Frampton 2018: 258.

110 CIA-RDP79R01012A005700050001-5, National Intelligence Estimate, Number 36: 1–55, "The Outlook for Egyptian stability and foreign policy," November 15, 1955.

111 Ibid.

112 WO 208/3965, Canal Zone Local Intelligence Committee, ISUM [Intelligence Summary] No. 7/54—1454, vol. IX, ISUM 12/54, "Covering the Period 11th November to 24 November 1954."

113 Ibid.

114 Ibid.

115 Ibid.

116 Frampton 2018: 263: See also Memorandum of a Conversation, Department of State, Washington, June 23, 1955; CIA-RDP79R01012A005700050001-5, National Intelligence Estimate, Number 36: 1–55, "The Outlook for Egyptian Stability and Foreign Policy," November 15, 1955.

117 Cited in Frampton 2018: 259.

118 Ibid.: 262.

119 Department of State, Central Files, 641.74/3–756, 175. Telegram from the Embassy in the UK to the Department of State, London, March 7, 1956.

120 Ibid.

121 Harris 1964: 236; for a contemporary report on the Brotherhood activities from outside Egypt cf., FO 371/125444, JE 1052/20, J. H. A. Watson July 9, 1957, attached brief "Egypt."

122 CIA-RDP78-02771R000500030002-9, "EGYPT'S ROLE IN THE MUSLIM WORLD," March 9, 1956.

123 Aburish 2004: 83–4; Sharaf 2015, IV: 998.

124 I am not arguing that Egypt became a democratic republic at this point. My contention, however, is that a façade of liberalization was attempted, so as to present Egypt as an inclusionary state.
125 Sharaf 2015, IV: 996.
126 Gordon 1992: 189.
127 Abdel Halim 2013, III: 495.
128 Al-Sisi 2003: 589–95.
129 Al-Sisi 2003: 594.
130 Abdel Halim 2013, III: 493–5.
131 Ibid.: 495–7.
132 Ibid.: 497.
133 Ibid.
134 Al-Sisi 2003: 598.
135 Ibid.: 598–600.
136 Mustafa (n.d.) https://bit.ly/3iaT01J (accessed March 16, 2021).
137 Nada and Thompson 2012: 3.
138 Ibid.: 17–25.
139 Nada and Thompson 2012: 25; al-Sisi 2003: 600.
140 Al-Sisi 2003: 600.
141 Nada and Thompson 2012: 25–7.
142 Nada and Thompson 2012: 25–6.
143 Adel Kamal 1989: 441.
144 Ikhwan-Wiki (n.d.), *Ahmad Abdel Majid*, https://bit.ly/2SF7xGE (accessed May 7, 2020).
145 Abdel Majid 1991: 43.
146 Jawhar 1977: 49–50; Ashmawi 1993: 47; Abdel Majid 1991: 45.
147 Abdel Khaleq 2004, XIV: https://bit.ly/30PVf1F (accessed July 22, 2020).
148 al-Sisi 2003: 598, 606–13.
149 Ikhwan-Wiki, *Hilal* (n.d.), https://bit.ly/35ZyyyE (accessed March 17, 2021).
150 Ibid.; see also Sharaf 2015, IV: 1000.
151 FO 371/125416, JE 1015/155 G, A, "Some developments in the internal situation in Egypt and Nasser's position," Foreign office, December 30, 1956.
152 FO 371/125416, JE 1015/155 G, "Reports since January 7 on the internal position in Egypt," Watson, January 15, 1957.
153 CIA-RDP79R01012A009800030005-8, National Intelligence Estimate, Number 36.1–57, Supersedes NIE 36.1-55, The Outlook for Egypt and the Nasser Regime, November 12, 1957.
154 FO 371/125416, JE 1015/155 G, "Egypt: Internal political situation, reports received up to June 24," 1957.
155 Ibid.
156 FO 371/125444, JE 1052/20, J. H. A. Watson July 9, 1957, attached brief "Egypt."

Chapter 6

1 Hawwash (1922–66), a working-class Brother who was Qutb's prison companion for the better part of the latter's ten-year imprisonment and who was strongly affected by Qutb's worldview. He was released in 1964, shortly after Qutb. Hawwash was accused of being the second-in-command of the organization, which is why he was sentenced to death together with six others and hanged alongside Qutb and Ismail. His wife, Fatima Abdel Hadi, a female activist of the Brotherhood, argues that Hawwash did not play a key role in the organization but was hanged on account of his ideas, which corresponded with Qutb's (Abdel Hadi 2011: 46, 51).

2 Ikhwan-Wiki, *Hawwash* (n.d.), https://bit.ly/3CPBeL0 (accessed March 18, 2021)

3 Al-Sisi 2003: 737.

4 Zollner 2011: 39 (italics in original).

5 Cf, Abed-Kotob 1995, 334; Kepel 1985, 26–38; Sivan 1990, 83–94; 117–29.

6 CIA-RDP79-00927A001300030001-6, Current Intelligence Weekly Summary, June 13, 1957; Abul Fadl 2012: 101.

7 Al-Sisi 2003: 605. For a list of the Brotherhood inmates in Tura at the time of the Massacre and the names of the victims, see Rizq 1979: 159–71.

8 Atiya Muhammad Aql cited in Rizq 1979: 63.

9 Abdel Khaleq 2004, XIV: https://bit.ly/30PVf1F (accessed July 22, 2020).

10 Al-Sisi 2003: 605–6.

11 Abdel Majid 1991: 43–5.

12 Ibid.: 46.

13 Ibid.

14 Ibid.: 46–8.

15 Ibid. See also Allam 1996: 119–20. (Fuad Allam, then an intelligence officer, substantiates this account, arguing that such activities took place in several provinces.)

16 Al-Sarwi 2004: 127.

17 Ibid.: 101–2.

18 Ibid.: 103.

19 Ikhwan-Wiki *Sharif* (n.d.), https://bit.ly/37XeXj8 (accessed March 24, 2021).

20 Cf, al-Sarwi 2004: 104; Mubarak 2017, https://bit.ly/2UAcxNJ (accessed June 11, 2020); al-Ghazali 1994: 33.

21 Ikhwan-Wiki *Awad Abdel ʿAl*, https://bit.ly/3Niy1sg (accessed March 24, 2021).

22 Al-Sarwi 2004: 105.

23 Ibid.: 102.

24 For a list of these organizations, see ibid.: 105–12.

25 Mamduh (n.d.), https://bit.ly/3IHKkuy (accessed March 25, 2021); Al-Sarwi 2004: 107.

26 Al-Sisi 2003: 609.

27 Al-Ghazali (1917–2005) was born in Beheira to a religious family. Her father was an Azhari scholar who died before she turned eleven. In 1934, al-Ghazali became a disciple of Huda Shaʿrawi and joined the latter's "Egyptian Feminist Union," formed along European lines. However, in 1935, the young Zainab took a different path when she devoted her life to Islamic activism, and in 1936 she founded the Society of Muslim Women. In 1948, she joined the Muslim Brotherhood, and in 1951, she married the *Ikhwani* businessman Muhammad Salem (see al-Ghazali 2012).

28 Mubarak 2017, https://bit.ly/2UAcxNJ (accessed June 11, 2020); Al-Ghazali 1994: 33.

29 Al-Ghazali 1994: 34–5.

30 According to her own memoirs, she had pledged allegiance to Hasan al-Banna in 1948 (al-Ghazali 1994: 27).

31 Al-Sarwi 2004: 18–19.

32 Mentioned in Chapter 3 for her ventures during the first dissolution of the *Ikhwan* in late 1948.

33 Al-Ghazali 1994: 32.

34 Ibid; Ikhwan-Wiki, ed. (n.d.), *Amal al-Ashmawi*, https://bit.ly/3awFCAf (accessed January 20, 2020); Abdel Hadi 2011: 55–65; al-Sarwi 2004: 149.

35 Al-Ghazali 1994: 35.

36 Abdel Khaleq 2004, XIV: https://bit.ly/30PVf1F (accessed July 22, 2020); Abdel Khaleq 1987: 113.

37 Ibid.: 65; al-Tuni 1975: 287–8.

38 Badiʿ (n.d.), https://bit.ly/2AnSJpP (accessed May 12, 2020).

39 Egypt arrests Muslim Brotherhood's top leader (2013) https://bit.ly/3KaPDo7 (accessed April 5, 2021).

40 Simmel 1906: 473.

41 Al-Ashmawi 1993: 47.

42 Al-Sarwi 2004: 18–19, 134, 160–3; for a similar story, see Afifi 2013, https://bit.ly/2WnjdjA (accessed May 11, 2020).

43 Ikhwan-Wiki (n.d.), *Mahmoud Izzat*, https://bit.ly/2xSlFoV (accessed May 11, 2020).

44 Rizq 1978: 47; al-Sarwi 2004: 134; Ashmawi 1993: 100.

45 Al-Arusi 1995: 252.

46 Ghusheh 2013: 53–54.

47 Ibid.

48 Ashmawi 1993: 49.

49 Abdel Majid 1991: 49–51.

50 Ashmawi 1993: 53, 56; Abdel Majid 1991: 49–50, see also Abdel Khaleq 2004, XIV: https://bit.ly/30PVf1F (accessed July 22, 2020). Zainab al-Ghazali, a close associate

of Ismail objects to this account. According to her story, Ismail's and her intentions were utterly educational "to create the Muslim society" and revenge was not part of their aims (Al-Ghazali 2012: 66).

51 Abdel Majid 1991: 50–2, 60.
52 Ashmawi 1993: 54; al-Ghazali 2012: 160.
53 Abdel Majid 1991: 52.
54 Ibid.; Ashmawi 1993: 58.
55 Abdel Majid 1991: 52, 58.
56 Ashmawi 1993: 54; Abdel Majid 1991: 59; al-Ghazali 2012: 160.
57 Al-Sarwi 2004: 145–6.
58 Abdel Majid 1991: 61–2, al-Sarwi 2004: 146; Ashmawi 1993: 57.
59 Abdel Majid 1991: 61; Ashmawi 1993: 57.
60 Ashmawi 1993: 54.
61 Ibid.: 65.
62 Ibid.: 54; Abdel Majid 1991: 58; al-Ghazali 2012: 160.
63 Abdel Majid 1991: 68; Ashmawi 1993: 58–64.
64 Adel Majid 1991: 68; Ashmawi 1993: 66.
65 Ashmawi 1993: 58–66; Abdel Khaleq 2004, XIV: https://bit.ly/30PVf1F (accessed July 22, 2020).
66 Gerges 2018: 243.
67 Raif 1986: 239; al-Khalidi 1994: 377.
68 Jawhar 1977: 49.
69 Al-Sarwi 2004: 150.
70 In addition to those two, the opposing group comprised Salah Shadi, Abdel Qader Hilmi, and Saleh Abu Ruqayiq, all of whom had been close associates prior to the repression of the *Ikhwan*. This group was also bound together by family relations.
71 Abdel Khaleq 2004, XIV: https://bit.ly/30PVf1F (accessed July 22, 2020).
72 Al-Khalidi 1994: 375.
73 Abdel Majid 1991: 71; Ashmawi 1993, 70.
74 Abdel Khaleq 2004: XIV: https://bit.ly/30PVf1F (accessed July 22, 2020).
75 Ibid.
76 Abdel Majid 1991: 71, 72; Raif 1986: 239, Abdel Majid quotes al-Hudaybi as telling the opposing faction "let the young men who want to work and attain martyrdom be, these are people who want to attain martyrdom, so let them attain it."
77 Ashmawi 1993: 68; al-Sarwi 2004: 150–1; Abdel Majid 1991: 54.
78 Abdel Majid 1991: 53; Ashmawi 1993: 68–9; al-Arusi 1995: 94.
79 Al-Khalidi 1994: 361, 372–3; Qutb 2007: 92; Calvert 2010: 202.
80 Qutb 2007: 85.
81 Ibid.: 88.
82 Qutb 2007: 87–92.
83 Al-Khalidi 1994: 372–3; Calvert 2010: 236.

84 Abdel Majid 1991: 70.
85 Abdel Majid 1991: 69–70.
86 Qutb, 2007: 98; Al-Arusi 1995: 99; Abdel Majid 1994: 69–70.
87 Qutb 2007: 100.
88 Abdel Majid 1991: 73.
89 Ibid.: 75–7.
90 Qutb 2007: 92–3, 95; Abdel Majid 1991: 82–6.
91 Al-Arusi 1995: 98.
92 Qutb 2007: 97–8.
93 Ibid.: 85–8, 96–7.
94 Ibid.: 96.
95 Qutb 2007: 101; Al-Arusi 1995: 99–101.
96 Qutb 2007: 87, 104.
97 Ibid.: 87.
98 Ibid.: 87, 104; Quran, 2: 194; see also Ashmawi 1993: 99.
99 Al-Arusi 1995: 101.
100 Qutb 2007: 104.
101 Qutb 2007: 129.
102 Ibid.: 104.
103 Ibid.: 104–5, 129.
104 The Central Treaty Organization was founded in 1955 and included the UK, Pakistan, Turkey, and Iran until 1979.
105 FO 371/183884, VG 1015/21, No. 55, Mr. Wilton, from Cairo to Foreign Office, September 10, 1965.
106 FO 371/183884, VG 1015/21, No. 58, from Cairo to Foreign Office, September 10, 1965.
107 Lajnat Kutub Qawmiya 1965: 4.
108 FO 371/183884, VG 1015/21, No. 58, from Cairo to Foreign Office, September 10, 1965.
109 FO 371/183884, VG 1015/38, D. J. Speares, December 1, 1965.
110 FO 371/190189, VG 1015/89, "The Trials of the Moslem Brothers in the U.A.R., 1965–6." 1967 (n.d.); see also FO 371/190187, 1015/51, (1016/66) Canadian Embassy, British Interests Section, Cairo, September 8, 1966.
111 See e.g. FO 371/157387, E 1015/9, MA/549/166, October 26, 1961.
112 El-Sadat 1978: 49, 165.
113 Allam 1996: 128; Sharaf 2015, IV: 1001.
114 For such a judgement, see FO 371/190188, VG 1015/53, "UAR: Internal Situation," September 8, 1966.
115 371/183884, VG 1015/21, No. 55, Mr. Wilton, from Cairo to Foreign Office, September 10, 1965.

116 Rizq 1978: 38, 48–9.
117 See e.g. Abdel Majid 1991: 127.
118 Rizq 1978: 43, Rizq mentions five names of young men who died under torture. See also FO 371/190189, VG 1015/89, "The Trials of the Moslem Brothers in the U.A.R., 1965–6," 1967 (n.d.).
119 CIA-RDP79T00826A003200180001-1, Current Intelligence Country Handbook, United Arab Republic (Egypt), OCI No. 1925/66, August 1966.
120 FO 371/183884, VG 1015/20, (1011/65) British Embassy Cairo, September 1, 1965; FO 371/190189, VG 1015/89, "The Trials of the Moslem Brothers in the U.A.R., 1965–6," 1967 (n.d.); Sharaf 2015, IV: 1000 (Sharaf claims that 5,000 members were arrested).
121 Allam 1996: 133; for a list of all verdicts see al-Sarwi 2004: 330–7.
122 Abdel Majid 1991: 201; Al-Arusi 1995: 233–41.
123 Abdel Majid 1991: 201; see also FO 371/190189, VG 1015/89, "The Trials of the Moslem Brothers in the U.A.R., 1965–6," 1967 (n.d.).
124 FO 371/190187, VG 1015/45, P. W. Unwin, August 31, 1966.
125 Abdel Majid 1991.
126 Jawhar 1977: 196–9; Calvert 2010: 262–3; Rizq 1978: 145–6.
127 Rizq 1978: 146.
128 Qutb 2007: 73.

Conclusion

1 FCO 17/224, "Recent Muslim Brotherhood Activity in the United Arab Republic" (n.d.) 1968.
2 CIA-RDP79R00967A000800010010-2, No. 8–68, "Special Memorandum, Nasser's Limited Options," April 15, 1968.
3 CIA, Special National Intelligence Estimate No. 36.1–67, "The Situation and Prospects in Egypt," August 17, 1967.
4 FCO 17/224, "Recent Muslim Brotherhood Activity in the United Arab Republic" (n.d.) 1968.
5 Ibid.
6 Al-Anani 2016: 87–8, 105–6.
7 Jung 2018: 225. See chapter two.
8 Zollner 2011: 16.
9 Al-Anani 2016: 110.
10 Abdel Halim 2013, I: 288.
11 NA 1954, I: 93–4.
12 Cited in al-Sisi 1981: 278–9.

13 FO 371/90115, JE 10110/15, 1019/27/51, No. 167, British Embassy, Cairo, May 2 1951.
14 Kepel 2014: 30; Willi 2021: 9; Weber 2013: 517; Mitchell 1993: xxv; Harris 1964: 235.
15 Ashmawi 1993; Al-Sarwi 2004; Abdel Majid 1991.
16 Cf. Willis 2021.
17 Qutb 2007: 97.
18 Ibid.: 99, 100; Ashmawi 1993: 77.
19 Qutb 2006: 139–40.

Bibliography

Abdel Aziz, Jumʿah Amin (2004), *Awrāq men Tārīkh al-Ikhwan al-Muslimin, Marḥalat al-Takwīn, al-Binā' al-Dākhilī 1938–1943* (Pages of the Muslim Brotherhood's history, the phase of construction, the inner structuring 1938–1943). Cairo: Dār al-Tawzīʿ wal-Nashr al-Islāmiya.

Abdel Aziz, Jumʿah Amin (2006a), *Awrāq men Tārīkh al-Ikhwan al-Muslimin, Marḥalat al-Takwīn, Istikmāl al-Binā' al-Dākhilī 1943–1945* (Pages of the Muslim Brotherhood's history, the phase of construction, the realization of the inner structuring 1943–1945). Cairo: Dār al-Tawzīʿ wal-Nashr al-Islāmiya.

Abdel Aziz, Jumʿah Amin (2006b), *Men turāth al-Imam al-Banna, Qaḍāyā al-ʿālam al-Islāmī* (From the tradition of the Imam al-Banna, the causes of the Islamic world) Cairo: Dār al-Tawzīʿ wal-Nashr al-Islāmiya.

Abdel Aziz, Jumʿah Amin (2006c), *Men turāth al-Imam al-Banna, Maqālāt Ḥawla al-Qaḍiya al-Filisṭīniya* (From the Tradition of the Imam al-Banna, articles on the Palestine case). Cairo: Dār al-Tawzīʿ wal-Nashr al-Islāmiya.

Abdel Hadi, Fatima (2011), *Riḥlatī maʿ al-Akhawāt al-Muslimāt, min al-Imām al-Banna ilā Sujūn Abdel Nasser* (My journey with the Muslim Sisters, from the Imam al-Banna to the prisons of Abdel Nasser). Cairo: Dār al-Shurūq.

Abdel Halim, Mahmoud (2013), *Al-Ikhwan al-Muslimin, Aḥdāth Ṣanaʿat ul-Tārikh, Ruʾyā men al-Dākhel* (The Muslim Brotherhood, Events that shaped the history, a view from inside) (vol. I–III). Alexandria: Dār al-Daʾwa.

Abdel Khaleq, Farid (1987), *Al-Ikhwan al-Muslimun fī Mīzān al-Ḥaq* (The Muslim Brotherhood in the righteous balance). Cairo: Dār al-Sahwā Lil-Nashr wal-Tawzīʿ.

Abdel Majid, Ahmad (1991), *al-Ikhwan wa Abdel Nasser, al-Qiṣah al-Kāmilah li-Tanẓīm 1965* (The Brotherhood and Abdel Nasser, the full story of the 1965 organization). Cairo: al-Zahrāʾ lil-ʾiʿlām al-ʿarabī.

Abdel Nasser, Gamal (1955), *Philosophy of Revolution*. Cairo: Mondiale Press.

Abdel Rahim, Muhammad Said (1989), *Rijal al-Da'wa al-Islamiyya al-Muʿāsirūn, Umar al-Tilmisani al-Murshid al-Thaleth lil-Ikhwan al-Muslimin* (Contemporary men of the Islamic call, Umar al-Tilmisani the third guide of the Muslim Brotherhood). Cairo: Dār al-Ḍiyāʾ.

Abdel Rauf, Abdel Munʿim (1988), *Arghamtu Farouq ʿala al-Tanāzul ʿan al-ʿarsh, Mudhakirāt Abdel Munʿim Abdel Rauf* (I forced Farouq to abdicate from the throne, the memoirs of Abdel Munʿim Abdel Rauf). Cairo: al-Zahrāʾ lil-ʾiʿlām al-ʿarabī.

Abed-Kotob, Sana (1995), "The Accommodationists Speak: Goals and Strategies of the Muslim Brotherhood of Egypt," *International Journal of Middle East Studies* 27, no. 3: 321–39.

Abou El Zalaf, Ahmed (2022), "The Special Apparatus (al-Niẓām al-Khāṣṣ): The Rise of Nationalist Militancy in the Ranks of the Egyptian Muslim Brotherhood," *Religions* 13, no. 1: 77.

Abu Al-fadl, Medhat (2012), *Qissatī ma' al-Jama'ah wa-Qisatuhum ma' al-'Askar* (My story with the group/movement, and their story with the military). Cairo: Maktabat al-Shorūq al-Duwaliya.

Abul Nasr, Muhammad Hamed (1988), *Ḥaqīqat al-Khilāf Bayna al-Ikhwan al-Muslimun wa Abdel Nasser* (The truth behind the dispute between the Muslim Brotherhood and Abdel Nasser). Cairo: Dār al-Tawzīʿ wal-Nashr al-Islāmiyya.

Aburish, Said K (2004), *Nasser: The Last Arab*. London: Duckworth Books.

Adel Kamal, Ahmad (1989), *Al-Nuqāt Fawq al-Ḥurūf, al-Ikhwan al-Muslimun wal-Tanẓīm al-Sirī* (The Dots above the Letters, The Muslim Brotherhood and the Secret Organization). Cairo: al-Zahrāʾ lil-ʾiʿlām al-ʿarabī.

Ahmad, Asʿad Sayyid (1977), *Al-Islam wal-Dāʿiya, al-Imam al-Murshid Hasan Al-hudaybi* (Islam and the missionary, the Imam and Guide Hasan al-Hudaybi). Cairo: Dār al-Anṣār.

Al-Anani, Khalil (2016), *Inside the Muslim Brotherhood, Religion, Identity and Politics*. New York: Oxford University Press.

Al-Arian, Abdullah (2014), *Answering the Call, Popular Islamic Activism in Sadat's Egypt*. New York: Oxford University Press.

Al-Arusi, Mahmoud Kamil (1995), *Muḥākamat Sayyid Qutb, Wathīqat Muḥākamat al-Shaykh Sayyid Qutb wa-Rifāqahu fī al-Fatra men 1959–1965* (The court case against Sayyid Qutb, the document from the court case against Sayyid Qutb and his colleagues in the period between 1959 and 1965). Shibīn al-Qanāṭer: Maṭbaʿat al-Jumhūrriya al-Ḥadītha.

Al-Ashmawi, Hasan (1977), *al-Ikhwan wal-Thawra* (The Brotherhood and the revolution). Cairo: al-Maktab al-Maṣrī al-Ḥadīth.

Al-Ashmawi, Hasan (1985), *Al-Ayām al-Ḥāsima wa-Ḥaṣāḍuhā, Jāneb men Qiṣat al-* ʿAṣr (The decisive days and its harvest, from the story of the era). Beirut: Dār al-Fatḥ.

Al-Baghdadi, Abdel Latif (1977), *Mudhakirāt Abd al-Latif al-Baghdadi* (The memoirs of Abdel Latif al-Baghdadi), vol. I and II. Cairo: al-Maktab al-Miṣrī al-Ḥadīth.

Al-Bahi, Ahmad (2011), *Asad al-Qanāl, al-Shahīd Yusuf Talʿat* (The lion of the Canal, the Martyr Yusuf Talʿat). al-Ismailiyya: Smart Media.

Al-Banna, Hasan (2004), *Majmu'at rasāil al-imām al-shahīd Hasan al-Banna* (The collection of the tracts of the martyr Imam Hasan al-Banna). Beirut: Al-Islamiyyah.

Al-Banna, Hasan (2013), *Mudhakirāt al- Daʿwa wal-Dāʿiyya* (Memoirs of the mission and the missionary). Cairo: Dār al-kalimah.

Al-Banna, Jamal (2009), *Khiṭābāt Hasan al-Banna al-Shāb ilā Abīh* (Letters from the young Hasan al-Banna to his father). Cairo: Halā lil-Nashr wal-Tawzīʿ.

Al-Baqouri, Ahmad Hasan (1988), *Baqāyā Dhikrayāt* (Remnants of memories). Cairo: Markaz al-Ahrām.

Al-Bess, Ahmad (1987), *Al-Ikhwan al-Muslimun fi Rīf Maṣr* (The Muslim Brotherhood in rural Egypt). Cairo: Dār al-Tawzīʿ wal-Nashr al-Islāmiyya.

Al-Bishri, Tariq (2002), *al-Ḥaraka al-Siyāsiya fi Miṣr 1945–1953* (The political movement in Egypt 1945–1953). Cairo: Dār al-Shurūq.

Al-Firmawi, Kamal (1976), *Yawmiyāt fi al-Sijn al-Ḥarbi* (Diaries from the Military Prison). Cairo: Dār al-Thaqāfah.

Al-Ghazali, Zainab (1994), *Return of the Pharaoh, Memoir in Nasir's Prison*, trans. Mokrane Guezzou. Leicester: The Islamic Foundation.

Al-Ghazali, Zainab (2012), *Ayām min Ḥayātī* (Days from my life). Cairo: Kunūz.

Al-Ghazi, Issam (2008), *Umar al-Tilmisani, min al-Tango fi ʿimād al-Dīn ilā Zaʿāmat al-Ikhwan al-Muslimin* (Umar al-Tilmisani, from tango in Imad al-Din to the leadership of the Muslim Brotherhood). Cairo: Halā Lil-Nashr wal-Tawzīʿ.

Al-Hajj, Jaber (1993), *Zilzāl al-taʾāmur al-Nāsseri bil-Ikhwan al-Muslimun* (The earthquake of Nasserite conspiracy against the Muslim Brotherhood). Zagazig: Dār al-Arqam.

Al-Hajj, Jaber (1977), *Al-Farāʿina al-Ṣighār fi Hīltun al-Nāṣiriya* (The small Faraos in the Nasserite Hilton). Cairo: Dār al-Iʿtiṣām.

Al-Hajj, Jaber (1987), *Fashal Ḥarakat Yūlyū bi-ʿadāʾihā lil-Tayār al-Islāmī* (The failure of the July Movement, due to its enmity to the Islamic current). Cairo: Dār al-Iʿtiṣām.

Al-Hajj, Jaber (1995), *Dhikrayātī min Fasād al-Malakiya ilā Istibdād al-Naṣiriya* (My memoirs from the corruption of the monarchy to the despotism of Nasserism). Cairo: Dār al-Iʿtiṣām.

Al-Harani, al-Sayyid (2014), *Mudhakirāt Jamal al-Banna* (The memoirs of Jamal al-Banna). Cairo: Dār Iktib lil-Nashr wal-Tawzīʿ.

Al-Jamal, Hasan (2000), *Jihad al-Ikhwan al-Muslimin fī al-Qanāt wa-Filisṭīn, Riwāyat Shāhed ʿAyān* (The struggle of the Muslim Brotherhood in the Canal and in Palestine, an account of an eyewitness). Cairo: Dār al-Tawzīʿ wal-Nashr al-Islāmiyya.

Al-Khalidi, Salah Abdel Fattah (1994), *Sayyid Qutb, min al-Mīlād ilā al-Istishhād* (Sayyid Qutb, from his birth to his martyrdom). Damascus: Dār al-Qalam & Beirut: al-Dār al-Shāmiyya.

Al-Kilani, Naguib (2006), *Mudhakirāt al-Duktūr Naguib al-Kilani* (The Memoirs of Doctor Naguib al-Kilani). Cairo: Kitāb al-Mukhtār.

Allam, Fuad (1996), *al-Ikhwan wa-Anā, min al-Manshiyya ilā al-Manaṣa* (The Brotherhood and I, from al-Manshiyya to the Platform). Cairo: al-Maktab al-Maṣrī al-Ḥadīth.

al-Majles al-Aʿlā lil-Shuʾūn al-Islāmiya (1965), *Raʾī al-Dīn fī Ikhwan al-Shayṭān* (The religion's stance on the Brothers of the devil). Cairo: al-Majles al-Aʿlā lil-Shuʾūn al-Islāmiya.

Al-Qaradawi, Yusuf (2000), *Muhammad al-Ghazali kamā ʿareftuhu, riḥlat niṣf qarn* (Muhammad al-Ghazali as I knew him, a journey of a half century). Cairo: Dār al-Shurūq.

Al-Qaradawi, Yusuf (2002), *Ibn al-Qarya wal-Kutāb, Malāmeḥ Sīra wa-Masīra* (Son of the village and the traditional school, characteristics of a biography and a trajectory). Cairo: Dār al-Shurūq.

Al-Qaradawi, Yusuf (2004), *Ibn al-Qarya wal-Kutāb, Malāmeḥ Sīra wa-Masīra* (Son of the village and the traditional school, characteristics of a biography and a trajectory). Cairo: Dār al-Shurūq.

Al-Qaradawi, Yusuf (2006), *Ibn al-Qarya wal-Kutāb, Malāmeḥ Sīra wa-Masīra* (Son of the village and the traditional school, characteristics of a biography and a trajectory). Cairo: Dār al-Shurūq.

al-Sabbagh (1989), *Mahmoud, Ḥaqīqat al-Tanzīm al-Khāṣ, wa-Dawruhu fi Daʿwat al-Ikhwan al-Muslimin* (The truth about the Special Apparatus and its role in the mission of the Muslim Brotherhood). Cairo: Dār al-Iʿtiṣām.

Al-Sabbagh, Mahmoud (1998), *Al-Taṣwīb al-Amīn limā Nasharahu baʿḍ al-Qaḍa al-Sābiqīn ʿan al-Tanẓīm al-Sirī lil-Ikhwan al-Muslimin* (The honest correction of what some of the former leaders have published on the Secret Organization of the Muslim Brotherhood). Cairo: Maktab al-Turāth al-Islamī.

Al-Sadat, Anwar (1957), *Revolt on the Nile*. London: Allan Wingate. See also El-Sadat.

al-Sarwi, Muhammad (2004), *Al-Ikhwan al-Muslimun, Miḥnat 1965, al-Zilzāl wal-Ṣaḥwah* (The Muslim Brotherhood, the tribulation of 1965, the earthquake and the awakening). Cairo: Dār al-Tawzīʿ wal-Nashr al-Islāmiyya.

al-Sarwi, Muhammad (2006), *Al-Ikhwan al-Muslimun fi Sujūn Maṣr min ʿĀm 1942–1975* (The Muslim Brotherhood in Egypt's prisons from the year of 1942 to 1975). Cairo: Dār al-Tawzīʿ wal-Nashr al-Islāmiyya.

Al-Sawwaf, Muhammad Mahmoud (1987), *Min Sijil Dhikrayātī* (From the record of my memories). Cairo: Dār al-Iʿtiṣām.

Al-Sharif, Kamil (1987), *Al-Muqāwama al-Siriya fi Qanāt al-Suez* (The secret resistance in the Suez Canal zone). Al-Mansura: Dār al-Wafāʾ.

Al-Sharif, Kamil and Mustafa al-Sibai (1984), *Al-Ikhwan al-Muslimun Fī Ḥarb Filisṭīn* (The Muslim Brotherhood in the Palestine war). Cairo: Dār al-Ṭibāʿa wal-Nashr al-Islāmiyya.

Al-Shawi, Tawfiq Muhammad (1998), *Mudhakirāt Niṣf Qarn min al-ʿAml al-Islāmī 1945–1995* (Memoirs of a half century of Islamic activism 1945–1995). Cairo: Dār al-Shurūq.

Al-Sisi, Abbas (1981), *Hasan al-Banna, Mawāqef fi al-Daʿwa wal-Tarbiya* (Hasan al-Banna, situations of missioning and education). Alexandria: Dār al-Daʿwa.

Al-Sisi, Abbas (1987), *Gamal Abdel Nasser wa-Ḥādith al-Manshiyya bil-Iskandariya 26 October 1954* (Gamal Abdel Nasser and the Manshiyya incident in Alexandria 26 October 1954). Alexandria: Dār al-Ṭibāʿa wal-Nashr wal-Ṣawtiyāt.

Al-Sisi, Abbas (2003), *Fī Qāfilat al-Ikhwan al-Muslimin* (In the caravan of the Muslim Brotherhood). Cairo: Dār al-Tawzīʿ wal-Nashr al-Islāmiyya.

Al-Tal, Abdullah (1990), *Kārithat Falasṭīn: Mudhakirāt Abdullah al-Tal Qaʾid Maʿrakat al-Quds* (The Catastrophe of Palestine: The memoirs of Abdullah al-Tal, the Commander of the Battle of Jerusalem). Minya: Dār al-Hudā.

Al-Tilmisani, Umar (1985), *Dhikrayāt lā Mudhakirāt* (Memories not memoirs). Cairo: Dār al-Ṭibā'a wal-Nashr al-Islāmiyya. Cairo: Dār al-Tawzī' wal-Nashr al-Islāmiyya.

Al-Tilmisani, Umar (2003), *Hasan al-Banna, al-Mulham al-Mawhūb, Ustādh al-Jīl* (Hasan al-Banna the inspired and talented, teacher of the generation). Cairo: Dār al-Tawzī' wal-Nashr al-Islāmiyya.

Al-Tuni, Shawkat (1975), *Muḥākamāt al-Dijwi* (The trials of al-Dijwi). Cairo: Dār al-Sha'b.

Al-Uqayl, Abdallah (2008), *Men A'lām al-Da'wa wal-Ḥaraka al-Islāmiya al-Mu'āṣira* (Amongst the protagonists of the contemporary Islamic mission and movement). Cairo: Dār al-Bashīr.

Aly, Abd al-Monein Said and Manfred W. Wenner (1982), "The Islamic Reform Movements: The Muslim Brotherhood in Contemporary Egypt," *Middle East Journal* 36, no. 3 (summer): 336–61.

Amin, Mustafa (1991), *Sana 'Ūlā Sijn* (First-year prison). Cairo: Dār Akhbār al-Yawm.

Amin, Mustafa (n.d.), *Sana Thālitha Sijn* (Third-year prison). Cairo: al-Maktab al-Maṣrī al-Ḥadīth.

Aminzade, R. and E. Perry (2001), "The Sacred, Religious, and Secular in Contentious Politics: Blurring Boundaries," in *Silence and Voice in the Study of Contentious Politics*, Cambridge Studies in Contentious Politics, ed. R. Aminzade, J. Goldstone, D. McAdam, E. Perry, W. Sewell, S. Tarrow et al., 155–78. Cambridge: Cambridge University Press.

Arjomand, Saïd Amir (2010), "Islamic Resurgence and Its Aftermath," in *The New Cambridge History of Islam*, ed. Michael Cook. Cambridge: Cambridge University Press.

Ashmawi, Ali (1993), *al-Tārīkh al-Sirī lil-Ikhwan al Muslimin, Mudhakirāt Ali Ashmawi Ākhir Qādat al-Tanẓīm al-Khās* (The secret history of the Muslim Brotherhood, the memoirs of Ali Ashmawi the last leader of the Special Apparatus). Cairo: Dār al-Hudā.

Ashour, Omar (2009), *The De-Radicalization of Jihadists, Transforming Armed Islamist Movements*. Abingdon: Routledge.

Ayubi, N. Nazih (1993), *Political Islam, Religion and Politics in the Arab World*. London: Routledge.

Azb, Khaled and Safaa Khalifa (2011), *al-Ightiyālāt al-Siyāsiya fi Maṣr, Dimā' fi Tārīkh Maṣr al-Mu'āṣer min Khilāl al-Wathā'iq wa-Maḥāḍir al-Taḥqiq* (Political assassinations in Egypt, blood in the contemporary history of Egypt through the documents and records of interrogation). Beirut: Dār al-Kitāb al-'Arabī.

Bayyoumi, Zakariya Sulayman (2012), *Al-Ikhwan al-Muslimun wal-Jamā't al-Islamiya fi al-Ḥayāt al-Siyāsiya al-Maṣriya 1928–1948* (The Muslim Brotherhood and the Islamic societies in the political life of Egypt, 1928–1948). Cairo: Maktabat Wahba.

Bergesen, Albert J. (2008), *The Sayyid Qutb Reader, Selected Writings on Politics, Religion, and Society*. New York and London: Routledge.

Borum, Randy (2011), "Rethinking radicalization," *Journal of Strategic Security* 4, no. 4: 1–6.

Bowyer Bell, John (2000), *The IRA 1968–2000, Analysis of a Secret Army*. London: Frank Cass Publishers.

Calvert, John (2010), *Sayyid Qutb and the Origins of Radical Islamism*. London: Hurst and Company.

Commins, David (2008), "Hasan al-Banna (1906–1949)," in *Pioneers of Islamic Revival*, ed. Ali Rahnema, 125–53. London and New York: Zed Books.

Cross, Remy and David A. Snow (2012), "Radicalism within the Context of Social Movements: Processes and Types." *Journal of Strategic Security* 4, no. 4: 115–30.

Davis, Eric (1983), "Ideology, Social Classes and Islamic Radicalism in Modern Egypt," in *From Nationalism to Revolutionary Islam*, ed. Said Amir Arjomand, 134–57. Albany: State University of New York Press.

Della Porta, Donatella (1988), "Recruitment Processes in Clandestine Political Organizations: Italian Left-Wing Terrorism." *International Social Movement Research* 1: 155–69.

Della Porta, Donatella (2013), *Clandestine Political Violence*. New York: Cambridge University Press.

Dessouqi, Abduh Mustafa (2012), *Lawa'ih wa Kawanin al-Ikhwan al-Muslimin men al-Ta'sis hata al-Intishar 1930–2009* (The bylaws and rules of the Muslim Brotherhood from its establishment until its proliferation, 1930–2009). Cairo: Muʾasasat Iqraʾ.

Duh, Hasan (1983), *25 ʿāman maʿ al-Jamāʿa, Murūran bel Ghāba* (25 years with the group/organization, passing through the woods). Cairo: Dār al-Iʿtiṣām.

Duh, Hasan (1989), *Ālām wa Āmāl ʿala Ṭarīq al-Ikhwan al-Muslimin* (Pains and hopes on the route of the Muslim Brotherhood). Cairo: Dār al-Iʿtiṣām.

Eisenhower, Dwight D. (1965), *The Whitehouse Years, Waging Peace, 1955–1961*. New York: Doubleday.

El-Awaisi, Abd al-Fattah M. (1991), "The Conceptual Approach of the Egyptian Muslim Brothers towards the Palestine Question 1928–1949." *Journal of Islamic Studies* 2, no. 2: 225–44.

El-Awaisi, Abd al-Fattah M. (1998), *The Muslim Brothers and the Palestine Question 1928–1947*. London: I.B. Tauris.

El-Awaisi, Abd al-Fattah M. (2010), "Jihadia Education and the Society of the Egyptian Muslim Brothers: 1928–49," *Journal of Beliefs & Values: Studies in Religion & Education* 21, no. 2: 213–25.

El-Sadat, Anwar (1978), *In Search of Identity*. New York: Harper and Row. See also Al-Sadat.

Eppel, Michael (2009), "Note about the Term *effendiyya* in the History of the Middle East," *International Journal of Middle East Studies* 41, no. 3: 535–9.

Erickson, Bonnie H. (1981), "Secret Societies and Social Structure." *Social Forces* 60, no. 1: 188–210.

Fanon, Frantz (2001), *The Wretched of the Earth*. London: Penguin Books.

Frampton, Martyn (2018), *The Muslim Brotherhood and the West, a History of Enmity and Engagement*. Massachusetts: The Belknap Press of Harvard University Press.

Gelber, Yoav (2001), *Palestine 1948, War, Escape and the Emergence of the Palestinian Refugee Problem*. Brighton and Portland: Sussex Academic Press.

Gerges, Fawaz A. (2007), "Egypt and the 1948 War: Internal Conflict and Regional Ambition," in *The War for Palestine, Rewriting the History of 1948*, 2nd edn., ed. Eugene L. Rogan and Avi Shlaim, 150–75. New York: Cambridge University Press.

Gerges, Fawaz A. (2018), *Making the Arab World, Nasser, Qutb, and the Clash that Shaped the Middle East*. New Jersey: Princeton University Press.

Gershoni, Israel (1986), The Muslim Brothers and the Arab Revolt in Palestine, 1936–39. *Middle Eastern Studies* 22, no. 3 (Jul.): 367–97.

Gershoni, Israel and James P. Jankowski (2002), *Redefining the Egyptian Nation, 1930–1945*. Cambridge: Cambridge University Press.

Ghanem, Ibrahim al-Bayyoumi (2011), *Wathā ʾiq Qaḍiyat Filisṭīn fi Malafāt al-Ikhwan al-Muslimin, 1928–1948* (The Documents of the Palestine cause in the files of the Muslim Brotherhood, 1928–1948). Cairo: Maktabat al-Shurūq al-Duwaliya.

Ghusheh, Ibrahim (2013), *The Red Minaret: Memoirs of Ibrahim Ghusheh (Ex-Spokesman of Hamas)*. Beirut: Al–Zaytouna.

Gist, Noel P. (1937), "Structure and Process in Secret Societies," *Social Forces* 16, no. 1: 349–57.

Gogmen, Dogan (2008), "Modernization Theory," in *Encyclopedia of Social Problems*, ed. Vincent N. Parrillo, 594. Thousand Oaks: SAGE Publications, Inc.

Gordon, Joel (1992), *Nasser's Blessed Movement: Egypt's Free Officers and the July Revolution*. New York and Oxford: Oxford University Press.

Haddad, Yvonne (2008), "Muhammad Abduh: Pioneer of Islamic Reform," in *Pioneers of Islamic Revival*, ed. Ali Rahnema, 30–63. London: Zed Books.

Hafez, Mohamad M. (2004), "From Marginalization to Massacres, A political Process Explanation of GIA Violence in Algeria," in *Islamic Activism, a Social Movement Theory Approach*, ed. Quintan Wiktorowicz, 37–60. Bloomington, IN: Indiana University Press.

Hafez, Mohammed M. and Quintan Wiktorowicz (2004), "Violence as Contention in the Egyptian Islamic Movement," in *Islamic Activism, a Social Movement Theory Approach*, ed. Quintan Wiktorowicz, 61–88. Bloomington, IN: Indiana University Press.

Halpern, Manfred (1963), *The Politics of Social Change in the Middle East and North Africa*, New Jersey: Princeton University Press.

Hammuda, Adel (1987), *Sayyid Qutb min al-Qarya ilā al-Mashnaqa* (Sayyid Qutb from the village to the gallows). Cairo: Sīnā lil-Nashr.

Hammuda, Hussein Muhammad Ahmad (1985), *Asrār Ḥarakat al-Ḍubāṭ al-Aḥrār wal-Ikhwan al-Muslimun* (The secrets of the Free Officers' movement and the Muslim Brotherhood). Cairo: al-Zahrāʾ lil-ʾiʿlām al-ʿarabī.

Hamrush, Ahmad (1984), *Qiṣat thawrat 23 Yūlyū, Kharīf Abd al-Nasser* (The story of the 23 July Revolution, the autumn of Abdel Nasser). Cairo: Maktabat Madbūlī.

Harris, Christina P. (1964), *Nationalism and Revolution in Egypt, the Role of the Muslim Brotherhood*. California: Mouton & CO.

Hathut, Hasān (2000), *al-ʿAqd al-Farīd 1942–1952, ʿAshr Sanawāt maʿ al-Imām Hasan al-Banna* (The Unique Decade 1942–1952, Ten years with the Imam Hasan al-Banna). Cairo: Dār al-Shurūq.

Haydar, Khalil Ali (1989). *Aḍwāʾ ʿālā Mudhakirāt Hasan al-Banna* (Lights on the memoirs of Hasan al-Banna). Kuwait City: Kāḍima lil-Nashr.

Hegghammer, Thomas (2020), *The Caravan, Abdullah Azzam and the Rise of Global Jihad.* Cambridge: Cambridge University Press.

Heyworth-Dunne, James (1950), *Religious and Political Trends in Modern Egypt.* Washington: published by author.

Hopwood, Derek (1993), *Egypt, Politics and Society 1945–90.* London: Routledge.

Husaini, Ishaq Musa (1956), *The Moslem Brethren, the Greatest of Modern Islamic Movements.* Beirut: Khayat's College Book Cooperative.

Jankowski, James (1980), Egyptian Responses to the Palestine Problem in the Interwar Period. *International Journal of Middle East Studies* 12, no. 1 (August): 1–38.

Jawhar, Sami (1976), *Al-Ṣāmiṭun Yatakalamūn* (The silent talk). Alexandria: al-Maktab al-Maṣrī al-Ḥadīth.

Jawhar, Sami (1977), *Al-Mawtā Yatakalamūn* (The dead talk). Alexandria: al-Maktab al-Maṣrī al-Ḥadīth.

Jordanova, Ludmilla (2019), *History in Practice*, 3rd edn. London: Bloomsbury.

Jung, Dietrich (2011), *Orientalists, Islamists and the Global Public Sphere: A Genealogy of the Modern Essentialist Image of Islam.* Sheffield: Equinox.

Jung, Dietrich (2018), "The Multiple Faces of Mustafa Kemal Atatürk: Authority, Iconography, and Subjectivity in Modern Turkey," in *Reframing Authority: The Role of Media and Materiality*, ed. Laura Feldt and Christian Høgel, 207–28. Sheffield: Equinox Publishing.

Jung, Dietrich and Ahmed Abou El Zalaf (2019), "Hasan Al-Banna and the Modern Muslim Self: Subjectivity Formation and the Search for an Islamic Order in Early 20th-Century Egypt," *Numen* 66, no. 4: 381–402.

Kamil, Abdel Aziz (2006), *Fī Nahr al-Ḥayāt* (In the life's river). Cairo: al-Maktab al-Maṣrī al-Ḥadīth.

Kassem, Maye (2004), *Egyptian Politics, the Dynamics of Authoritarian Rule.* Colorado: Lynne Rienner Publishers, Inc.

Kedourie, Elie (1980), *Islam in the Modern World and Other Studies.* London: Mansell.

Kenney, Jeffrey T. (2006), *Muslim Rebels, Kharijites and the Politics of Extremism in Egypt.* New York: Oxford University Press.

Kepel, Gilles (1985), *The Prophet and the Pharaoh, Muslim Extremism in Egypt.* London: Al Saqi Books.

Kepel, Gilles (2014), *Jihad, The Trail of Political Islam.* London: I.B. Tauris.

Kerr, Malcom H. (1975), *The Arab Cold War, Gamal ʿAbd al-Nasir and his Rivals 1958–1970.* London: Oxford University Press.

Khafaji, Abdel Halim (2006), *ʿindamā Ghābat al-Shams* (when the sun disappeared). Cairo: Dār al-Tawzīʿ wal-Nashr al-Islāmiyya.

Khatab, Sayed (2001), "Al-Hudayb's Influence on the Development of Islamist Movements in Egypt," *The Muslim World* 91, no. 3/4 (Fall): 451–79.

Khatab, Sayed (2002), "Citizenship Rights of Non-Muslims in the Islamic State of Ḥākimiyya Espoused by Sayyid Quṭb," *Islam and Christian–Muslim Relations* 13, no. 2: 163–87.

Khatab, Sayed (2009), "The Voice of Democratism in Sayyid Qutb's Response to Violence and Terrorism," *Islam and Christian–Muslim Relations* 20, no. 3: 315–32.

Khayal, Muhammad Abdel Hakim and Mahmoud Muhammad Al-jawhari (1993), *Al-Akhawāt al-Muslimāt, wa Binā' al-'Usra al-Qur'āniya* (The Muslim Sisterhood, and the construction of a Quranic family). Alexandria: Dār al-Da'wa.

Khosrokhavar, Farhad (2010), "The Muslim Brotherhood in France," in *The Muslim Brotherhood, the Organization and Policies of a Global Islamist Movement*, ed. Barry Rubin, 137–47. New York: Palgrave Macmillan.

Krämer, Gudrun (2010), *Hasan al-Banna*. Oxford: One World.

La Rue, George M. (2002), "The Capture of a Slave Caravan: The Incident at Asyut (Egypt) in 1880," *African Economic History*, no. 30: 81–106.

Lajnat Kutub Qawmiya (1965), *Jarā'im 'Iṣābat al-Ikhwan* (the crimes of the Brotherhood gang). Cairo: al-Dār al-Qawmiya lil-Ṭibā'a wal-Nashr.

Leiken, Robert. S. and Steven Brooke (2007), "The Moderate Muslim Brotherhood," *Foreign Affairs* 86, no. 2: 107–21.

Levenberg, Haim (1993), *Military Preparations of the Arab Community in Palestine, 1945–1948*. London: Frank Cass and Co. Ltd.

Lia, Brynjar (2010), *The Society of the Muslim Brothers in Egypt, the Rise of an Islamic Mass movement, 1928–1942*. Reading: Garnet Publishing ltd.

Lockman, Zachary (2011), *Contending Visions of the Middle East, the History and Politics of Orientalism*. New York: Cambridge University Press

Louis, Roger (1985), *The British Empire in the Middle East 1945–1951, Arab Nationalism, The United States, and Postwar Imperialism*. New York: Oxford University Press.

Mahmoud, Ali Abdel Halim (1997), *Wasā'il al-Tarbiyya 'ind al-Ikhwan al-Muslimin, Dirāsa Taḥlīliya Tārīkhiya* (The methods of education in the Muslim Brotherhood, an analytic and historic study). Cairo: Dār al-Tawzī' wal-Nashr al-Islāmiyya.

Malthaner, Stefan (2017), "Radicalization: The Evolution of an Analytical Paradigm," *European Journal of Sociology* 58, no. 3: 369–401.

Mansfield, Peter (1971), *The British in Egypt*. New York, Chicago and San Francisco: Holt, Rinehart and Winston.

Mansour, Ahmad (2004), *Husayn al-Shafi'i, Shāhed 'alā 'ahd Thawrat Yulyū* (Husayn al-Shafi'i a witness to the July Revolution). Beirut: al-Dār al-'Arabiya lil-'Ulūm.

Maréchal, Birgitte (2008), *The Muslim Brothers in Europe, Roots and Discourse*. Leiden: Brill.

Marsot, Afaf Lutfi al-Sayyid (2007), *A History of Egypt, from the Arab Conquest to the Present*. New York: Cambridge University Press.

Marx, Gary T. (1974), "Thoughts on a Neglected Category of Social Movement Participant: The Agent Provocateur and the Informant," *American Journal of Sociology* 80, no. 2: 402–42.

Mashhur, Mustafa (1987), *Ṭarīq al-Daʿwa* (The path of the mission). Cairo: Dār al-Ṭibāʿ wal-Nashr al-Islāmiya.

Mayer, Thomas (1982), "The Military Force of Islam: The Society of the Muslim Brethren and the Palestine Question, 1945–48," in *Zionism and Arabism in Palestine and Israel*, ed. Ellie Kedourie and Sylvia G. Haim, 100–18. London: Frank Cass.

Melucci, Alberto (1996), *Challenging Codes Collective Action in the Information Age*. Cambridge: Cambridge University Press.

Mesbar Studies and Research Centre (2014), *Ḥaqīqat Tanẓim al-Ikhwan, Ārāʾ Kibār Kutāb Maṣr fi al-Ikhwan* (The truth about the Brotherhood organization, the viewpoints of Egypt's greatest writers on the Brotherhood in Egypt). Dubai: Mesbar Studies and Research Centre.

Mitchell, Richard P. (1993), *The Society of the Muslim Brothers*. London: Oxford University Press.

Moussalli, Ahmad S. (1992), *Radical Islamic Fundamentalism, The Ideological and Political Discourse of Sayyid Quṭb*. Beirut: American University of Beirut.

Muhammad, Abdel Wahab Bakr (1982), *Al-Jaysh al-Miṣrī wa Ḥarb Filisṭin 1948–1952* (The Egyptian Army and the Palestine War 1948–1952). Cairo: Dār al-Maʿāref.

Muhammad, Muhammad Abd al-Jawad and Mashhur, Mustafa Mashhur (2005), *Ḥayāt Mustafa Mashhur kamā ʿāshathu Usratuhu* (The life of Mustafa Mashhur as lived by his family). Cairo: Dār al-Tawzīʿ wal-Nashr al-Islāmiya.

Muhammad, Muhsin (1987), *Man Qatala Hasan al-Banna* (Who killed Hasan al-Banna?). Cairo: Dār al-Shurūq.

Muhyiddin, Khaled (1992), *Wal-Ān Atakalam* (And now I speak). Cairo: Markaz al-Ahrām.

Munson, Ziad (2001), "Islamic Mobilization: Social Movement Theory and the Egyptian Muslim Brotherhood," *The Sociological Quarterly* 42, no. 4: 487–510.

Mårtensson, Ulrika (2015), "'Islamic Order'": Semeiotics and Pragmatism in the Muslim Brotherhood?" *Journal of Islamic Research* 9, no. 1: 35–57.

Nada, Youssef and Douglas Thompson (2012), *Inside the Muslim Brotherhood, Youssef Nada*. London: Metro.

Naguib, Muhammad (1984), *Mudhakirāt Muhammad Naguib, Kuntu Raʾīsan li Maṣr* (Memoirs of Muhammad Naguib, I was president of Egypt). Cairo: al-Maktab al-Miṣrī al-Ḥadīth.

Naguib, Muhammad (2011), *Kalimatī lil-Tārīkh* (My word to history). Cairo: al-Maktab al-Miṣrī al-Ḥadīth.

Nasr, Seyyed vali Reza (1994), *The Vanguard of the Islamic Revolution: The Jama'at-I Islami of Pakistan*. London: I.B. Tauris.

Neumann, Peter R. (2013), "The Trouble with Radicalization," *International Affairs* 89, no. 4: 873–93.

Osman, Ghada (2011), *A Journey in Islamic Thought, the Life of Fathi Osman*. London, New York: I.B. Tauris.

Pargeter, Alison (2016), *Return to the Shadows, the Muslim Brotherhood and An-Nahda since the Arab Spring*. London: Saqi books.

Qamiha, Jaber (2009), *Dhikrayātī maʿ Daʿwat al-Ikhwan fi al-Manzila wal-Daqahliya* (My recollections with the mission of the Brotherhood in al-Manzila and al-Daqahliya). Cairo: Markaz al-Iʿlām al-ʿArabī.

Qaud, Ibrahim (1985), *Umar Al-Tilmisani Shāhed ʿalā al-ʿAṣr, al-Ikhwan al-Muslimun fi Dāʾirat al-Ḥaqīqa al-Ghāʾiba* (Umar al-Tilmisani a witness on an era, the Muslim Brotherhood in the circle of an absent truth). Cairo: al-Mukhtār al-Islāmī.

Qutb, Sayyid (2006), *Dirāsāt Islāmiyya* (Islamic studies). Cairo: Dār al-Shorūq.

Qutb, Sayyid (2007), *Limādha Aʿdamūnī ?* (Why did they execute me?). Cairo: Manshūrāt Nūn.

Radwan, Fathi (1986), *72 Shahran maʿ Abd al-Nasser* (72 months with Abdel Nasser). Cairo: Dār al-Ḥurriya lil-Saḥāfa wal-Tibāʿa wal-Nashr.

Raif, Ahmad (1986), *al-Bawāba al-Sawdā*ʾ (The black gate). Cairo: al-Zahrāʾ lil-ʾiʿlām al-ʿarabī.

Raif, Ahmad (1990), *Sarādīb al-Shayṭān* (The catacombs of the devil). Cairo: al-Zahrāʾ lil-ʾiʿlām al-ʿarabī.

Ramadan, Abdel ʿAzim (1993), *Al-Ikhwan al-Muslimun wal-Tanzīm al-Sirrī* (The Muslim Brotherhood and the Secret Organization). Cairo: Al-Hayʾah al-Maṣriyah al-ʿāma lil-kitāb.

Rich, David (2010), "The Very Model of a British Muslim Brotherhood," in *The Muslim Brotherhood, the Organization and Policies of a Global Islamist Movement*, ed. Barry Rubin, 117–36. New York: Palgrave Macmillan.

Rizq, Jaber (1978), *Madhābiḥ al-Ikhwan fi Sujūn Nasser, Asrār Rahība Tunshar li-Awal Mara* (The massacres of the Brotherhood in Nasser's prisons, horrible secrets published for the first time). Cairo: Dār al-Iʿtiṣām.

Rizq, Jaber (1979), *Madhbaḥat al-Ikhwan fi Limān Ṭura* (The massacre of the Brotherhood in Liman Tura). Cairo: Dār al-Iʿtiṣām.

Rizq, Jaber (1991), *Hasan al-Hudaybi, al-Imam al-Mumtaḥan* (Hasan al-Hudaybi, the tried Imam). Cairo: Dār al-Liwāʾ.

Rodinson, Maxime (1968), "The Political System," in *Egypt since the Revolution*, ed. P.J. Vatikiotis, 87–113. London: George Allen & Unwin.

Rogan, Eugene L. (2009), *The Arabs, A History*. London: Penguin Books.

Rubin, Barry (2010), "Introduction," in *The Muslim Brotherhood, the Organization and Policies of a Global Islamist Movement*, ed. Barry Rubin, 1–3. New York: Palgrave Macmillan.

Sadiq, Ali (1987), *Al-Ikhwan al-Muslimun bayna Irhāb Farouq wa Abdel Nasser* (The Muslim Brotherhood between the terror of Farouq and Abdel Nasser). Cairo: Dār al-Iʿtiṣām.

Saleh, Ibtisam Yahya and Abduh Mustafa Dessouqi (2009), *Fatā al-Jihad, Mudhakirāt Abd al-Rahman al-Bannan* (The youngster of Jihad, the memoirs of Abdel Rahman al-Bannan). Cairo: Dār al-Nashr lil-Jāmiʿāt.

Sattar, Noman (1995), "'Al Ikhwan Al Muslimin' (Society of Muslim Brotherhood) Aims and Ideology, Role and Impact," *Pakistan Horizon* 48, no. 2: 7–30.

Scruton, Roger (2007), *The Palgrave Macmillan Dictionary of Political Thought*, 3rd edn. Basingstoke: Palgrave Macmillan.

Sedgwick, Mark (2010), "The Concept of Radicalization as a Source of Confusion," *Terrorism and Political Violence* 22, no. 4: 479–94.

Selak, Charles B. (1955), "The Suez Canal Base Agreement of 1954," *The American Journal of International Law* 49, no. 4: 487–505.

Selznick, Philip (1952), *The Organizational Weapon, a Study of Bolshevik Strategy and Tactics*. New York: McGraw-Hill Book Company, Inc.

Shadi, Salah (1987), *Safahat men al-Tarikh, Ḥasad al-'Umr* (Pages from history, the harvest of life). Cairo: al-Zahrāʾ lil-ʾiʿlām al-ʿarabī.

Shadi, Salah (1988), *Al-Shahīdān Hasan al-Banna wa-Sayyid Qutb* (The two martyrs, Hasan al-Banna and Sayyid Qutb). Cairo: Dār a-Wafāʾ.

Shalabi, Rauf (1978), *Al-Shaykh Hasan al-Banna wa-Madrasat al-Ikhwan al-Muslimun* (The Shaykh Hasan al-Banna and the school of the Muslim Brotherhood). Cairo: Dār al-Anṣār.

Sharaf, Sami (2015), *Sanawāt wa-Ayām maʿ Gamal Abdel Nasser* (Years and days with Gamal Abdel Nasser) vol. I–V. Cairo: al-Maktab al-Maṣrī al-Ḥadīth.

Shʿir, Muhammad Fathi Ali (1985), *Wasāʾil al-Iʿlām al-Maṭbūʿa Fi Daʿwat al-Ikhwan al-Muslimin* (The printed media in the mission of the Muslim Brotherhood). Jidda: Dār al-Mujtamaʿ lil-Nashr wal-Tawzīʿ.

Simmel, Georg (1906), "The Sociology of Secrecy and of Secret Societies," *American Journal of Sociology* 11, no. 4: 441–98.

Sivan, Emmanuel (1990), *Radical Islam: Medieval Theology and Modern Politics*. New Haven, CT/London: Yale University Press.

Soage, Ana Belén and Jorge Fuentelsaz Franganillo (2010), "The Muslim Brothers in Egypt," in *The Muslim Brotherhood, The Organization and Policies of a Global Islamist Movement*, ed. Barry Rubin, 39–55. New York: Palgrave.

Thornhill, Michael T. (2006), *Road to Suez, the Battle of the Canal Zone*. Stroud, Gloucestershire: Sutton.

Toth, James (2013), *Sayyid Qutb: The Life and Legacy of a Radical Islamic Intellectual*. London: Oxford University Press.

Vatikiotis, Panayiotis Jerasimof (1978), *Nasser and His Generation*. London: Croom Helm.

Vatikiotis, Panayiotis Jerasimof (1985), *The History of Egypt, from Muhammad Ali to Mubara*, London: Weidenfeld and Nicolson.

Vidino, Lorenzo (2010), *The New Muslim Brotherhood in the West*. New York, Chichester and West Sussex: Columbia University Press.

Weber, Max (1949), "'Objectivity' in Social Science and Social Polity," in *The Methodology of the Social Science*, ed. Max Weber, trans. Edward A. Shils and Henry A. Finch. New York: The Free press of Glencoe.

Weber, Peter C. (2013), "Modernity, Civil Society, and Sectarianism: The Egyptian Muslim Brotherhood and the *Takfir* Groups," *Voluntas: International Journal of Voluntary and Nonprofit Organizations* 24, no. 2: 509–27.

Weismann, Itzchak (2015), *Abd al-Rahman al-Kawakibi, Islamic Reform and Arab Revival*. London: A Oneworld Book.

Weismann, Itzchak (2017), "A Perverted Balance: Modern Salafism between Reform and Jihād," *Die Welt Des Islams* 57: 33–66.

Wickham, Carrie Rosefsky (2002), *Mobilizing Islam, Religion, Activism, and Political Change in Egypt*. New York, Chichester and West Sussex: Columbia University Press.

Wickham, Carrie Rosefsky (2013), *The Muslim Brotherhood, Evolution of an Islamist Movement*. Princeton, New Jersey and Woodstock, Oxfordshire: Princeton University Press.

Wiktorowicz, Quintan (2004), "Introduction: Islamic Activism and Social Movement Theory," in *Islamic Activism: A Social Movement Theory Approach*, ed. Quintan Wiktorowicz, 1–33. Indiana: Indiana University Press.

Willi, Victor J. (2021), *The Fourth Ordeal: A History of the Muslim Brotherhood in Egypt, 1968–2018*. Cambridge: Cambridge University Press.

Yavuz, M. Hakan (2004), "Opportunity Spaces, Identity, and Islamic Meaning in Turkey," in *Islamic Activism: A Social Movement Theory Approach*, ed. Quintan Wiktorowicz, 270–88. Indiana: Indiana University Press.

Zahid, Mohammed and Michael Medley (2006), "Muslim Brotherhood in Egypt and Sudan," *Review of African Political Economy* 33, no. 110: 693–708.

Zahmul, Ibrahim (1985), *Al-Ikhwan al-Muslimun, Awrāq Tārīkhiya* (The Muslim Brotherhood, historical papers). France: n.p.

Zaki, Muhammad Shawqi (1954), *Al-Ikhwan al-Muslimin Fī al-Mujtama' al-Masrī* (the Muslim Brotherhood in the Egyptian Society). Cairo: Dār al-ʿahd al-Jadīd.

Zald, Mayer N. (2008), "Culture, Ideology and Strategic Framing," in *Comparative Perspectives on Social Movements, Political Opportunities, Mobilizing Structures, and Cultural Framings*, ed. Doug McAdam et al., 261–74. Cambridge: Cambridge University Press.

Zarzour, Adnan Muhammad (2000), *Mustafa al-Sibai, Al-Dāʿiya al-Mujadid* (Mustafa al-Sibai the renovating missionary). Damascus: Dār al-Qalam.

Zollner, Barbara (2007), "Prison Talk: The Muslim Brotherhood's Internal Struggle during Gamal Abdel Nasser's persecution, 1954 to 1971," *International Journal of Middle East Studies* 39, no. 3: 411–33.

Zollner, Barbara (2011), *The Muslim Brotherhood, Hasan al-Hudaybi and Ideology*. New York: Routledge.

Official Documents:

NA (1954), *Maḥkamat al-Sha'b, al-Maḍbaṭa al-Rasmiya li-Maḥāḍir Jalasāt Maḥkamat al-Sha'b* (The People's Tribunal, the official Transcripts from court hearings from the People's Tribunal) (vol. I–VI consisting of 9–25 November). Cairo: Idārat al-Nashr wal-Tawzī'.

Internet Database:

Abdel Khaleq, Farid (2004), *Shāhed 'alā al- 'Aṣr, al-Ikhwan kamā yarāhum Farid Abdel Khaleq* (Witness of an epoch, The Muslim Brotherhood as seen by Farid Abdel Khaleq): I https://bit.ly/33ZG1GB (accessed December 12, 2019); VII https://bit.ly/31jRVvk (accessed February 2, 2020); XII https://bit.ly/3ePTqGW (accessed July 22, 2020); XIV https://bit.ly/30PVf1F (accessed July 22, 2020).

Afifi, Ali (2013), *Shādāt wa-Ru'ā 'ālā Ṭarīq al-Da'wa* (Testimonies and views on the path of the mission). https://bit.ly/2WnjdjA (accessed May 11, 2020).

Akef, Mahdi (2008), *Murāja'āt ma' Murshid al-Ikhwan Muhammad Mahdi Akef* (Reviews with the Leader of the Brotherhood, Muhammad Mahdi Akef). al-Hiwar Tv: II https://bit.ly/3eJVT6C (accessed April 22, 2020);III https://bit.ly/3bvmsup (accessed April 22, 2020).

Akef, Mahdi (2017–18), *Ṣafaḥāt min al-Dhikrayāt: Riḥla fī Dhikrayāt Mahdi Akef* (Pages of memoirs, a journey into the memoirs of Mahdi Akef), on Arabi21.com: I https://bit.ly/34fVEdf (accessed December 12, 2019); II https://bit.ly/2YIxDuo (accessed December 12, 2019); III https://bit.ly/2PCjeM6 (accessed December 12, 2019); IV https://bit.ly/2t3zwpt; V https://bit.ly/3uHOyPq (accessed February 11, 2019); VI https://bit.ly/3sCbD3H (accessed February 11, 2019); VIII https://bit.ly/3h3luKb (accessed February 11, 2019); XVII, https://bit.ly/2XLPZf6 (accessed June 9, 2020); XIX https://bit.ly/2Un3b7W (accessed June 9, 2020); XXI https://bit.ly/30pYaza (accessed June 9, 2020).

Al-Antabli, Ashraf Eid (n.d.), *Al-Mustashār Munir al-Dilla, Ramz al-Taḍḥiya wal-Fidā'* (The counselor Munir al-Dilla, the symbol of sacrifice and redemption). https://bit.ly/2u7KMl6 (accessed November 26, 2018).

al-Banna, Hasan (n.d.), *Qaḍiyatunā* (Our cause). https://bit.ly/35ZIIsR (accessed January 16, 2020).

Al-Uqayl, Abdullah (n.d.), *Kamil al-Sharif (1926–2008)*. https://bit.ly/36mLvNn (accessed December 12, 2019).

Ashmawi, Saleh (n.d.), *Labayki Falastin* (Palestine, Your wish is my command), in *Jarīdat al-Ikhwan al-Muslimin* (The newspaper of the Muslim Brotherhood), June 14, 1947. https://bit.ly/2MvsBwi (accessed December 26, 2019).

Badi, Muhammad (n.d.), *al-Murshid al- ʿĀm lil-Ikhwan, Sīra wa-Masīra* (The general guide of the Brotherhood, biography and trajectory). https://bit.ly/2AnSJpP (accessed May 12, 2020).

Egypt arrests Muslim Brotherhood's top leader (2013). https://bit.ly/3KaPDo7 (accessed April 5, 2021).

Hajji, Tariq (2018), *Tārīkh ʿUnf wa Irhāb, al-Ikhwan al-Muslimin* (A history of violence and terror, the Muslim Brotherhood). https://bit.ly/2uTWwbz (accessed September 19, 2019).

Ikhwan-Wiki (n.d.), *Ahmad Hassanein, Rajul al-Mahām al-Ṣa ʿba* (Ahmad Hassanein, the man for the difficult operations). https://bit.ly/2Peh6uT (accessed December 12, 2019).

Ikhwan-Wiki (n.d.), *Ahmad Abdel Majid*. https://bit.ly/2SF7xGE (accessed May 7, 2020).

Ikhwan-Wiki (n.d.), *Al-Amr al- ʿAskarī bi-Ḥal al-Ikhwan al-Muslimin li-Sanat 1948* (The military commandment for dissolving the Muslim Brotherhood, for the year 1948). https://bit.ly/2O2RAYJ (accessed January 27, 2020).

Ikhwan Wiki (n.d.), "*al-Duktūr Muhammad Farid Abdel Khaleq*" (Doctor Muhammad Farid Abdel Khaleq). https://bit.ly/2RPw50a (accessed July 21, 2020).

Ikhwan-Wiki (n.d.), *Al-Ikhwan wal-Qaḍiya al-Filisṭīniya* (The Brotherhood and the Palestine question). https://bit.ly/2M5mvlY (accessed December 18, 2019).

Ikhwan-Wiki (n.d.), *Amal al-Ashmawi*. https://bit.ly/3awFCAf (accessed January 20, 2020).

Ikhwan-Wiki (n.d.), *Awad Abdel ʿAl*. https://bit.ly/3Niy1sg (accessed March 24, 2021).

Ikhwan-Wiki (n.d.), *Mahmoud Abdel Halim, Namūzaj al-Qiyāda wal-*Jundiya (Mahmoud Abdel Halim, a model of leadership and soldiery). https://bit.ly/2RcnRhG (accessed January 21, 2020).

Ikhwan-Wiki (n.d.), *Muhammad Hilal*. https://bit.ly/35ZyyyE (accessed March 17, 2021).

Ikhwan-Wiki (n.d.), *Mahmoud Izzat*. https://bit.ly/2xSlFoV (accessed May 11, 2020).

Ikhwan-Wiki (n.d.), *Muhammad Abdel Fattah Sharif*. https://bit.ly/37XeXj8 (accessed March 24, 2021).

Ikhwan-Wiki (n.d.), *Muhammad Yusuf Hawwash*. https://bit.ly/3CPBeL0 (accessed March 18, 2021).

Ikhwan-Wiki (n.d.), *Said Ramdan*. https://bit.ly/3ARa713 (accessed February 2, 2022).

Ikhwan-Wiki (n.d.), *Tārīkh al-Ikhwan al-Muslimin fi al- ʿIrāq* (The history of the Muslim Brotherhood in Iraq). https://bit.ly/392opOa (accessed December 23, 2019).

Ikhwan-Wiki (n.d.), *Tārīkh al-Ikhwan al-Muslimin fi Djibouti* (The history of the Muslim Brotherhood in Djibouti). https://bit.ly/34BKqQC (accessed December 19, 2019).

Ikhwan-Wiki (n.d.), *Tārīkh al-Ikhwan fi Filisṭīn* (The history of the Brotherhood in Palestine). https://bit.ly/3aqWTd1 (accessed March 4, 2020).

Ikhwan-Wiki (n.d.), *Qism al-Akhawāt al-Muslimāt* (The department of the Muslim Sisters). https://bit.ly/2uerNFK (accessed January 20, 2020).

Mubarak, Umar Qasir (2017), *al-Shahīd al-Shāb Abdel Fattah Ismail Ḥajar al-Zāwiya li-Tanẓīm 65* (The young martyr Abdel Fattah Ismail, the cornerstone of Organization 65). https://bit.ly/2UAcxNJ (accessed June 11, 2020).

Mamduh, Alaa (n.d.), *al-ʿālem al-Mujāhid al-Shaykh Fathi al-Rifʿi* (The striving scholar, Shaykh Fathi al-Rifai). https://bit.ly/3IHKkuy (accessed March 25, 2021).

Mustafa, Ahmad Farid (n.d.), *Mudhakirāt Muhājir ilā al-Madīna al-Munawarah* (Recollections of an emigrant to the enlightened city). https://bit.ly/3iaT01J (accessed March 16, 2021).

Picture of a Brother in a sack (1954), https://bit.ly/34RQYMM (accessed April 20, 2020).

Sunan Abi Dawud (The traditions of Abi Dawud), English translation: Book 14, Hadith 2602. https://bit.ly/3aAjq8f (accessed January 23, 2020).

Index

www.ingramcontent.com/pod-product-compliance
Lightning Source LLC
Chambersburg PA
CBHW050430280326
41932CB00013BA/2063
* 9 7 8 0 7 5 5 6 4 6 6 4 7 *